Dear Wain,
All the very best on your
" "

# Unthinkable

journey!
Scott
Rigsby

# UnThinkable

2.4-MILE (3.9 KM) SWIM | 112-MILE (180 KM) BIKE | 26.2-MILE (42.2 KM) MARATHON RUN

THE TRUE STORY ABOUT THE FIRST DOUBLE AMPUTEE TO COMPLETE THE WORLD-FAMOUS HAWAIIAN IRONMAN TRIATHLON

SCOTT RIGSBY

WITH JENNA GLATZER

Tyndale House Publishers, Inc.

CAROL STREAM, ILLINOIS

Visit Tyndale online at www.tyndale.com.

Visit the author's website at www.scottrigsby.com.



*Unthinkable*



Edited by Dave Lindstedt

Designed by Ron Kaufmann



---

**Library of Congress Cataloging-in-Publication Data**

Rigsby, Scott.
Unthinkable / Scott Rigsby, with Jenna Glatzer.
p. cm.
Includes bibliographical references.
ISBN 978-1-4143-3315-1 (hc)
ISBN 978-1-4143-3314-4 (sc)
1. Rigsby, Scott. 2. Athletes with disabilities—United States—Biography.
3. Amputees—United States—Biography. 4. Wheelchair sports. 5. Ironman triathlons.
6. Sports—Religious aspects—Christianity. I. Glatzer, Jenna. II. Title.
GV697.A2R547 2009
796.092—dc22 [B] 2009025769

---

Printed in the United States of America

18 17 16 15 14 13
9 8 7 6 5

*This book is dedicated to*
*my brother Tim,*
*the real Ironman of our family*

# CHAPTER 1

"Please, mister, get this trailer off me! Please help me!"

I didn't remember saying that, but he sure remembered hearing it. The man had tears in his eyes as he filled in the gaps in my memory, explaining that I had grabbed his arm when he came over to ask what he could do.

He was the driver of a truck that was behind the eighteen-wheeler that had sideswiped our pickup, causing me to go flying off the side of our truck's toolbox and bounce up and down the hot asphalt of the roadway for 324 feet. When the pickup finally stopped, what was left of my right leg was trapped under a trailer carrying three tons of lawn-mowing equipment, and my back was a mass of third-degree burns from scraping along the pavement.

I was just a kid at the time—eighteen years old, fresh out of high school and working a summer landscaping job with a couple of my best friends. It was a great way to work on my tan and my muscles while making some spending money—and I liked the work. We had a boss we called "Unc," an African-American in his late sixties with a grandfatherly manner, who looked out for us. The housing authority of Camilla, Georgia, had hired us to mow lawns in the city's housing projects and some smaller surrounding communities.

When we drove to the smaller towns, three guys would ride in the cab of the truck, and three guys would hop into the back and sit on the toolbox with their backs resting against the cab. Once we were all aboard, we would drive to our location for that day. On July 23, 1986, we headed to Norman Park, a small, unincorporated town near Moultrie, Georgia. I drove the truck that morning—way too fast for Unc's taste, as usual. Having grown up watching movies such as *Smokey and the Bandit* and *Cannonball Run* and television shows such as *The Dukes of Hazzard*, whenever I went somewhere, I always wanted to see how fast I could get there.

My friends and I liked working in Norman Park because it was a bit of a distance from Camilla—by the time we finished the job and made it back to the housing authority office, it would be about time to break for lunch. We always drove at or just under the speed limit on the way back because we were kids and were getting paid by the hour. Plus, you can't hit a road sign with a bottle at high speeds. Yes, we were mischievous, but not malicious.

Whenever we rode in the back of the truck, we played games to see how many road signs we could hit. My competitive nature would take over, and soon we would be throwing cinder blocks, and then larger objects, until Mike McClain—always the voice of reason on our crew—would suggest that maybe throwing a table at a sign might be a little over the top.

Once we arrived back at the Camilla Housing Authority, we'd partake of our favorite event of the day: eating. With the metabolism of eighteen-year-olds, we ate anything and everything in sight. We would head to Guy Watson's house, which was within walking distance, and we'd scarf down soft drinks, pizza, and any other food that had not been properly hidden.

We'd also watch television, but not just any television. It

had to be *Bodies in Motion*, a half-hour fitness and aerobics workout show on ESPN. The star of the show was an Olympic athlete named Gilad Janklowicz, but that's not what kept us glued to the television. No, we tuned in to see Gilad's assistants—the most amazingly beautiful women—exercising in skimpy spandex outfits. These women put Olivia Newton-John and her *Physical* video to shame.

But even though *Bodies in Motion* was an intellectually and culturally stimulating program, it could sustain our knowledge-seeking minds only so long before our food coma kicked in. Then we'd fade peacefully into a thirty-minute nap, and I'd dream about blades of grass gently swaying in the breeze until it was time to head back to work. All in all, it was a glorious summer experience.

That particular day, we finished our morning work and went to the store to get some cold drinks and snacks. After we loaded up on enough junk food to put a dent in our $3.35-per-hour paychecks, it was time to head to Guy's house for lunch. I hopped back into the driver's seat, and my right hand had a firm grip on the steering wheel when Unc said, "Why don't you let someone else drive?"

It didn't bother me. I loved and respected Unc—he loved us and we were his boys. He was a great manager because he was tough but fair. I'm not sure if Unc knew how to read or write very well, but that wouldn't have changed my opinion of him. I was proud that he had a managerial role. Growing up in the South could not have been easy for him, yet he showed no bitterness or prejudice against white folks.

Often, he was thinking ahead about what he wanted to tell us, and he would get so caught up in his words that he would mix up our names. He'd say, "Now, Tommy, . . . I mean Mike, . . . I mean Guy," and then he would pause and collect his thoughts. "Now, Scott, I wantcha ta go over there, and cut the grass on dat part of dat dem buildings." That was our Unc.

We shared the driving duties all the time, and I knew that Unc wanted a slow pace on the way home.

"Tommy, you drive us on home," he said. Tommy Hilliard was a couple of years younger than Mike, Guy, and I were—a good farm kid from a great family. His mom ran the Camilla Housing Authority. Although he was the youngest, Tommy was probably the best driver of us all.

I often replay in my mind that moment of getting out of the driver's seat. It was such a small event, but it changed the course of many lives. I have to believe that Unc and Tommy must have reflected on that decision as well. Unc was right to let Tommy drive. I always drove way too fast because patience was not one of my virtues.

Being behind the wheel was a circus act for me. I was an early practitioner of multitasking. My mouth would run double the speed of the vehicle while I stuffed my face full of chips and washed them down with a cold drink and somehow reached to turn the channel on the radio. My talking or deejaying didn't annoy anyone—the others were too gripped with fear by my haphazard attention to the road. Tommy, on the other hand, was patient and careful when driving.

Who knows how different things might have been if I had stayed at the wheel?

Tommy slid into the cab for the leisurely drive back to Camilla. I hopped in the back of the truck and slammed my dirty, grass-covered shoulders right next to my best friends, Guy Watson and Mike McClain. I sat on the left side of the truck behind the driver's seat, Mike was in the middle, and Guy was on the right. Tommy, Unc, and Demetrius—the other member of our crew—rode in the cab. Jacked up from the sugar of a Snickers bar and the caffeine of a Mountain Dew I had inhaled, I proceeded to give my friends an earful of my philosophies of life.

Guy was one of the best and funniest storytellers I had

ever met, with a particular aptitude for impressions. His parents, "Mr. Bill" and "Miss Janie," were like a second set of parents to me. I had known Mike since eighth grade, when he and his family moved to Pelham, a town near Camilla. He was a great athlete because what he lacked in size and strength, he made up for in intelligence. His thinking was calculated and methodical. Okay, there were a few times when he didn't make the best decisions, but that was usually when he'd had too much of the spirit (and I don't mean the holy one). Between Guy's constant humor and my reckless abandon, Mike brought a good balance of levelheadedness to our version of the Three Musketeers.

We proceeded down the highway, checking occasionally to make sure that Tommy was not going faster than the speed limit and reminding him quietly that getting back to the office sooner meant we would have to do more work. Unc made the most of every minute that he had us.

Shoulder to broad shoulder, we were squished together on the lid of the toolbox with our legs dangling in the bed of the truck. The wind whipped around our heads as we bounced and swayed along the country road with the summer sun baking the backs of our necks—blissful, except when we would encounter the occasional June bug at forty-five miles per hour, hitting the backs of our heads like a tiny baseball.

"Ouch! That's gonna leave a mark! You wanna know the first thing that came to that June bug's mind when he hit me? His butt!" I would say as I cackled like a laughing hyena. I have been told that my laugh is also loud, vociferous, and contagious. Once I get started, it's hard to stop until the tears get rolling.

When I got tired of yapping, I relaxed and listened on my gigantic Walkman to one of my all-time favorite rock bands, an Australian group called Models. I still remember the lyrics perfectly:

Hey, hey, honey, when I'm without you,
I get a chill up and down my spine. . . .

A quintessential summer tune to fit the mood. There we were, three buddies enjoying our final summer together. We were getting a sweet tan, building our muscles, having great banter, and loving the pride that came from earning a little money by the sweat of our own brows. We were headed to different colleges soon, and deep down we knew things would never be the same after that. This stage of our lives was ending, but for now, there was nothing better than being on the back of that truck after a solid day's work out in the blazing sun, feeling the good kind of tired and the good kind of dirty. We smelled like manual labor, freshly cut grass, and the gasoline and oil of the mowers.

Being red-blooded teenage boys, our conversations ranged from verbal insults that were really terms of endearment to reminding one another of the many foolish and embarrassing decisions we had made to, inevitably, our favorite subject: girls.

These serious topics—well, they were serious to us teenage boys—were interrupted only by the more analytical and thought-provoking discussions of what might be the proper trajectory to give us the greatest opportunity to hit the most road signs using the fewest number of bottles.

Meanwhile, up in the cab of the truck, Unc would be seated with a toothpick in his mouth and one arm hanging over the ledge of the passenger-side window. That was the way Unc always rode. Either he was hard of hearing or he had decided there were bigger issues that he could address, but he never said anything to us about the bottles.

It's not that we ever consciously thought about how dangerous it was or that we were destroying government property or the consequences if we were caught—we were just being boys, keeping ourselves entertained. Boys are immortal and bulletproof, right?

That July day, an eighteen-wheeler had been following us for at least ten miles at a safe distance, but then it started to creep up closer behind us. If we noticed it at all, we didn't think much of it at the time.

"Hey, Scott, let me listen to your Walkman," Guy said, leaning across Mike to reach for it.

"Gumby," I said back. That was Guy's nickname, from Eddie Murphy's character on *Saturday Night Live*. "I just got this new tape. I want to listen to it first."

"Fine." He turned his back to me, tossing his legs over the side of the truck with his feet dangling toward the edge of the road as if he would leap off at any second. It was a very dangerous way to ride and certainly the easiest way to get knocked off, but like me, Guy was fearless.

And I, I feel so hot, and the pain won't stop
Tearing at this heart of mine. . . .

My mind wandered to the driver of the eighteen-wheeler behind us. I wondered what it would be like to have a career like that. Growing up in the late seventies and early eighties, I'd watched a show called *B. J. and the Bear*. It was about B. J. McKay, a trucker who traveled in a red and white Kenworth K100 cabover semi with his pet chimpanzee, Bear—named for the famed college football coach Paul "Bear" Bryant. They were always getting in trouble with the local sheriffs as well as uncovering corruption. It seemed like a very exciting job—and apparently one filled with flirtatious, buxom, blonde, lady truckers.

Here I was, about to start my journey into figuring out what to do with my life, and this guy had already made his decision. Why truck driving? I wondered if it was a good job and as adventure-filled as it seemed on television. I wondered if he had kids at home and a wife cooking him a fancy dinner.

In just another two months, I was going to begin reinventing myself. At college, you get to wipe out your entire academic and social past and get a "do over." I wished I had listened to my mom and applied myself better in school—I regretted that I hadn't followed Mike's example and made better grades. Mike was the salutatorian of our graduating class and voted most likely to succeed. Guy was a good student also.

With a chance at redemption, maybe I would turn into a real intellectual in college. Not likely, but anything was possible. And maybe I'd get out of my dating rut, too. I was really fortunate to go to a high school where there were lots of beautiful girls. Rival high schools loved to play us because we had the prettiest cheerleaders and girls in the stands. But I was too shy and insecure to ask them out, so many times I settled for playing it safe and staying in the "friend zone."

I grew up on films like *Making the Grade*, *Weird Science*, *Sixteen Candles*, *The Breakfast Club*, and *St. Elmo's Fire*. I dreamed of being the good guy in the movie who got the pretty girl at the end. In college, I hoped, I would find the courage to be proud of who I was and what I had to offer. Plus, college girls all had shiny hair and short skirts and slim waists. At least that's what I'd heard. I'd find out for myself soon enough.

Relationships were on my mind because I had just broken up with my girlfriend, one of the few really pretty girls I had ever worked up the nerve to ask out. She was six feet tall, with long brown hair, and had won a modeling contest earlier in the summer. Instead of being proud of her success, I was sad and jealous and afraid she would leave me. Two weeks earlier, we'd gotten into a fight and called it off. That was okay, though, because there was another girl I had set my sights on. I was going to call her when we got to Guy's house.

Well, come a little bit closer now;
I've got something to say to you. . . .

My girlfriend and I had had a tumultuous high school relationship filled with insecurity, jealousy, and immaturity. I spent most of my time worrying about how I could get her to like me more and fearful that she would one day leave me. I hated dating and the fear that was brought on by it. I would rather play it safe and go out with friends.

Serious dating was rare in high school unless you were "going with someone" or "hanging out." Mostly, my friends and I just drove around town, meeting in parking lots to talk to girls from other schools and trying to buy beer with other high school kids who were also driving around with no particular destination.

Now that I think of it, it was kind of a pre-mating ritual for us guys. Like bantam roosters strutting their stuff to see who could attract the most attention, we would show up in our nicest clothes, best-combed hair, and—yes—even jewelry to impress the young ladies. We'd make a big deal out of finding these pretty girls and trying to impress them. Most of the time, we'd egg each other on to go ask out one of these elusive creatures, and then we'd take turns chickening out.

Unless you've traveled extensively, when you live in a small town you get a sense that the world is very tiny and that you're a big deal if you have more than the next guy has. The reality was that the rich kids' parents had either inherited their money, worked very hard for their wealth, or they were up to their eyeballs in debt.

On the football team, guys would sometimes wear shirts underneath their pads, and the rich kids would show off by wearing Polo or Flying Scotsman shirts—their way of saying, "I'm going to trash this really expensive shirt because I have so much money it doesn't matter."

The guy who most incited my jealousy had that kind of money. He was a doctor's son and our rival high school's starting quarterback. Even his name sounded cooler than mine: Mattison Dunaway. When I saw my ex-girlfriend in his car, it made me even more enraged. I thought, "I'll show her!" Later that week, I called Mattison and told him he could have her—I wanted nothing to do with her. *See how cool I can be?* I thought.

I had liked the fact that my girlfriend was so tall that I had to look up to kiss her. I would probably miss that. And she had a really nice complexion. The more I thought about it, the more I thought that breaking up was kind of a bummer.

Out of mind out of sight—
Gotta keep my body tight. . . .

As the music blared in my ears, I noticed something that bothered me. The eighteen-wheeler behind us was getting closer and closer, its speed increasing as if the driver had floored the accelerator. He got so close, I thought he was going to run into the back of us, but at the last moment, he shifted his massive vehicle into the oncoming lane of the two-lane country road. That wouldn't have been so scary except that we had just passed the break of a curve with plenty of signs indicating that this was a no-passing zone, and when I glanced over my shoulder at the road ahead of us, I saw that we were approaching a spot where the roadway narrowed between two guardrails as it passed over a little creek.

Surely he doesn't mean to pass us now, does he?

Maybe he thought we were going too slow, or maybe he hadn't liked our earlier bottle throwing, but it became clear that he did indeed intend to pass us. I grabbed on to the rusty old toolbox under me, thinking that he was a little too close for comfort.

As we closed in on the narrow bridge ahead, I looked at the trucker in his side window and then glanced at his cargo. He was pulling a load of phosphorus, probably for fertilizer. My stomach tightened with the hunch that he wasn't going fast enough to get past us in time.

At that very moment, he seemed to realize that both vehicles weren't going to fit on the bridge. He would have to move his truck closer to the double yellow line in the middle of the road. When he did, a perfect storm ensued. His right front cargo jack was even with our trailer's left front tire. When the truck driver moved closer to our vehicle, his cargo jack punctured our trailer tire, causing it to blow out, careening our three-ton trailer into the guardrail with full force.

*Hold on!*

We all rocketed off the toolbox and into the air. My body flew over the side of the truck, and I grabbed on for dear life. *Hold it, hold it. . . . You can do it.*

As I struggled to pull myself back into the truck, I thought, *All those hours of lifting weights, all that time getting stronger—where's my superhuman strength?* I fought with everything I had in me.

*I can do this. . . . I have to do this. . . .*

But I couldn't. We were going too fast and my legs were being dragged on the road. I lost my grip.

My buddy Mike grabbed Guy around the neck and kept him from falling off the other side and being crushed between the side of our truck and the guardrail. He then frantically reached out for me, but I was gone.

As I dropped off the side of the truck, my body was flung backward into the narrow corridor between the pickup and the eighteen-wheeler, but my right leg did not clear the trailer. Instead, it became stuck in a brace that was attached between the two trailer wheels. Once my leg was caught, my body smashed against the pavement and I was dragged along the hot Georgia asphalt farther than the length of a football field. Each contact with the road tore more flesh off my back.

The fact that I lived through the accident doesn't make any sense at all. My head should have been split open ten times over. As it was, I must have struck my head on the pavement at least once, because later at the hospital, I had a bald spot and a gash on the back of my head. The doctors diagnosed a concussion, but that would prove to be the least of their worries.

Brooks Mulliford, who was driving the truck behind the truck that hit us, later told me that I was reaching for the huge ropes that were securing the large lawn mowers. "It seemed like something—or someone—was holding your head up off the pavement, keeping you alive," he said.

I'd love to tell you I had all sorts of profound thoughts during what should have been my last moments on earth, but in those nine seconds, all I could think was, *What's going on? How did I get here? Where am I? Help!*

Mike frantically beat on the pickup's back window to tell Tommy to stop. By the time he did, my leg was pinned underneath the trailer and I was unconscious. My friends thought I was dead. Their fear must have been almost unbearable, but when it happened they didn't hesitate in the face of such a shock. Mike ran to me and Guy went to go find help. Then, to everyone's great relief, I opened my eyes. The first thing I remember seeing was Mike's face, looking ghost-white. I hadn't yet made sense of what had happened, but I knew my body felt wrong.

*Hey! Who hit me? What was his jersey number?*

While playing high school football, I always tried to hit people as hard as I possibly could. For the most part, I hit people within the sound of the whistle, but there were a few occasions—okay, several occasions—when I hit an opponent rather late. I soon learned, however, that what the Bible says is true: "You will reap what you sow." So, yes, I got hit plenty of times in return and was almost knocked out a few times as well. Another truth I learned is that you often reap *much* later than you sow, and *more* than you sow.

During those brutal hits on the football field, you're stunned and your head feels numb. You hear a ringing, and it's not the angel Gabriel playing his harp. There's a funny little expression to describe this feeling: They say you got your "bell rung." Well, that's how I felt at first out there on the road, like I had my bell rung.

Whenever I felt that way in a football game, I'd spend the rest of the game trying to get back at the guy who had tackled me—which was exactly what I wanted to do now; I wanted to know who had caused the accident so I could go tackle him. I tried to get up and look for the guy, but my head was lying in Mike's lap.

*What happened? Why is he looking at me that way? Why is he sweating so much?*

Through the ringing, I heard Mike say, "We've been in an accident, and help is on the way." He's sensible that way. He pushed me back down gently and told me to lie still. The guys took their shirts off and put them under me on the pavement and tried to keep me cool.

One time, when I was playing Little League baseball, I got nailed in the nose by a fastball from James Jackson. James had a cannon for an arm and would later become the starting quarterback for the University of Georgia Bulldogs. When he hit me, blood went everywhere and I had tons of people looking after me. That time, someone found me some ice and I was fine after a few hours, but this felt different. This was my best friend looking down at me, and he looked scared. Why did he look so scared? I wondered if someone was going to get me an ice bag.

*Am I hurt?*

Mostly what I remember was feeling hotter than I ever had

in my life. I was lying on asphalt that had been cooking in the Georgia heat all day, and my body was one giant open wound. It felt as if my entire body were on fire, and I was as dirty as if I'd been in a dust storm. The humidity didn't help as the dirt and sweat clung to me in a sweltering blanket.

As I faded in and out of consciousness, I heard the chirpy, nervous voices of everyone debating what to do. If they took the lawn mowers off the trailer one by one, I'd bleed to death. Even if they could get a helicopter to rush me to a hospital, it would be useless unless it had a crane to pull the trailer off me. What we really needed was a large vehicle to lift the weight off me—something like a tow truck. But for all they knew, the nearest tow truck could be in the next county.

Still, despite the severity of my injuries, many things were happening in my favor. The rim of our flatbed trailer's wheel was pinning my right leg to the ground, and its weight was acting as a tourniquet. Brooks Mulliford had had some paramedic training, so he was helping and telling the boys what to do. We were in a very rural part of southwest Georgia, where it could have been miles to the nearest phone, but we ended up between two houses and someone was home when Guy knocked on the door to use the phone. In this era before cell phones, we needed a landline to call an ambulance. Also, the nearest hospital could have been almost an hour away—but we happened to be within twelve miles. When you're bleeding to death, every minute counts. The one thing I still needed to save my life was a tow truck to pull the trailer off me.

And then a tow truck showed up.

Let me tell you, tow trucks don't just appear out of nowhere in Moultrie, Georgia. And here's the crazier part: The guy pulled up, said, "Do you need help?" and after he pulled the trailer off me, he drove away. To this day, I have no idea who he was. I've met the EMTs, nurses, doctors, and everyone else associated with my accident, but no one was ever able to track down the tow truck driver. He didn't show up to take credit even when the newspapers turned their attention to my accident that week.

Who was he? What was he doing there? Where did he go? He was like Michael Landon in my personal *Highway to Heaven* experience.

After calling for an ambulance, my friends called my mom. How do you break this kind of news to someone's mom? They didn't, exactly.

All they said was, "Mrs. Ruth, there's been an accident, and we think Scott's leg is broken. We're going to take him to the hospital in Moultrie." So my mom took a book and some stationery with her—she figured it might be a long evening if the doctor had to put a cast on my leg.

The coincidence is that when I was a sophomore in high school and playing spring football, I went out for a pass and Mike tackled me. When I jumped up, I realized my thumb was broken—the only time I'd ever broken a bone. My mom got the call, and off we went to the doctor for a cast. So, when my friends told her that my leg was broken, she was thinking about that experience. She had no idea what she was really in for.

When the EMTs arrived and examined me, they told my friends to go look for my heel bone on the road. What does a heel bone look like, anyway? And how would you recognize it amid all the trash and torn-up clothes strewn along the way? It was important to find that piece of bone because I wouldn't have a foot without it—nothing like putting people under pressure! They never did find it.

I don't remember being put into the ambulance or the ride to the hospital. Maybe they gave me pain medicine to endure it.

When my mom got to the hospital, the doctor made her lie down on a hospital bed, and he put up the side rails before he would speak to her of my condition. Then he told her the truth, in harsh terms: "Your son has been hurt from one end of his body to the other." He told her that I had already lost a leg, I had lost a lot of blood, and they didn't know yet what kind of internal injuries I had. They weren't even sure if I was going to live or die.

My mom called my dad, told him what had happened, and said to be sure to have someone drive him over. He called my cousin, Dean Daniels, but didn't explain anything to Dean. He just said, "I need you to drive me to Moultrie."

Dean was thinking, *He's a grown man. Why does he need me to drive him?* but he went to pick him up anyway. During the car ride, my dad told Dean that I'd been in a serious accident and that I might not make it. It was a very quiet ride the rest of the way.

My first memory in the hospital is seeing Dean's face, even before I saw my parents.

"Man, I really messed up, didn't I?" I said to him. "How bad is it?"

"It's bad," he admitted, "but you're going to make it, Scott. You're going to make it."

He later told me that he didn't believe what he was saying. I was sedated at that point and feeling no pain so I had no idea my life was in jeopardy, but it was painfully clear to everyone else. No one knew the extent of my internal injuries, and it was anyone's guess as to whether any of my major organs had been damaged.

"If you're going to do something, do it right," I said to Dean. "I did a darn good job, didn't I?"

"You sure did."

When my mom came to see me, two nurses escorted her, one on each side, in case she fainted. She did not want to see my legs or my back and is still very glad that she never saw that gruesome sight.

Taking X-rays proved to be a challenge because pebbles

and gravel and dirt were actually falling out of my back and clanking on the glass of the X-ray machine. I could hear the *tink-tink-tink* as they rained down. Cleaning out the embedded debris from my body was excruciating, and it took several tries. (My entire back looked as if someone had taken a cheese grater to it and sliced off the first couple layers of skin.)

Following that, I lost consciousness again. The next thing I remember is waking up in a very white room and having no idea where I was.

I heard a man nearby say, "We're going to have to amputate his right leg. We should amputate both of them; it would be better."

*Was that guy talking about me? Did he say that he was going to remove my legs? I have only one scar on my body. I'm a weight lifter! I'm a runner! You leave my legs alone!*

I said it in my head before I could say it out loud. My brain felt like it was floating in Jell-O, and I struggled to regain enough wakeful strength to argue. I was unaware that the bottom half of my right leg was already effectively gone. From the middle of the shin on down, it was just barely hanging on, and there was no way to save it.

"Wait a minute! Wait a minute!" I yelled. "Who said that?"

I sat up in bed, a feat my mom says should have been impossible. One leg was shredded, and my other thighbone was broken, but I summoned all my energy to find out what in the world was going on.

The doctor appeared and placed my X-rays on a lighted board behind him. Next to him, my father was holding my mother and they were both looking at me.

"Son, there's no getting around it," the doctor said.

"What do you mean? You're going to take off both my legs?"

"We may have to, to save your life."

*You can't take my legs!* I thought. *I am not a guy with no legs. That's not who I am.* I was the picture of fitness and health—a football player who spent his summers voluntarily pushing manual mowers all day rather than using the ride-on ones. Then I would go to the gym and work out with weights before I ran several miles.

What the doctors had told my parents was that there was zero percent chance of saving my right leg, and only a 20–30 percent chance of saving the left one. My parents thought it would be too devastating for me to lose both legs.

"If there is a chance of saving one, I want to try," my dad told the doctors, despite their recommendations to amputate both legs. And with that, a surgeon carted me away to sever my right leg about five inches below the knee, only a couple of hours after I had been running around with my friends.

My dad had to sign the paperwork for the surgery. I can't even imagine what a difficult decision that was for him. My mom supported his decision, but that's really a choice no parent wants to make.

Sometimes, something happens in life that's just so big that everything leading up to it is "Before" and everything that follows is "After." The accident was mine. The next time my friends would see me in the hospital, half my leg would be gone. Nothing was ever going to be normal again.

# CHAPTER 2

The hospital had given my parents a private room as their personal waiting area. My sister Emily remembers my father crying in her arms when she arrived—the first and last time she ever saw him cry. No one knew if I was even going to come out of surgery alive, and if so, what kind of shape I'd be in for the rest of my life. Here I was, the baby of the family, and maybe now I'd always be a "baby." Maybe I wouldn't be able to walk, or drive, or even bathe myself.

The fact that I was unconscious much of the time from my head injury and the pain medication postponed those worries for me until after the initial shock wore off. At the time, my family and friends bore the brunt of the worrying. They say the mood was very somber in the hospital that day, with many people feeling guilty for not having been able to prevent the accident. Mike, especially, felt guilty because he had reached out to grab Guy first, instead of me.

As the anesthesia wore off, I hoped what I'd heard last had been only a dream. It took all the nerve I had to check my leg. It really was gone. A part of my body was simply not there anymore. And it was that doctor's fault!

The next time I saw his face, I recognized him—the horrible man who had ruined my life. Maybe I ought to get up and tackle him.

"You're the doctor who cut off my right leg," I said.

"No, you did that in the wreck," he said. "I just sort of finished up the edges."

Once I was considered stable, I was transferred to Emory Crawford Long Hospital in Atlanta, where there were two specialists who would try to reconstruct my left leg and build me a new foot. One of the doctors, Dr. George Cierny, was among the few orthopedic surgeons in the world who specialized in the evaluation and treatment of orthopedic infections. He was in charge of mending my broken femur, making me a new heel bone, and treating any complications. His bedside manner left room for improvement—he was tough and straightforward—but his expertise was top-notch.

The other specialist, Dr. Foad Nahai, is internationally recognized as an innovator in the field of plastic surgery. He has developed and refined many procedures. Dr. Nahai was in charge of the skin and muscle grafts needed to close my wounds and attach the soft tissue back to my foot. He would go on to coauthor seven books and publish more than 135 scientific articles on all aspects of plastic surgery. Considering my circumstances, I was in the most capable hands possible.

The first time the doctors came in to meet me, I yelled as they exited the room, "Rambo ain't got nothing on me! Rambo ain't got nothing on me!" I'm sure my friends were taken aback by my outburst. Maybe it was the fighter in me that was desperately holding on to the dying dream of a perfect body.

Over time, with bone fragments painstakingly chiseled from my back, sections of top-layer skin taken from my thighs, and part of the right latissimus dorsi muscle from my lower back, the doctors surgically reconstructed my foot and ankle. With each procedure, pieces of my spirit were left behind on the operating table.

My entire self-image was wrapped up in my body. After a bully at school had beaten me up in the fifth grade, I made it my mission to get bigger so no one could intimidate me again. I counted on my body to be the equalizer, to make me feel as if I measured up to the other guys. I was blinded by the illusion that all around me were kids who drove BMWs and had fancier clothes and houses than I did. That really wasn't true, but it was a persistent lie that must have been planted and nurtured somewhere in the shaping of my self-worth.

I placed a lot of significance on what other people thought about me, and my work seemed to pay off when girls commented on my body. I'd think, *I'd better keep working at this so I don't lose it*. Those compliments meant so much to me—they meant I was someone worthwhile. Of all the parts of my body, my legs were my pride and joy. I thought back to the pretty girls who had told me I had nice legs.

Now who was I?

My first instinct was to deny what was happening. *This isn't real,* I thought. *My legs are going to be fine. The doctors are wrong. They don't understand I'm invincible.* Then I decided, *Okay, they weren't lying. My right leg really is missing, but it will grow back. Starfish can regenerate their limbs, so why can't I?*

But deep down, I knew this was forever, and forever no longer looked very appealing to me. Nothing about my life was going to be the way I had planned it. I had no faith in myself, no confidence beyond my athletic ability—and even that wasn't exactly great. I was like the guy in the movie *Rudy*: short on talent, long on heart. My goal had been to ask the football coach at Valdosta to let me join the practice squad and be a live tackling dummy. *Who knows? Maybe I could get good enough to make the team someday and at the very least play one down.* But now I wouldn't ever get that chance. My friends were going on to college, and I was going to sit in a hospital room trying to stay alive.

Everything in the first few weeks after the accident is a haze, probably due to the combination of a concussion, pain medication, and the endorphins that kicked in when my body went into shock after the trauma. I remember waking up one time and thinking I was in a mobile trailer home. I remember the surrealism of seeing my entire body covered in Silverdine, a white ointment that helps burns to heal.

At one point, I realized with dread that my shoes were missing. My favorite sneakers, which I was wearing at the time of the accident.

"Hey, what happened to my sneakers?" I asked.

Someone told me that one of them was dragged off and the other had to be cut off.

My checkerboard Vans. Gone. I'd probably never find another pair.

Friends came to visit and sent so many flowers that my room looked like a florist shop. My mom was moved by that, seeing how many kids came to see me every day.

I remember a sea of faces, but I'm not sure who was there. My old girlfriend came by several times; even though we had broken up and I had already taken a friend of hers out on a date, we got back together while I was recovering.

My siblings, in-laws, and cousins took turns keeping vigil at the hospital, along with my parents. My older brother Tim is mentally and physically disabled and doesn't walk or talk, so someone always had to be home with him. My cousin Deanie took that role, without even needing to be asked. For weeks, she watched Tim by herself. My sister Emily made up a visitation and task schedule for my other cousins and sisters. They tried hard to keep the pressure off my parents so they could be by my side as much as possible.

I didn't go to the bathroom for a few days after the accident, as far as I know. Then I woke up in the middle of the night needing to go, and it was a whole new challenge. I had never been in a situation where I couldn't get up freely and go relieve myself when I needed to, but now here I was, with one leg amputated and the residual limb in a pressure bandage, the other leg and ankle in a halo device, and tubes up my nose and all over my body. No one had told me I would have to use a bedpan, and I panicked.

My mother was next to me, and I desperately told her, "Get the nurse. Get the nurse!"

But the nurse didn't make it in time, and I defecated all over the bed. Lying there in my own filth, I had never felt so utterly and completely helpless. Eighteen years old, and my mother and a nurse had to wipe my bottom and wash me up and change the sheets. With open wounds all over my body, some spots worn all the way to the bone, the last thing I needed was excrement getting anywhere near the wounds.

Of course, the nurse was used to this—probably half her patients had accidents in their beds—but it was mortifying to me. I felt terrible that I had made this woman have to do something so foul. I started to cry, and just wept and wept until I dry heaved.

My mom said, "It's okay. You didn't mean to do it. We'll work on it for next time."

But this was the moment of truth for me. It all came crashing down that the Scott Rigsby I had always been was gone. This new guy couldn't even go to the bathroom on his own. I didn't want to be this guy. How could God have let this happen to me? *I even went to church for you on days when I could have been playing sports. I have tried to be a good person, and you let this happen to me! How could you let this happen? Aren't you supposed to be in control? What, were you asleep while this was happening? You let the only thing that I was proud of get taken away from me! And this is your will for me? You turn me into a useless amputee?*

The nurses changed my bandages twice a day. Because the skin was so delicate and they wanted to avoid further damage, they'd take half an hour just inching the bandages off my back and bottom. Then they'd pour on hydrogen peroxide and put on new bandages. The whole time they were working, I had to hold myself up on a triangle apparatus over my head while keeping my left leg immobile in the halo device.

Twice a day, my screams would clear out the third floor waiting room. It was so upsetting to listen to that everyone would go to a different floor's waiting room until I was finished. At the end of each session, I would pass out from exhaustion.

A hospital is no place to rest, though. It felt as if every five minutes someone was checking my temperature, testing my blood, putting on more antibiotic cream, or checking my blood pressure. I got a shot in my arm every night so I wouldn't develop blood clots. A nasty nurse would wake me every night to ask if my bowels had moved. I considered screaming into her stethoscope. It seemed so backward to mess with a person so much when they're trying to heal. Can't a guy get some sleep?

The pain was agonizing and constant. Medications went into my body through a catheter so they'd work faster, and I had a morphine line that my parents controlled. Whenever the pain became unbearable—which was just about all the time—they'd push a button, and the machine would deliver more morphine straight into my veins. It didn't take long for me to get addicted. My parents pushed the button for me every twenty minutes like clockwork.

Then the doctors switched me to Percocet, which was such a step down from morphine that it felt like baby aspirin to me. My life in those first few weeks was all about pain management. I think I watched some television; I might have read some books; but really, my brain was consumed with getting through each day, waiting for a day when the pain would subside.

The guys who had been in the truck with me were also consumed with my pain. Mike and Guy had gone back to work the day after my accident, but both burst into tears shortly after they got there and agreed that they couldn't finish out the day. They came to see me in the hospital instead, which was awful. My screaming echoed in their consciences, a loud reminder that they hadn't been able to save me.

*It's not your fault.* I hope I told them, but I may have just thought it.

My accident changed so many people's lives. Because my parents were with me in Atlanta all the time, my brother Jim quit his job and moved back home to take care of the farm. Although the hospital staff was very good about letting my parents stay beyond visiting hours, and sometimes overnight, they couldn't live at the hospital. So my father's cousin and her husband invited them to stay in their home in Atlanta every night. They got a chance to recoup for a little bit, but then they came back to me every day.

In the first six weeks, I think I had eight surgeries. Many were to deal with problems from previous surgeries or to prepare for future surgeries. My left thighbone (femur) was broken, and the bone nearly stuck out of the skin. The pressure of the bone pushing against my skin created a cavity that filled with infected fluid. As the fluid increased, so did the size of my leg. As my leg swelled, the infection started to spread. The doctors needed to put a rod in my leg, but they couldn't do that while I had a serious bone infection. To combat it, they cut open the side of my thigh to release the pressure, drain the fluid, and put in antibiotic beads. Then came another surgery to take the beads out before the doctors could cut my leg open again to put the rod in.

What no one realized at the time was that my quest for big muscles almost killed me. I had worked so hard to get bigger, to bulk up and look muscular. When it seemed that I had maxed out what I could accomplish by lifting weights, I had secretly begun taking anabolic steroids. For a few months, I had ordered them by mail. Building a great body seemed to be the one thing I could do right, so I had taken it to extremes. Narcissism got the best of me, and before long, I was taking pills and injecting steroids every day.

"Mom, come check out my muscles!" I had said one day.

She was sitting on the couch at the time and said, "Oh, come on, I can see you from here. Don't make me get up."

"I want you to measure them."

"You *what* now?"

"With a tape measure. Come here, measure my biceps for me."

Even though she thought I was being silly, she got up from the couch and measured my arms. I was so proud of my progress. I remember thinking, *I bet I have bigger muscles than my cousin now.*

I hadn't told anyone I was taking steroids except for one of my close friends who was a gym rat and a steroid user also. But just before the accident, my mom had opened a package that arrived in the mail for me. She sent the steroids back to the company with a letter warning them never to ship to our address again. Little did she know that I was also buying them locally and had been taking them since the start of the summer.

In fact, the day of my accident, I had a bottle of steroids in the glove compartment of my car. For some reason, my mom never found them. My brother Jim must have discovered them and thrown them out, wanting to save my parents any further heartache.

I knew guys at my school who had taken steroids, and

they were excellent athletes. Nothing bad ever happened to them. Although I didn't see how it could be relevant, when I was asked about it, I admitted to the doctor that I had been taking them.

"Well, that makes sense. That's why nothing we're giving you is working," Dr. Cierny said. "The steroids make it harder for you to fight infection, and your body is rejecting the donor bone."

Shame pierced through me. I wished the doctor would keep it our secret, but he was right to tell my parents.

I was confined to a bed made for burn patients. It was like a waterbed except filled with circulating air and sand to prevent pressure sores. I couldn't wear clothing, so they had me in a makeshift, Tarzan-style loincloth. Once, when the mother of one of my friends came to visit me, I said, "Look, they have me strapped down here." I wanted to show her my catheter, and my mind was so mixed up from the drugs that I whipped off the covers and actually exposed myself to her. I'm lucky that she made light of the moment, because . . . seriously, I flashed my friend's mother!

That was only slightly less embarrassing than the fact that my sisters—who each gave up a week's vacation at their jobs to take turns staying with me in the hospital—were now wiping my butt. One of my main goals was never to poop on myself again. *Think ahead,* I told myself. *Remember to call for a nurse to transfer you over to the bedpan before you really have to go*. It's sad that this was such an important goal. Only a month before, I had been thinking about what my college major was going to be, and now all I cared about was getting a bedpan in time.

When I was well enough to sit up, I began going to the physical therapy room and sitting in a whirlpool to soak my wounds. It was torture. Mike McClain and my childhood friends Bryant Rykard and Wey Rooks came to visit me in physical therapy. I had just finished my whirlpool treatment, and I wasn't sure which of us was more traumatized. It was the first time they had seen my amputated right leg with its seam of metal staples closing the end and my left ankle looking like a huge mound of sutured flesh on a barely recognizable foot.

Slowly, I made the transition from being bedridden to gaining some mobility in a wheelchair. My healing was the result of care from excellent nurses such as Kelly Chastain and an out-of-this-world therapist named Denise. She was mean as the devil and stubborn as any mule. I remember weeping and screaming so hard that, when I looked up, the other therapists had wheeled their patients out of the room and there were only the two of us left.

"Okay, Sunshine, you are going to finish your exercises," she would say. There were days I plotted her death, but if not for her tough love, I would not have the mobility I do today. I will always remember her investment in me.

Dr. Cierny told me the truth about what he saw for my future: He didn't think I'd ever run again. He thought I might walk okay, but he didn't try to pretend that I was going to have a normal, limitless life. Sometimes I don't know why doctors feel the need to do that; even false hope is some form of hope. I wanted to believe that all this pain was going to be a memory one day and that I would go back to being what I had been.

All the while, mail poured in at unprecedented rates. The staff kept telling us that they thought I was setting a record: No patient had ever received that much mail at the hospital before. My mom remembers that my dad was about as excited over the mail as I was. He wanted to open it all for me.

"I'll just take a knife and open it, and you can read it," he would say.

The irony of this phenomenon was that my dad had often ridiculed me for having so many friends. He was the opposite of gregarious. I, on the other hand, tried to be the Dale

Carnegie or Will Rogers of southern Georgia—as long as it wasn't on the playing field.

One of the cards came from the son of the truck driver who had caused the accident. Inside the card was a twenty-dollar bill. I think it was all he had. Maybe he was my age or younger and felt bad about what had happened. I don't know. People never really know how to react in these types of situations. They just do the best they can.

Along with the cards, there were flowers and balloons, cakes and candy, stuffed animals and posters, and lots of visits from pretty girls. If you ever want to get a lot of presents and visitors, losing your leg is apparently a good way to do it. My friend Jamie Williams came to visit me with her roommate from Georgia Tech. Jamie later said I could not stop babbling about her cute roommate. (Some things never change, no matter how difficult the circumstances.)

It did lift my spirits to see that my friends and people who didn't know me but knew my parents were thinking about me so much, and I tried hard to keep a smile on my face for them when they were allowed to visit. They tell me that I seemed like the same old Scott, that they thought my spirits were as good as ever. My friend Susan Warren said that if the accident had to happen to someone in our class, she was kind of glad it had happened to me because I was the one who could handle it. She was sure that my sense of humor and tough will would get me through this, and I tried to show her and everyone else that they were right.

Sometimes, the smiles and laughter were genuine, and other times I was really feeling sorry for myself and felt hopeless. Each day, it became clearer to me that this was real—my leg wasn't coming back. These terrible scars were not going away, and I would have to live with this grotesque man-made left foot. I wasn't going to "get better" in this hospital and go home "fixed." And it seemed as if my foreseeable future was going to be filled with pain, illness, and surgeries. To me, being an amputee meant leading a very limited and probably depressing life . . . and this was only the beginning.

There was one other amputee at my hospital, an African-American who had lost both his legs after a spinal injury. His name was Arnold. Among my fellow patients, he was my best friend. He would roll around the hospital like a speed racer. He had been in the hospital long-term and did his very best to keep my spirits up. Whenever I had to have an operation, he would wheel himself to my room to say, "You can do this. If I can get through this, so can you. You're going to do great."

I think he looked on me as his personal responsibility. It's good he did, too, because I had never known an amputee before. At least this gave me someone to talk with and relate to. I once told him that when I got legs, I would carry him around. He was such a great friend.

Then Arnold got tired of all the rules at the hospital and moved to an apartment across the street, even though the nurses tried to convince him he would have better care if he stayed put. But hospitals can make you crazy—it's hard to be without any privacy or personal space for a long period of time. I was feeling it too.

Finally, the doctors decided it was time to send me home to continue my recovery. Someone had announced over the loudspeaker at my school's football game that I was scheduled to come home the next day, and as we turned the corner to my house, we saw that the yard was lined on both sides with cars—all my friends were there to welcome me back. I should have been excited to see everyone, but I was terrified of their reaction.

*Oh man, I really don't want everyone to see me looking this bad. I look horrible. What will they think?*

No one cared what I looked like. People were simply happy to see me and see me alive. Friends, family, and townspeople were so kind to me. Small towns like Camilla get ridiculed at times for their size, way of life, and beliefs, but these people stood by me in the good times and the bad. They had put a hospital bed in the dining room and food on the table, and a nurse stood guard to do the things my mother felt incapable of doing.

Mike and another friend connected their arms into a cradle and carried me into the house. I had lost a lot of weight by that point, so I wasn't as heavy as I had been. Hospital food can do that to you.

"You feel like a sack of potatoes," Mike said.

My friends optimistically threw me a homecoming party, and the people at my school took up a collection to buy me a VCR. I don't know how much VCRs cost in 1986, but they were expensive because they were still newfangled technology. Thank goodness I had one, though, because I was soon back to my old bed in the hospital.

On day four of my return home, I spiked a fever, so my dad took me to the doctor. He confirmed an infection and said I needed to go back to Emory Crawford Long Hospital.

"We've got to go to Atlanta," Dad told my mom.

"Right now?" she asked. She was in the middle of shelling butter beans at the time, making supper and washing the laundry. It really upset her routine to drop what she was doing and leave it unfinished like that, so from then on, every time she walked in the door, she made sure to get the laundry done first. "I didn't want him to ever catch me like that again," she explained.

We got into my dad's truck and headed back to Atlanta. Along the way, a truck with a semitrailer went around us. It sent me into a panic attack, giving me visions of the accident and how I had been dragged down the road with my leg hanging off. My whole body shook, and I felt like I couldn't breathe.

"Get away from that truck!" I yelled, tears streaming down my face. I put my hands over my head and cried hard.

"Now, Son, there's nothing I can do about it," my dad said. "And we've got two hundred miles to go. You're going to have to calm down now. I can't drive like this."

My mom gave me a Valium from her purse to get me through the rest of the trip, and soon we were back on the second floor at Crawford Long, back to the nurses and doctors who had become a second family to my parents and me. They pumped me up with antibiotics and set up my new VCR. I had nothing better to do than to watch every video that came down the pike that year. Good or bad, I watched them all. I long for the day when I can get on *Jeopardy* and be quizzed on 1980s movie trivia. I cannot be defeated.

Over the next several months, I was able to go home from time to time, but never for long. On one of those trips home, in December, I went to a high school basketball game with my girlfriend. She told me, "This isn't going to work out."

Now, that relationship was never supposed to be anything more than a teenage romance anyway, but her words crushed me. My greatest fear had come to pass: I was no longer lovable.

The reality was that our little romance had simply run its course. It was ending, the same way relationships end every day. At that point in my life, though, she was my connection to my former self, my whole self. The accident had made everything much more intense, and I had been leaning on her for support. People get their hearts broken, and it's always lousy when that happens, but I was already on the edge between life and death. I had enough to deal with just trying to get through the pain and fight off the infections. A heartbreak on top of it was too much to handle.

I tried to be strong and support her decision. "Well, good luck with whatever you do in life. I wish you all the best," I said with all the calmness I could fake.

*Who's ever going to love me again?* I thought.

I couldn't see anything beyond my broken-down body. No one knew if I would walk again or be stuck in a wheelchair permanently. And I was pretty sure that no woman was ever going to want a guy like me—missing one leg and the other one deformed.

*That was probably the last woman who will ever love me,* I thought. *I'm not brilliant, I'm not wealthy, I'm not model good-looking, and now I'm not even physically whole. My life really is over.*

Whenever I'd had troubles in the past, I'd gone running as a way to deal with things, to take my mind off my problems and work them out. Now I was lost. I longed for some kind of normalcy. Once, in the middle of the night, I sat on the edge of my bed and pretended to run. I pumped my arms hard up and down and moved as if I were running in place. My cousin Bruce was spending the night to watch over me, so I stayed as quiet as I could to avoid waking him; but I cried so hard I thought I was going to throw up.

I could not run away from this problem. My legs were gone. I would have to look into the face of my demons.

# CHAPTER 3

My accident and what happened next aggravated the cracks in my relationship with my family, and with my father in particular. To this day, the two of us haven't fully recovered from the aftermath of my accident. It saddens me, but we have never really understood each other.

My father is a farmer, with sun-weathered skin and the coarse hands that come from a lifetime of lifting feed and heavy equipment. Every day, he wears boots and khaki work pants, a white T-shirt and a work shirt, and a John Deere baseball cap. He still lives on the cattle farm in Mitchell County, Georgia, about twelve miles outside Camilla, where he has lived his entire life.

That property has been in the family since my father's great-grandfather, Confederate soldier Thomas Wiley Rigsby, had walked back from the Civil War and settled there, in the middle of three thousand acres of farmland. Thomas Rigsby's son was a pastor who started a church in Mitchell County—the same church I attended, on average, three days a week, from the time I was conceived. My mother, even while pregnant with me, rarely missed a church service.

Before my dad had a car, he walked to school and rode horses. He made it through the Great Depression, and his goal was to become a good provider—which he achieved. My dad has plenty of faults, as we all do, and there is almost nothing we actually agree about, but he is the most honest, hardworking man I have ever met. If he has breath in his lungs and strength in his body, he is going to work and make sure his family's needs are met. I never knew what it was to be in need or to want for something that was essential.

I always knew that my dad loved my mother. She was the only woman he had ever kissed. My dad weighed cattle that were to be sold at the local stockyard, and one day a lady propositioned him. Being a man of great integrity, he drove straight home and told my mom what had happened to him. There is nothing more important in this world to him than his faith, his family, and the honor of his good name.

I never felt that my dad liked me very much, but I wasn't sure whether that was my fault or his. In his mind, due to a strong and very practical work ethic, you do what you have to do to put food on the table, no complaining, and you don't get caught up in foolish dreams and ambitions. My sisters were all "daddy's girls," and they and my brother Jim seemed to step in line easily with my dad's lifestyle. Whatever he told them to do on the farm, they did. I, on the other hand, wanted as little to do with farm life as possible. I wasn't interested in any cow that was not cooked to perfection and sitting on my dinner plate, and I think they resented me for it.

My dad is not a complex man. He is a man of few words and allows his actions and deeds to speak for themselves. He doesn't have a filter for his words. His speech can be curt and biting, but you will always know where he stands. Although his stubbornness was at the root of many of our fights, I inherited the same stubborn tenacity. When I was finally able to channel this trait in a positive way, it saved my life.

My mother is my best friend. She is a delicate-looking brunette with beautiful skin, and she also grew up on a farm in the same kind of community as my dad's, not far away. Unusual for girls who grew up on farms in those days, she graduated from a two-year college. She taught first grade for one year at the same school where my father's mother was a schoolteacher, and that's how my parents met. To top it off, my dad is a twin, and his twin brother married my mother's sister.

My parents married in 1947, and in ten years, they had five kids: four girls and a boy. Then my mom had two miscarriages before giving birth to their sixth child, my brother Tim. Tim was born deaf, with multiple physical and mental handicaps, and was not supposed to live past five years old. Taking care of Tim took up most of my mother's energy, and she wasn't planning to have any more kids, when—surprise!—I came along. Lucky number seven. My friends say that they never know what I am going to do next. Well, I guess I started this unpredictability at an early age.

My mom sewed most of my sisters' blouses, skirts, and dresses; and she was a terrific cook who liked to "fatten people up." I'd probably weigh six hundred pounds if I still lived under her roof. She has a petite frame, and her weight fluctuates a bit based on how many M&M'S she's been eating—her only vice.

Her name is Ruth, and she was legendary in my circle of friends. If I thought they might be lying, all I'd have to ask was "Ruth's word?" They were so afraid of going to hell that they couldn't lie on her name. They could lie to me, but toss my mom into the mix, and it was, "Okay, fine, I did it!"

If you have ever read the biblical story of Ruth, and if you knew my mom, you wouldn't fault me if I said that God also had my mom in mind when he wrote that book. She is not a woman who has ever been wrapped up in superficial things such as fine clothes or jewelry, but she has elegantly worn a noble character for almost eighty-three years. My dad has always been able to lean on her wisdom with confidence, and he knows that in her eyes he holds great value.

My mom is not simply a good woman; she is a great woman. When others brought her harm, she chose to forget it and responded in love. My mother had her birthright stolen from her on my grandfather's deathbed, when my uncle changed the will. But I've never heard my mother speak badly of her brother, and whenever he or his family were ill, she went to visit them. She is a hard worker as well as one of the most resourceful people I know. And she may be married to my dad, but her first love has always been Jesus. That's my mom.

Growing up, I never knew if I was rich, middle class, or poor. But I knew there would always be clothes on my back, food on the table, and a shelter over my head. My parents made sure of that. My dad had built our house, with the help of a local carpenter. It was a modest four-bedroom, two-bath ranch—maybe two thousand square feet—all paneled in wood, with hardwood floors and a view of the city's water tower. A thief would be very disappointed if he broke into that house, because I can't think of a single expensive thing in it. My parents didn't put any value in "things." All their value is placed in relationships, family, community, and lots and lots of hard work.

There's a twenty-year age gap between my oldest sister, Elizabeth, and me, so we didn't all grow up together. By the time I was old enough to notice, my sisters were off to college and getting married and having kids of their own. They would visit us as often as they could, and usually they were pregnant or nursing. It was traumatizing for me as a kid to have one of my sisters unceremoniously lift her shirt and breast-feed while we were having a conversation. I would say, "Whoa, do you see me over here?" Those are not my fondest memories, but I did like having the company of my nephews and nieces as they got older.

Most of the time, I felt very lonely when I was a kid, even though I had friends, because it sometimes felt as if I were an only child. I dearly love my brother Tim, and I always have. Tim was the only one close to my age—he was four when I was born—but he's never heard or spoken a word in his life. Which is not to say he doesn't communicate. He does, some. We have a very crude communication system that mostly consists of hand signals and Tim's grunts. In spite of his severe physical disabilities and some mental disabilities, he is intelligent. For instance, he knows when his favorite television shows are coming on, and he knows to make noise to alert us to change the channel.

When I was a baby, the pediatrician said I was a better physical therapist than anyone my parents could have hired for Tim, because he wanted to imitate me. In the four years before my arrival, Tim hadn't been mobile at all—he had never been able to crawl, let alone walk. But when I started crawling, Tim would use his hands to scoot along on his bottom and follow me around.

But then I progressed like a normal baby does—standing, walking. As soon as I was able to walk from room to room, it seemed as if Tim's spirit was broken because he couldn't walk. He couldn't follow me around anymore. My mom says he was depressed for a long time after that and was totally unresponsive.

We went to church three times a week: Sunday mornings and evenings, and Wednesday nights. We used to all go, until Tim's noises got to be too disruptive, and then my mom and dad would alternate staying home with him. My parents and all my siblings were devout Christians, who seemed content to help on the farm. They're the type of people who obey the speed limit and iron their pillowcases. I became the black sheep at an early age.

I complained about working on the farm, I cursed like a sailor, I thought I was a NASCAR driver the day I got my license, and I was generally unappreciative of what I had as well as of those who had given it to me. When I finally became a teenager, I was completely and thoroughly a spoiled brat. My world was me, and I thought that everything should revolve around me.

In a way, I was like Joseph in the Bible. I wasn't the smartest, best looking, or the most talented, but people said I had that "it" factor—even at an early age, I dreamed of being great and doing something great. I really don't know how my family was able to tolerate me, and I can completely understand why Joseph's brothers sold his arrogant self into slavery. It's a good thing my parents and family were Christians, or this story might not have ever been told.

When I say I grew up in a Southern Baptist church, it really started in the womb. As I said before, I was in that church three times a week, even before I made my appearance in the world. Some pregnant women play Mozart to their babies-to-be. I was serenaded with hellfire and brimstone sermons. It's a wonder I wasn't born prematurely because of a strong fear that I might go to hell if I didn't repent of my sins immediately.

My impression of God when I was a young child was that he was stoic and a very temperamental, angry guy. If you did something wrong—maybe refuse to brush your teeth or eat your vegetables, God could strike you down at any moment. I thought of God as the "Soup Nazi" on *Seinfeld*. You said your prayer or "placed your order" to his cosmic kitchen, and then if you ordered correctly and by his rules, you would get your serving. If you gave him any attitude or didn't follow his rules, you might be starving for a long time, unless you could get someone else to order for you while you tried to work yourself back into his good graces. My mom's prayer was my "backup order" in case my own didn't work. Every night, my little mom would kneel on the hard floor of my room and bow her head to pray with me before I went to bed.

She is such a genuine person, one who always puts the needs of others before her own. About the time I was born, her mother and sister were both battling cancer at the same time, and she wanted to be by their sides, so my sisters and cousins often looked after me in a motherly fashion. She says they spoiled me.

When I started walking, my mom wanted my grandmother to see me, but she said she didn't want me to see her in the hospital.

"When I get home," my grandmother said. "I'll see him walk then."

No one had the heart to tell her that the doctors had said she wouldn't be going home. She never got to see me again. Aunt Elvie, my mother's only sister, died that same year, leaving her husband and two daughters, Clair and Deanie, behind. They were thirteen and seventeen then. We all spent a lot of time together, and my mom became the closest thing they had to a mom.

At age five, I was the first kid in the family to go to kindergarten. Two of the neighbors' kids, Bobby and Reagan Bass, were going to the same school, and we carpooled together. Their mother, Miss Daphine, drove us in the morning, and one of my parents picked us up in the afternoon. I had a great time at school. I have always had an outgoing personality, and I made friends with great ease. School became difficult for me only when one of my parents picked me up and the schoolkids saw Tim. He would stare out the window, and the kids noticed there was something different about him. I wanted to tell them, "He's just like us. He laughs and cries. He's happy and sad."

How could I make them understand? I was torn. I didn't want to answer any questions. They were overwhelming.

Sometimes kids would say hurtful things such as, "What's wrong with him?" or "Why does he look that way?" My emotions ranged from anger to helplessness to embarrassment. *Why can't I do anything to make people see that he is a really great guy with a mind of his own, but he just looks different from us?* I would wonder.

In a way, this early life experience helped prepare me for the looks, stares, and behind-the-back comments I would get after my accident.

My parents sent me to a private school, Westwood, even though all my siblings had gone to public school. It was a time of integration in the South, and things were very turbulent in the local public school. Classroom sizes mushroomed, and my parents worried that I would not get a good education unless they sent me to the town's private school—which cost almost as much as sending me to college.

There were only thirty-five kids in my grade, and my parents felt good about that kind of individualized attention. They couldn't have afforded private school tuition for all my siblings, but they did it for me, the baby of the family. As the Joseph of my family, I was once again showing off my coat of many colors while my siblings worked.

My father willingly paid for private schooling, but he was never interested in connecting on an emotional level. He was driven more by a sense of duty, though he always tried to be a great father. In his mind, that meant, "I am faithful to your mother, and I keep a roof over your head, food on the table, and clothes on your back." Often, when my sisters came to visit, he would sit and read a book the whole time they were there, never looking up for more than a few seconds to pay any attention to them.

As a kid, I loved competitive sports, both playing and watching. And that was convenient, considering sports were such a major part of growing up in small-town Georgia. You either played sports or you watched from the bleachers—those were your choices, assuming you weren't aiming to be a social misfit. Whatever sports I didn't play well, I still liked to watch. And when there weren't games to watch at school, there were usually games to watch on television.

I'd get so emotionally involved watching college football on television that I'd cry if my favorite teams—Florida State University and the University of Georgia—lost. I've had to temper that through the years, so I no longer put quite so much faith in the performances of eighteen-year-old kids. It was too difficult to control my moods when they were tied so closely to whether my teams were winning or losing.

My cousin, Dean Daniels, lived within walking distance from my house, so I would walk to his house to shoot baskets or throw a football. Aunt Veda always kept Dean active in sports, so I would tag along to watch. I didn't like to leave my parents at home, but someone had to watch Tim, and my mom wasn't much of a sports fan.

When I wasn't in school, I often had to figure out how to play by myself. My dad was always working, and my mom was taking care of half the people in the world, so I'd make my own adventures. I spent hours upon hours in the woods by myself, with only my dogs to keep me company. Like a typical Southern country kid, I got a rifle and a shotgun as Christmas presents. I carried them into the woods, where I would walk around and shoot bottles. For kids who grow up on a farm, it's the norm rather than the exception to be armed. At least, that's the way it was in the 1980s. The last thing you'd want to do is get bitten by a snake or see a pack of wild dogs attack one of the farm animals. You'd shoot them before they could kill you or your goats, sheep, or cattle.

At Westwood, several of the farm kids were packing heat. When we'd go to football practice, there was no telling how many guns were in the parking lot. We would not have taken a foreign invasion lightly. Every boy at my school had seen *Rambo* and *Red Dawn* way too many times.

A lot of my friends were into hunting, but that really wasn't my thing. Sometimes I felt that I had been born in the wrong place. In my heart, I was a city boy living a farm life.

I did like our bull, though.

When I was in sixth or seventh grade, my dad went to Texas and bought a big Brahma bull that he named Henry, after the bull's original owner, Henry Koontz. Henry—the bull—had a black face, a black-and-white peppered body, and floppy ears. He was from a good bloodline for producing good calves. He had a massive hump on his shoulders, big round horns on his head, and a flat back, and he was as gentle as they come. You could actually go right up and pat him. He was our pet.

One day, I was in a field hanging out with Henry when he leaned his horns down as if he wanted me to climb on him. My dad nodded and said, "Go ahead and crawl up on his head."

I patted him a bit and put my knees on his horns, and he raised me up as if his head were an elevator and threw me over his hump. I landed straddling his back, not at all hurt. I turned around on his back and he didn't budge. I was actually riding a one-ton Brahma bull! You see that only in rodeos, and the guy stays on the bull's back for eight seconds—if he's lucky.

*That's weird,* I thought. *He couldn't have meant to do that.*

I jumped down to the ground, and Henry leaned down again, offering his horns.

*Is he playing a game with me?*

Again, I put my knees on his horns, and again, *whomp!* He picked me up and tossed me over his hump onto his back. I turned around and straddled his back again, and we repeated the process a few more times until I was convinced that he was a very special bull. Henry was the kind of animal that comes along once in a lifetime.

My friends got a big kick out of this sight. Someone called Channel 10, the local NBC station in Albany, Georgia. Just to show you how much was happening in small-town Georgia, the news team drove twenty-five miles to our farm to tape a news segment about Henry throwing me over his hump. Then I was on the cover of *Georgia Cattlemen* magazine, sitting on Henry's back with my dog, Duke. It was my first taste of celebrity, and how sweet it was.

People actually started driving to our farm from all over southwest Georgia so they could have their kids and grandkids pose for pictures on top of Henry. It made my dad proud to have such a fine animal drawing that kind of attention.

I didn't have a gentle way with all the farm animals, though. I remember helping my dad vaccinate the cattle, or some chore like that, and at the time I thought it was a total waste of my time. I remember a bull calf charged at me and tried to run me over. In anger, I picked up the stick end of a shovel and hit him so hard across the nose it knocked him out cold. This 700- or 800-pound bull calf went lights out.

I looked at my dad, but I cannot repeat what I said first. It was not nice, and I should have had my mouth washed out. That's what Mother would have done if she had been around when this happened.

But what I said next was, "I think he might be dead!"

I figured I was in big trouble, and I hated to see my dad angry. Losing a calf meant losing hard-earned money, which was irresponsible. Luckily, the not-dead calf got up a few minutes later and ran off as if nothing had happened.

I got into plenty of hijinks in school, too. In those days, the principal and the coaches could take off their leather belts and give you swats across your backside if you were caught misbehaving—which I was, lots of times. I was good at running my mouth. The principal, who was also my football coach, was legendary for his whippings. He would set your backside on fire with just two or three swats with his very thick leather belt, depending on the severity of your offense.

One time, when I was in middle school, I used a fair amount of profanity and Coach Lowe heard me. It was the end of the day, and he said, "When you come in tomorrow, I'm going to give you a swat with my belt for each of those words."

All I thought was, *Wow, is he really going to bring a calculator?* Yes, that's the reason I stayed in trouble.

The next morning, I said to myself, *I'll show him*. I put on eight pairs of underwear. We are not talking boxer shorts. We are talking tight Fruit of the Loom briefs. *Go ahead and do your worst, you old geezer.*

Problem was, he had so much on his mind that he forgot all about little ol' potty mouth me. But I couldn't forget; I had to hide the fact that I was walking around all day with eight pairs of underwear under my jeans. I was not only uncomfortable with those stupid things but downright hot. Going to the bathroom during the day was no piece of cake either. Any swipes of Coach Lowe's belt would have been much easier to endure than all the underwear.

I did get my whipping later, though. A busload of us football players were riding alongside another team's bus, and they flipped us the middle finger as they passed, so we flipped them off right back. Our coach saw us and told the bus driver to pull over.

Even though it wasn't a Christian school, we prayed before games, and Coach Lowe didn't let us use profanity or behave badly.

"Line up!" he told us, and we cringed as he took off his belt.

When I didn't study, I was a C-plus student. When I really worked hard, I could pull down B-pluses and A-minuses. Whenever my grades began to slip, all it took was a threat from my parents to pull me off the football team to get me back in line. During my junior year, they made good on their threat and made me drop out of football because I had a D.

"I don't care if you get a C, but you're not going to get a D," my mom said.

"If I get my grades back up, can I get back on the team?" I asked, and she agreed. After what seemed like the longest two weeks of my life, I rejoined the team, having missed two games. I never let that happen again. Even though I didn't understand why studying was so important, I loved football more than I hated hitting the books, so I did what it took to get to my goal.

During middle school and my first two years of high school, I was a happy, upbeat kid with plenty of friends. We'd all grown up together, from first grade through high school, so we all knew each other pretty well. It didn't occur to me until adolescence that my family didn't have much of anything compared to the other kids' families, at least when my siblings were growing up. My parents shared one car, our clothes were handmade or hand-me-downs, and everything was done as cheaply as possible.

Things were a little easier for my parents by the time I was born because they had decided to stick to just the cows and had rented out the rest of the farmland, which proved more lucrative. Still, times were never easy, and my parents were the sort who always lived below their means.

My father worked the land and borrowed against it, and he always paid back his loans. His priority was to make sure we had the essentials in life, and that was it. He sure didn't care if I had a new $50 pair of shoes or a Polo shirt. But I cared.

During my last two years of high school, I became self-conscious and insecure about what I didn't have, particularly because I was in a private school with kids who for the most part had much more than I did. I wanted to measure up to their clothes, their cars, their houses, but I never did. I couldn't measure up in height, either, which always bothered me. I felt short, small, and too skinny—not at all powerful looking.

A bully knocked me down in fifth grade because I was small. It took only one punch to the face, and I went down. I went home and told my dad, and he didn't say or do anything. I didn't have a twin brother, like my dad did, to watch my back, and I didn't have a dad who would back me up, either. That day, I vowed that I would literally die before I was bullied again. The experience left a chip on my shoulder that never left me.

While in high school, I looked for ways to make extra money so I could afford to buy myself some really nice things. One of my favorite odd jobs was working in the school lunchroom during home basketball games. I worked the games for the middle school teams, the high school girl's team, and the high school boy's team. It was a great job for me because I got a chance to meet a lot of people from other schools, and I liked that they kind of had to talk to me—after all, I was the guy with their food. My buddy Todd Edwards and I made sandwiches and conversation and earned a little money.

In the summer of 1984, I also worked as a janitor and all-around handyman at my school. It was easy work and Coach Lowe was a great boss. Whatever needed to be done, whether it was painting, mowing the lawn, or general maintenance, I did it.

Along the same lines, I signed up to be the manager of the track team. I actually created the position, and our track coach, Noel Martin, okayed it out of sheer humor. I carried the equipment, went to all the track meets, and got to meet the girls on the other track teams. I made lots of wingmen out of guys from other schools. I introduced them to our pretty girls, and they returned the favor. Meeting people was at the top of my priority list. The more friends I made, the happier I felt.

When I was sixteen, I got my driver's license, and my dad let me drive his farm truck, a Ford F-150. My friends nicknamed it "Gray Thunder." Within a few months, though, my parents decided it would be cheaper and easier to buy me my own car than to have to take me back and forth to school in their one shared car, so they bought me a Chevy Cavalier. My dad would never have let me drive a foreign car, even if someone had given me one for free. I don't think my older siblings got their own cars at that age, because my parents hadn't been in a position to be able to do that.

To me, the Cavalier was a nice car, and I appreciated that my dad had worked so hard to provide it. The dealership had included the same awesome sound system they normally put into new Corvettes, and I took some of the money I earned and added speakers and an amplifier, so people could hear me coming down the street before they saw me. R.E.M., The Cure, The Outfield—all the current sounds of the day traveled with me around town.

After my junior year, in the summer of 1985, I worked for the Camilla Housing Authority for the first time. My buddies Mike and Guy had already worked there the previous summer and thought it was a pretty cool job, so I joined them. They were right. I liked the work.

Attitudes about race were beginning to change where I lived, but I had been brought up believing that African-Americans were basically lesser people. When my dad hired a black man to work on the farm, he didn't let him come into the house to eat lunch with us. I remember one time asking him why.

"He wants to stay out there," my dad said. "He doesn't want to come in with us."

That didn't sound right to me, but it was a common attitude. I got a kick out of the fact that, in our work with the housing authority, we were a bunch of white kids from a private school mowing lawns for an almost exclusively African-American housing project.

By the end of the summer, I had managed to get myself very, very grounded because my mom caught me in a drunken stupor.

My girlfriend had just broken up with me. I'd gone out with some friends and decided to drink my troubles away. I was so far gone that one of my friends had to drive my car home, and a third friend followed behind us to pick up the guy who dropped me off. When my mom unlocked the door for me, she looked outside and said, "Who's in the other car?"

I took one step inside the door, and—*Timber-r-r-r-r!*—I fell straight forward, face-first onto the floor. I picked myself up, mumbled some silly excuse, and walked off to go to bed.

My mom followed close behind, looking at me strangely.

"What's wrong with you?" she asked.

"Nothing's wrong with me!"

She figured I was either sick, narcoleptic, or drunk—and the first two didn't seem likely. She leaned in to smell my breath.

"Have you been drinking?" she asked.

I paused to consider the question. "I think I have."

We agreed to talk about it in the morning, and when the next day came, I put my arm around her and apologized. I knew that she viewed my behavior as a reflection on her parenting and that I had embarrassed her. I didn't like hurting her, and I knew I deserved the grounding I got-which lasted for *months*.

That doesn't mean I stopped drinking, mind you. But I at least tried not to fall flat on my face again in front of my mom.

I remember fondly some of my friends spending the night at my house around this time, and my mom came into the room to read us a Bible-based devotional. These were some of my wildest buddies—guys who could peel the paint off the wall with profanity-laced rants and who were used to getting drunk on the weekends, sleeping with as many girls as they could. I wasn't any different from those guys, but I respected my mom and I was afraid of God. I was amazed when they listened intently as south Georgia's version of Mother Teresa read a devotional, prayed for them, and kissed them on the cheek as if they were her own sons.

During my senior year, when a lot of the other kids were working out their life plans, I didn't have much of a direction in mind, except that I knew I wanted to go to college. That was the natural next step, and it's what all my friends were doing. Guy and I were planning to go to Valdosta State, and Mike was going to the University of Georgia. We talked about it a lot while we mowed lawns that summer. But then the accident changed my plans.

As the summer drew to a close, I was still in my hospital bed, battling infections and barely getting by. My friends came, one by one, to say good-bye to me as they headed off to college. You could see the guilt in their eyes. They all felt wrong about going to college and leaving me behind. But what else were they supposed to do?

When I told them I wanted to hear all about their college experience, I was lying. I felt left out and miserable, alone in that bed every night when I was supposed to be going to fraternity parties and having the time of my life.

For a good long while, I cursed the truck driver who had caused the accident. I wished for terrible things to happen to him to punish him for the way he had stolen my life from me. My oldest brother was seething with fury, too, and wanted to go after the man. In the end, the trucker got a $55 fine for improper passing. That was it. He was an independent contractor for a multimillion-dollar company, and they took the financial hit for it, but the man who personally caused the accident was off the hook for the price of a round of golf. Every time I thought about it, I wanted to scream.

But he wasn't there for me to scream at, so I took out a lot of my frustration on my father. I don't remember most of the things I said to him, but I know they were ugly. I was a broken-down kid whose dreams had been shattered and who was in a lot of pain, and between my traumatic brain injury (TBI) and the painkillers, it seemed my internal censor was broken. A lot of the things I would have only *thought* before now came tumbling out of my mouth. I remember telling my dad, in his own house, "If I had a gun, I would shoot you."

Today, doctors understand a lot more about traumatic brain injuries and can treat them, but in 1986, no one even evaluated my head injury or talked to us about what the long-term effects might be. It would take five or six years before we figured out what kinds of things were caused by the injury. For now, it was pretty clear I didn't have full control over my actions.

I was angry about having to continue to live with my parents. Angry that I wasn't going off to college as I was supposed to. Angry that I was still under my father's thumb. For so long, I had been looking forward to getting away from farm life and striking out on my own. And now I was going to be stuck on the farm indefinitely, once I got out of this hospital bed. It wasn't my father's fault, of course, but he represented a lot of my loss.

Sometimes he let me have my fit, and sometimes he yelled back at me, but I know he's never forgotten or forgiven me for those times.

The pressures were getting to him, too. What he expected was that now he was going to have two permanently disabled sons. Tim required so much care as it was that we were rarely able to go out as a family, and now he was worried that I might need to be cared for my whole life too. He couldn't say that to me, though, because my spirits were already in the gutter. And he's not the type of man to talk about his feelings to anyone else, anyway.

I tried to envision a bright future ahead, I really did. But it didn't look like a possibility anymore. At church, the pastors had always talked about how God has a plan for everybody. I grew up believing that, the same way I believed that trees have leaves.

"I know you must have a plan for me," I said to God. "But I sure don't know what it is."

# CHAPTER 4

I spent Christmas in the hospital that year, and although I had been fitted with a prosthetic leg by then, my only real mobility was when I was using a walker or a wheelchair. Some Christmas—my girlfriend had dumped me, my friends were all full of college stories, and my body flat-out refused to heal properly.

The bone fragments from my back that the doctors had used to create a heel for what remained of my left foot just weren't happy to be there. The seam in the middle of my foot, where the skin graft met my real skin, kept opening up and oozing fluid and getting infected. The doctors warned that I could easily lose the foot if it ever got injured again, because there wasn't enough foot left to heal. I felt like I was battling my own body to keep it together. *Heal, you lousy foot! Haven't I been through enough?*

Before my accident, I had been so lucky. Despite all the dumb things I'd done, I had never been seriously injured. A broken thumb had been my only battle wound, but now I was broken from one end to the other. Although the scars on my back were slowly improving, I would always carry marks to remind me and others that something bad had once happened.

My brain struggled to build new neural pathways, and I came to the realization that I had actually lost days of my memory. The three days after the accident were almost a complete blank, and my memories of the days after that were spotty. After my many surgeries, if my mother wasn't at the hospital when I came out of recovery, I'd call her.

"Hey, Mom. How's it going?"

"Fine, Scott."

"I had another surgery today."

"I know. You just talked to me."

"I did?"

Even if she and I had talked for an hour, I didn't remember any of it, and I'd want to have the same conversation all over again.

Around January of 1987, I began walking with crutches for the first time, but I still used my wheelchair if I had to go a long distance. My reconstructed left leg wasn't ready to hold any weight yet, so I walked on the prosthetic leg while I held my other leg off the ground. It appeared to many people as if I had only broken my ankle. It would take a year for the bone graft to heal enough for me to start walking again on the reconstructed foot. It was difficult at first to walk with my prosthesis and to carry all my weight on that one leg. I couldn't walk for very long, but as I began to get stronger, it forced me to develop exceptional balance.

The reconstruction of my left foot and ankle proceeded in stages—and each stage required several surgeries. One surgery would be to insert antibiotic beads to fight the recurring infections. The next surgery would be to take the beads back out. Then the doctors would do some work to try to improve the mobility, function, and appearance of my foot. And then back to another round of antibiotics.

After each surgery, I was able to go home for longer stretches at a time. I wasn't quite out of the woods, but the infections were less dire and spaced further apart. Going home wasn't nearly as exciting as it might have been, though, considering that my friends were all away at college. I mostly watched television, the same as in the hospital, and I was grumpier than ever.

Spring break 1987 arrived, and my friends came back to town for a while. We did our best to make believe it was old times again. Almost every year during high school, we had gone to Panama City, Florida, together during spring break. With its beautiful white sand beaches, water sports, daily pool parties, and abundance of alcohol, it was probably the most popular spring break destination in the United States. In fact, it was so popular that MTV set up camp there to cover all the crazy festivities that went on during the week. We would hang out on a four- or five-mile strip of highway where kids would drive around and meet one another and drink and flirt. Sometimes it would take two hours to drive from one end of the strip to the other, but we didn't mind because of all the pretty girls we saw.

When we were younger, we had gone with my friends' parents. When we reached driving age, we drove down there by ourselves. Now, one of my buddies from high school had moved to the beach and was going to the local community college. He said we could stay with him and not have to worry about renting a hotel room.

My parents decided it was a good idea for me to get away with my friends. Mike would be there to take care of me, they figured, and maybe it would help my spirits. I'm betting they really needed a break from me, too.

I had some worker's compensation money because my injury had occurred on the job, and though I hadn't yet received a personal injury settlement, I had some insurance money as well. It was plenty for a week's worth of spending money at the beach.

As we drove to Panama City, I thought about all the times we had cruised the strip and met girls. I looked down at my legs and thought, *How am I going to explain this?* It wasn't so much the prosthesis that bothered me; it was the other leg, the one that was supposed to be normal. But it wasn't normal at all. It looked like a bad science experiment, and I was very embarrassed about it. The cast was no longer on my leg, but my ankle and foot were still wrapped as if I had only sprained my ankle. If only.

It turned out I didn't have to do much explaining at all. I wore baggy chinos or jeans most of the week, and when someone asked why I was on crutches, it gave me a chance to tell my story and make plenty of new friends—many of whom just happened to be female. It also helped that Valdosta State College's spring break coincided with prom weekend at some of the local high schools, so there were kids partying everywhere. The girls were drunk; the boys were drunk; and in the madness of it, a girl ran up and kissed me. My leg didn't seem to bother anyone.

We all stayed as obliterated as possible—especially me. I think I was off the pain medications at that time, but who knows? I was never one to obey the directions on a label that say things like, "Don't drink alcohol while taking this medicine," or "Don't operate heavy machinery." I was missing my legs, for crying out loud, and I was going to drink and operate all the heavy machinery I wanted.

Imagine the sight of me trying to hobble along on the beach, shirtless, with my crutches, my fake leg, and my bad leg—drunk. The crutches would sink right into the sand. It's hard enough trying to navigate a beach when you've been drinking, but toss in a prosthetic leg on one side and a wrapped ankle on the other, and it's not a pretty sight.

I remember sitting down on a beach chair and asking some pretty girls to rub lotion on my back so my scars would not get too much sun. Most of my burns had faded and I had only two really noticeable scars by then. Oddly enough, the young ladies found them . . . well, very masculine. I had been self-conscious about them, but mostly people saw them as a badge of courage.

My friends didn't treat me any differently than usual. If I was being a jerk, my friends called me on the carpet about it. If I had a down moment, they didn't coddle me; they simply proceeded with business as usual. They still made fun of me and messed with me at any given opportunity. I had a few pity parties, but when no one else would show up, I figured I'd better just get on with life or I was going to miss out on even more than I already had.

At the end of the break, it was back to my parents' farm and back to my mundane existence again. All I could think about was that I should have been in college like my friends and that I couldn't wait to get away. I threw myself into working out and stayed up to the minute with all the small-town high school drama.

In the fall of 1987, one year after I was supposed to have gone to college, I enrolled at Valdosta State College. I really liked going to class—not so much for the learning aspect as for the social aspect. After being cooped up in my parents' house for a year and limited to the small-town social scene, it was refreshing to meet and talk with so many new and interesting people.

Though I enjoyed my classes, I struggled academically. I really had no clue about the profoundly damaging effects of a traumatic brain injury such as I had sustained in the accident. I wanted to do well in college. My plan was to study hard and make great grades. This was my clean slate, my chance at redemption in this area of my life. I invested the time and the effort, but the results were average at best. I couldn't figure out what was wrong with me.

I dealt with my disappointment by focusing on what I did do well: networking and making friends. Put me anywhere and I'll make friends. It's always been easy for me to meet people and strike up conversations.

Maybe it's because I spent so much time in the hospital, where you meet all kinds of people and learn to share with whomever they put next to you. You also come to realize that sickness is not a respecter of people—we've all been sick at some time in our lives. In the hospital, I met millionaires and paupers, and we were all equal when we were lying flat on our backs fighting injury, sickness, and disease.

One of my goals at Valdosta was to join a particular fraternity. Many of the guys from my high school were members, and they seemed to like it, so I participated in their "rush week." It was a very Southern fraternity, with a Confederate cannon in the front yard of the frat house. General Robert E. Lee was their spiritual leader. They were known as the fraternity of "Southern Gentlemen." I wanted people to associate me with being a Southern gentleman, so I didn't think very deeply about what any of that meant to people from other parts of the country. I just liked the guys I had met; they were popular with the young ladies on campus, and I knew they could party.

I didn't get into the fraternity on my first try. One of the brothers held a grudge against one of my old high school buddies, so he kept me out. It was a secret ballot, so he could hide his cowardly act. Interestingly enough, this would be my first exposure to, but certainly not my last experience with, real-world politics, personal agendas, and vendettas. I needed to take the high road, as I had always been taught, so I still showed up to congratulate the guys with whom I'd gone through rush and who had been accepted to be pledges.

My attitude impressed the brothers, and they decided to give me a "wild card bid," which allowed me to become one of their pledges—a new member who has to go through an initiation or a hazing period before becoming a full-fledged member.

With most fraternities, there is a grace period during which the brothers focus on making sure the pledges make their grades, get to know their pledge brothers, and make a sweat equity investment into the fraternity. After the grace period is over, they begin to treat the pledges horribly, as I had the pleasure of learning firsthand. But the more abuse they dished out, the more I thought, *They're not going to beat me. I'll show them what I can handle*.

Want to see me drink? *I'll show you how much I can drink*. Want me to pick up women? *I'll have women in my bed every week*. Want me to start a fight and act rowdy in public and get arrested? *Dare me*.

Once, when the police came to break up a house party, I walked outside and decided to steal the police car. Drunk as could be, I opened the driver's door and was about to get in and take off. Fortunately, my plans were stopped by one of the more clear-thinking brothers. He grabbed me and said, "Don't you do that!"

Every time I looked at my reconstructed foot, it reminded me that I was not a normal guy and that I was never going to have a normal life. The tragedy was that nobody knew that this makeshift leg was the source of so much emotional pain and that abusing alcohol was my way of coping. I think I took these extreme measures to prove to everyone and myself that I could still be Big Man on Campus, leg or no leg. I became the stereotype of a misbehaving frat boy.

My fraternity brothers were known for being rowdy, yet even they came to a point where they thought I was over the edge. I was hitting on some of their girlfriends and had the filthiest mouth of all. You know you're in trouble when the biggest, baddest troublemakers are saying, "*That* guy is out of control!"

Public drunkenness got me into trouble numerous times, and I'd often pass out wherever I landed. If I wasn't drunk, I was running my mouth off to people who, if they had chosen to, could have inflicted some serious pain on me. After one party, I had to drive some brothers home, and a police officer gave me a hard time. I told him, "I'm only a designated driver. Leave me alone."

He didn't like my back talk and told me to get out of there, which I was actually trying to do. But I couldn't ignore his attitude toward me, and I continued mouthing off. He was nice enough to give me a ride to the jail and put me up for the night.

I never feared getting arrested or getting hurt from a potential fight. I figured whatever pain was inflicted on me couldn't even come close to the pain I had already experienced or the pain I was living with at the moment. *So give me what you've got, or shut your mouth!*

I had never even seen marijuana before I went to college, but I started getting stoned whenever I had the chance. My friends often had to apologize for me and sidestep fights that I caused. During my first year of college, if there was trouble at a bar or a party, I wasn't far from it. I was a nice, friendly, gregarious guy, but I also had a very dark side.

Every spring, my fraternity had an "Old South Week," when members would dress up in Confederate uniforms and march through campus. My belief at that time was that this week was about celebrating our Southern heritage; the fact that it could also be seen as prejudice didn't occur to me. I didn't feel remorse about my participation until I saw some of the facial expressions on the African-American students. Some of my friends from class and the cafeteria were looking at me and wondering, *Who is this guy we like so well?*

What if Unc had seen me in that uniform? I was torn because I cared about the guys in the fraternity and I was proud of my Southern heritage, but this wasn't the way to show it. I honestly don't think that my fraternity brothers had thought much about what we were doing—or how many painful memories our actions caused.

That spring, my friends and I made our annual pilgrimage to Panama City, and I got into enough trouble that I thought I might be permanently banned from the spring break mecca. I drifted from one alcohol-induced blackout to another. It was by far the biggest party I had been semipresent for. When I was a kid, I had seen the movie *Animal House*, and now I was making my own version of it. It was great to see all my high school buddies again, but after that weekend, there was very little I could actually recall that we had done together. Most of the weekend was spent in my own downward spiral.

In 1988, I took some summer classes. I liked school, so why quit attending? During the summer, I met one of the local beauty queens. She was way out of my league, but I was sweet and funny, so she took a liking to me anyway. Some girls said I was handsome, but I think being funny can take you a long way.

I really wanted to impress this girl on our first date, so I took her to a nearby lake and prepared a meal for her, and we ate by candlelight. I had planned to take her home afterward and kiss her good night, but the next thing I knew, I was in her apartment sleeping with her. Where do you go from there?

I didn't want this to be a one-night stand, and she wasn't the type of girl to sleep around. So I called her and said, "I really like you. I hope you're not upset about what we did yesterday, because I'd really like to see you again."

We continued dating that summer and practically lived together. I didn't have any moral convictions about premarital sex. I had friends and I slept with them—I thought it was fun. But it felt different with her. There was something more serious, more real about our relationship. And yet I couldn't let myself go and fully enjoy being with her because something was haunting me.

I would wake up at her place and look at myself in the mirror and not recognize myself. They say that married people sometimes start to look like each other, and I think that's because they have a mind-body-spirit connection. A pastor once explained it in a way that made sense to me: Take a red piece of construction paper and a blue piece of construction paper and glue them together. Then try to pull them apart. When you pull them away from each other, they each have bits of the other color stuck to them—some red on the blue and some blue on the red. This is what happens whenever you sleep with someone: You take something of that person with you, and that person forever has something of you.

This pastor didn't try to lecture the congregation and say, "Don't sleep with people before marriage," but he explained the results, based on his many years of counseling couples. When you bring sex into a relationship, with no understanding or commitment, it causes confusion and you lose pieces of yourself. You're not just putting your bodies in the same bed; you're connecting them spiritually, and you don't get to take that back.

It got to the point where I couldn't look at myself in the mirror anymore. I would get dressed in the dark by only the dim light of a night-light rather than see myself in this strange reflection.

What was this relationship? Was it love or simply a summer romance?

Whenever we had sex, I made sure the lights were out because even though my wounds were healed physically, emotionally they were still fresh. I was very self-conscious about my foot. My rebuilt, deformed, freakish foot. I was so worried about how my girlfriend would feel when she saw it, and how she would react, that I had never shown it to her. We had been together for months, but this was a boundary I couldn't cross, and it hurt me to realize that I couldn't be that open with a person I had been so open with.

Eventually, I pulled out my accident photos and showed her what had happened to me, though I still couldn't summon up the nerve to show her what my foot really looked like after all those surgeries. Not long after that, we broke up, and she ended up marrying one of my fraternity brothers.

At the end of the summer, my friends and I had a Labor Day blowout extravaganza. I ended up causing fights, climbing over a fence to escape from security guards, and passing out face-first in my bed while my friends wondered what in the world was happening to me. Just another day in my crazy life—except that this time it led me to do some real soul searching. As I started tossing clothing into the washing machine a few days later, I picked up the pants and shirt I had ripped when I clawed my way over the fence. *What was I thinking? What am I doing?*

Something in me felt different, but it was an awkward feeling of change that I wasn't sure I liked. I wanted to go back to simply having fun and not thinking about the consequences, but I couldn't. It was as if I'd grown a conscience by accident.

I felt as if someone were chasing me and gaining ground on me no matter how far I ran. The first highs I had experienced from alcohol, drugs, sex—and even from spending money—were no longer to be found. It now took greater amounts of alcohol or a different type of drug, but the high was never the same as the first one. Sex became just another mundane, physical act without love. Every gift I bought for myself left me wanting more to make the package complete. No matter how many preppy outfits I bought, they could not fill the void inside me or cover the ugliness I felt. Something had to change—drastically.

*I need to get my act together. I'm going to be a good Christian,* I told myself. I made a whole list of things I was going to change: I would get back to church more often, I would quit smoking dope, I would not sleep around anymore, I would drink less, and I would stop cursing. I didn't actually get around to doing all those things, but I improved.

Unfortunately, I found it impossible to act like a "good Christian" or to live a religious lifestyle. There was no power, fulfillment, or freedom in living a life of dos and don'ts. It seemed I could never do enough good things to feel good, or keep from doing bad things enough to keep me from feeling bad about myself. I was caught between two worlds: a life of instant gratification that was now no longer gratifying and an unknown new life of anticipated peace.

Around this same time, I was finally awarded a personal injury settlement. It was somewhere near $600,000, but after the lawyers got their cut and I paid some bills, the amount I finally received was about $350,000. It didn't seem like enough for having my body permanently broken. It was as if I was told, "This is what your livelihood is worth." If someone offered you $350,000 to chop off one of your legs and leave the other one mangled, would you want it?

My legs were worth more than that. This was my whole life, forever downgraded because of the accident, and now this check was supposed to make things okay again? My leg is gone, but I get some money, so all's well, right? I was bitter about the money. It felt tainted to me.

My hideous left foot was my biggest shame, and it stole my greatest joy: athletics. If I tried to do anything active, the skin around my foot and ankle would split open and get infected. It looked less and less likely that it was ever going to heal enough so I could run again or play sports. I still loved watching sports, though, both on television and in person.

After a football game, I went to a fraternity party at the University of Georgia with some friends, and one of them led me toward a bedroom for more alcohol—or so I thought. In the room, there was a nerdy-looking guy with gorgeous college girls hanging all over him.

*What in the world is going on here?* I thought. *What kind of secret does this guy have to attract all these beautiful girls?*

We were introducing ourselves and drinking and hanging out when one of the guys closed the bedroom door and turned to the friend I was with. "Is he cool?" he asked.

"Yeah, he's cool," my friend said.

That's when the nerdy guy brought out a giant pile of cocaine. *So that's how he gets the girls.*

I looked at the cocaine and thought hard. I'd heard it said that someone can get addicted trying it just once.

*I've been drunk plenty of times, and I've been stoned plenty of times. Am I going to take the next step? Because this is the next step. And with my personality, if I take this step, there may not be any coming back.*

It was like a blaring alarm clock waking me from a deep sleep.

"Thanks, guys, but I think I'm going to head out. I'll leave you to your fun."

I walked out of that room and down a lonely highway back to where I was staying. I walked and talked with God.

It might sound weird that I was still chatting with God even as I lived this wild lifestyle, but that was my habit. I still went to church on Sundays, no matter what I had done the day before, no matter if there was a girl I barely knew in my bed that morning. I figured that going to church was what I was supposed to do as a Christian, and I thought if I kept going there, maybe one day life would make sense. Maybe I would find that peace I was so desperately searching for.

I fantasized about this peace as something like the feeling you get after you make a wise decision, or when you help someone in need, or when your mind is at ease because there isn't anything to worry about. But this peace would transcend even the bad times. This peace would allow you to find hope beyond your circumstances, give you confidence when facing insurmountable odds, and assure you that someone with great intentions was guiding your steps toward a positive destination.

Being a Christian was part of my heritage, but not really something I thought about actively. I was a Christian out of duty, but there was no devotion. I knew more Bible verses than anyone I knew. If someone misquoted the Bible, I would correct him or her, even if I was stoned or drunk. I knew a great deal about Jesus, but I didn't know Jesus personally. I had grown up in a culture that was permeated with religious activity and putting on airs—the appearance of God without the reality and power of God. There was a lot of talk about God, but no real evidence of change in people's lives.

What's more, I had grown up believing that God was someone to be feared. It's hard to have a personal relationship with someone you're afraid of, someone who might at any moment decide to zap you because you're expendable. At that moment, however, I wasn't afraid of God anymore. I wanted his help.

So on the walk home from that party, I started talking to God like never before. I told him, "I am totally screwed up. I am so far from being the person I want to be. I don't want to be this person anymore. I really need your help, because I have tried to clean up my act and do what I thought were the right things, but I have been failing miserably. I don't have a purpose, plan, or destiny for myself—maybe you do."

I didn't get an answer that night. I hoped God had heard me.

Over the next few months, I felt like I was flailing around haphazardly. I didn't have any particular ambition or goal in school; I had no idea what I wanted to do with my life; and what's worse, I didn't know what kind of person I wanted to be.

Even as I told myself I was going to clean my act up, there was nothing to replace it with. The problem was that I had associated some kind of happiness with all the things I was trying to quit. Even if it was temporary and not rooted in anything of value, I did get pleasure from being drunk, sleeping with women, smoking dope, and spending money foolishly. I had very little else that gave me joy.

So, on the one hand, being a party boy was fun. On the other hand, when I went to bed at night, I didn't have any peace.

That's what finally led me to talk with Steve Singletary, a minister who worked with Campus Outreach, a nonprofit, nondenominational Christian ministry group with branches on small college campuses throughout the South. Its purpose is to help college students grow in maturity in their relationship with Jesus. It didn't have a building like the denominational churches—the Catholics had their own center, the Baptists had a huge student union, but this was just a small group.

I knew Steve through some other students. He had been bugging me all year to come to his Bible study group, but I didn't want to. I'd been to plenty of Bible study groups before, and I could recite verses with the best of them. However, I thought enough of Steve that, in the spring of 1989, I asked him to go to lunch with me.

We sat together in a little sandwich shop in Valdosta, Georgia, and I told him how I was feeling. I told him that I had a whole list of reasons why I should be happy—my college was paid for, I had made it into the fraternity I wanted to join. There were so many boxes I could check off: "I have good friends, I have money from my settlement, and I'm having fun, but when I go to bed at night, I don't have any peace. For one night, I would love to be able to put my head on the pillow and just find peace. Not the kind of random happiness that comes and goes but real, lasting peace."

Steve asked me what I thought peace was like, and I said, "An assurance that God is going to take care of me—that all the pain and regret about my past would be washed away and my overwhelming fear about the future would be settled. I really want to experience that, and I'm not sure why I haven't. I've been going to church for twenty years, I've read the Bible tons, and I don't know why I can't find peace."

That's when he looked across the table at me, leaned in a little, and said, "Let me ask you a question: Why do you think you're a Christian?"

From the tone of his voice, I knew he wasn't trying to judge me or condemn me; he was asking in all sincerity. But it sounded like the stupidest question anyone had ever asked me, and I was downright offended. Me? Why do I *think* I'm a Christian? Did this guy not understand that I had been in a church since I was a zygote? Didn't he hear me when I told him that my mom used to teach in a church and my dad was a Baptist deacon? Who did he think he was, questioning my faith? The audacity of this man!

I wanted to get up and walk away because, at that point, I decided I was the most Christian person who had ever walked the face of the earth, except Jesus himself and maybe my mom—and who needed Steve Singletary, anyway? Not me! Clearly the man was crazy. But before I stomped off in righteous indignation, I decided to give him the right answer.

With a pious tone, I shot back at Steve, "I believe that Jesus Christ is the Son of God, and he died on the cross for my sins, and through his death, I can have eternal life."

*Humph. Take that, Steve.*

"Good," he said. "The Bible says in James 2:19 that even the demons believe in Jesus and they shudder at his name."

I sat there dumbfounded. I had just given this guy a well-practiced, intellectual answer to why I was a Christian, and it meant nothing. The Bible refers to God's Word as a sword, and I now painfully understood what that meant.

"Even the demons believe in Jesus . . ." When Steve quoted that verse to me, it was as if a sword had split me down the middle and exposed me for the person I was. My intellectual belief in Jesus was on a par with that of a demonic spirit. Was I no better than a demon?

It was like the moment when someone tells you Santa Claus doesn't exist. All your young life, you believed that a man in a red suit brings you presents on Christmas, and suddenly, it's like you've been the victim of a big practical joke. At that moment, I felt like someone had played an awfully big joke on me, too. But I was ready to listen.

"Then, can you tell me what it means?" I asked. "What does it mean to become a Christian?"

"Well, let's start from the beginning," he said. "Life is not a cosmic mistake. You were designed and planned. God knitted you together in your mother's womb; he knows the hairs on your head. Before the beginning of time, he planned to create you, and he has a plan and a purpose for you. He set eternity in the hearts of men; all people are created to live forever."

Then he talked me through what the Bible says Christianity is all about, which is that it's not good enough to have just an intellectual belief in Jesus but that I had to receive what Jesus had done for me on the cross. He had died for my sins, and I needed to receive his gracious gift of eternal life.

I was still confused. Had I ever "received" Jesus? Well, I wasn't sure, because I wasn't really sure what that meant. So I asked Steve.

"Receiving Jesus means trading in your imperfect life for his perfect life," he said. It meant giving him control of my whole life and letting go of my own control and desire to live a selfish, self-directed life. That required a lot of trust because it meant admitting that I was not doing the best job I could be doing and that God could orchestrate my life better than I could. It also meant I had to admit that simply living a "good" and "moral" life wasn't enough for me to have a personal relationship with God.

Even if I spent the rest of my life doing good works, I would have to pay for my mistakes and wrongdoings—or someone else would pay for them for me. Jesus was offering me a new life and a clean slate. It didn't mean that I wouldn't sin anymore, rather that he had already dealt with it. Jesus had taken care of my debt, and now if I would give him control of my life, he would show me how to live.

Then Steve asked me a weird question.

"Michael Jordan is the best basketball player in the world today, right?"

"Sure he is. He might even be on his way to being the best ever," I said.

"Well, then let me tell you a story," he said. And he began painting a picture for me:

> Imagine you were given tickets to see Michael Jordan play. You fly to Chicago, all expenses paid, and you're sitting in the stands with your popcorn and Coke, waiting for the game to start. The Bulls come out and they're warming up, but Michael Jordan hasn't come out yet. You think, *That's weird. I wonder what's up?* The game is about to start, and he still hasn't appeared. Then two men

in trench coats, wearing earpieces, come over to you and signal you out of your seat.

"We need you to come with us," they say, and they flash what look like Secret Service badges at you.

They take you to a room in the back, and lying over a folding chair is a jersey with number 23 on it, Michael Jordan's number. You look at it and think, *Wow! I'm going to get to meet Michael Jordan! I didn't know this was included in the package. Maybe he'll even give me that jersey and sign it for me.*

But before you can get too excited, a man says, "We have some news for you. Michael Jordan was killed in a plane crash last night."

You're crestfallen, thinking you can't believe you flew all the way here to get such bad news. And then the man tells you, "We need somebody to take his place."

"That's a tall order," you say. "He was the best player on the face of the earth. How are you going to replace him?"

The man says, "*You're* going to replace him."

"I'm sorry, I don't think I heard you. Did you say that *I'm* going to replace him? No, I didn't even play high school basketball. I really didn't even play recreational basketball. I can't possibly replace the best player on earth."

"Not only are you going to play in his place, but if you don't win the game, you're going to die."

"This is crazy!" you argue, but they flash their guns to show you how serious they are. Then they hand you the jersey.

After a few seconds of sweating it out, you realize that you really have to play. If you don't get out on the court, you're going to die—so you might as well try. You put on the jersey and go out there, but the jersey doesn't miraculously transform you into Michael Jordan. You're still the same person who could barely sink a basket against your little nephew. You try to play the game to the best of your ability, but you're fumbling around about as badly as you expected.

At halftime, your team is losing badly, and you're feeling dejected. Then you hear a voice whisper to you from behind. You turn around to see who's trying to get your attention, and there he is—Michael Jordan! Or at least the spirit of Michael Jordan. He says, "You're not going to be able to play this game like it is meant to be played, much less win it. But I know how to play, and if you will allow my spirit to come inside you and play through you, I'll be able to play the game the way it's supposed to be played. Not only that, but I can win this game through you."

You figure you don't really have a choice. He's the best, he is offering to help, and the alternative is not a great one. You tell Michael that you trust him enough to let him inside and to go ahead and play through you. But because you don't fully trust what's happening, at first you continue to have trouble on the court. You're not truly allowing him full control of your actions, so there's a lot of push/pull where he and you are in conflict about what move to make next. However, the more you surrender, the more he plays to his ability, and finally, you are able to give him total control and you win the game.

"That crude analogy says that the game of life is being played right now, and it requires perfection," Steve said. "We can't play to perfection in our own ability, and that's why we need Jesus to take control and allow his ability to play through us in our lives. He is the only one capable of playing perfectly; therefore, the more we allow him to live through us, the more we live our lives in his ability. What does that look like in the real world? It looks like forgiving somebody who doesn't deserve to be forgiven, being kind to someone who doesn't deserve kindness. It allows us to operate in a spirit of peace, love, joy, patience, and kindness. These virtues will characterize our playing style if Jesus is in control. We can't fully display these gifts unless we have him operating through us. That's the supernatural power of Jesus when he is playing the game. That's the way he rolls."

I felt amazed, relieved, and frustrated at the same time. In twenty years, why had no one ever told me this before? It felt as if the missing piece of the puzzle had finally come into view. All my life, I had believed that Jesus existed, that he died for my sins, and that he rose from the dead—a pretty impressive feat and one no one else has yet been able to claim in any other religion. But no one had ever told me about receiving Jesus before, and now it seemed so simple. High school could have been so much better!

A verse I had read, John 1:12, says, "To all who received him, to those who believed in his name, he gave the right to become children of God." How had I missed that "receive" part? I couldn't believe the years I had wasted in ignorance.

I wanted to be a child of God. I wanted it more than anything I could remember wanting. I'm sure that if Steve had asked me right then and there to pray with him to receive Jesus as my Lord and Savior, I would have done it—but he didn't. He said good-bye and left me to mull it all over. So I did for about two weeks, and all I kept thinking about was our conversation and how enlightening it had been to me. It gave me a sense of optimism to think that maybe God would do something great with my life, something I hadn't yet envisioned.

The following week, I showed up at Steve's Bible study, where thirty or forty people met in the student union building at Valdosta State College. I sat in the back and listened halfheartedly, praying that he would shut up. *I need to get saved, bro! What if Jesus comes back, and you're still babbling about whatever? Hey, man, you're killing me! Wrap it up!*

After another ten minutes or so, I got more desperate. *God, if you will please let me live long enough to get to the end of whatever it is that Steve is talking about, I will walk right up there and say that I am a sinner and I am lost and I want to be saved. Could you maybe speed this along?*

Finally, after what felt like the longest sermon in the world, Steve stopped speaking, and I did what I had promised myself I would do. I marched to the front of the room and said, "I am lost and I need Jesus to save me. I know Jesus died on the cross for my sins, and I believe that through his death I can have eternal life. But I want to not only believe what he did for me but to receive him as my Lord and Savior. I want his Spirit to play the game of life for me. Please pray with me."

I don't remember the words I prayed. The words weren't important. God doesn't care about whether or not you get the words exactly right. It was the attitude of my heart that mattered. What was in my heart was to finally connect with God personally by receiving Jesus, not simply to get a home in heaven but to have the abundant life Steve had talked about. "Jesus, I have trust and faith in you that I can have that," I prayed.

Later, after I had left the Bible study, I asked one of my buddies to pray with me again, in case I hadn't gotten my message across the first time. I got on my knees and again told the Lord that I wanted him to forgive me all my sins—past, present, and future—because I was pretty sure I was going to mess up many more times. I said, "It's no longer my will; it's your will. I want to quit living for me and start living for you." That was pretty clear, wasn't it? Jesus was bound to have understood my message that time. I went home feeling warmth in my heart and the special sort of joy you feel as a child the day before your birthday, anticipating all the wonderful things to come.

That night, May 10, 1989, when I put my head on the pillow, I had peace.

# CHAPTER 5

When I awoke the next morning, I put on my best clothes because I felt like a million bucks inside and out.

*Wow, this is what it feels like to wake up with peace. It's amazing!* I thought.

I felt like I could take on hell with a water pistol, and the first thing I wanted to do was to share my good feeling with everybody I saw. As I walked around campus that day, I told people, "There's great news. I'm a Christian!"

Everyone looked at me as though I had lost my marbles. But I wanted to shout it from the mountaintops, and I just about did. I had found the love I had been looking for all my life, and everything suddenly seemed brighter and more joyful. Black and white had gone color.

Most people who knew me didn't get it—I had been calling myself a Christian all my life, so why was I now reannouncing it? What was with this ticker-tape parade over something I'd already been all my life? I tried to explain the difference to people, but they didn't always understand. A lot of people probably wondered, *How long is this phase going to last?*

I didn't blame people for this way of thinking. I don't

know about the other parts of the country, but it seems that in the South these types of religious experiences are a common occurrence. . . . Wait a few months, and the so-called salvation experience would be over—the victorious Christian soldier would be defeated and be back to his or her old, unrepentant ways and imprisoned in the old lifestyle. But I was certain in my mind and heart that this wasn't going to happen to me.

I couldn't wait to tell my fraternity brothers about my big awakening. We had a regular Sunday night meeting at the house, and at the end of each meeting, the officers would ask if anyone had anything else to add. Sometimes, guys would tell funny stories about the crazy things they had done or something harmless but embarrassing that one of the brothers had done that week. I eagerly waited my turn, and then I got up and said, "This week, I became a born-again Christian, and I wanted to tell you about it."

You could have heard a pin drop. It was as if I had told them I was really a space alien or that I had grown a tail. But I continued, oblivious to a lack of encouragement. I told them that I had been searching for peace in so many places, things, and people, but I had finally found it in a relationship with God through his Son, Jesus.

Looking back, I'm sure some of the brothers thought I had found some really good drugs, and they might have even been envious of me. Most of their jaws dropped to the floor, and those who didn't think I had lost my mind were simply baffled by the sheer nerve it took to say something so off-the-wall and outlandish in such a setting.

When I finished delivering my testimony about relinquishing my old life and committing to what must have been viewed as an equally over-the-top life of piety, they applauded me—but it was sort of like the applause the office workers give to Jerry Maguire after he announces his "mission statement" of taking on fewer clients. It was the "it takes guts to be that much of an idiot" kind of applause. In all the years this fraternity had been in existence, I'm sure that no one had ever stood up and said the things I said.

My declaration caused my fraternity brothers to watch me even closer than they watched the lowly pledges. "Is this guy for real?" they asked. "Is he going to embarrass us all over campus?" "I hope he doesn't become one of those campus preachers who yell at everyone and condemn them to hell."

When I got back to the apartment I shared with one of my fraternity brothers, he told me, "Good for you for saying all that today."

"Are you a Christian, too?" I asked.

"I'm a backslidden Christian," he said.

A week or so later, he brought a couple of beautiful girls over to the apartment and invited me to go out drinking with them. This would be the first real test of my newfound faith.

"No, thanks. I'm going to stay in and study tonight," I told him.

"Okay, whatever."

A few hours later, one of the girls came back with him. She was drunk. My roommate tried to sleep with her, but she wouldn't have anything to do with him. After my roommate passed out, the girl came into my room. We talked and laughed, and it didn't take long before she and I were in bed together.

I had slept with other girls in the past, but this time was different. I felt sick to my stomach. I got up, put on my shorts and my shoes, and walked out the door. *What did I just do? What's wrong with me? I'm the same old Scott.*

I walked all the way across campus in only my shorts and shoes, weeping like I was about to attend a funeral, just letting it roll. The tears could not flow fast enough. I was so upset that I started to vomit, but I was able to stop myself. I knocked on a friend's door, but he wasn't home, so I went to my buddy Jeff's dorm room. He was a good ol' boy from a small town in Alabama. I beat on the door until he opened it for me.

Jeff was a former bodybuilder who loved God with a passion. I knew him from the campus ministry. When he opened the door to his room, I walked right past him, fell on my knees by his bed, and started boo-hooing like a baby. This was a meltdown of epic proportions. I sobbed into his sheets, I sobbed all over his pillow, and I sobbed some more.

Being a manly man, Jeff didn't know quite what to do with me. He gave me an awkward pat on the shoulder while he tried to figure out who had died or which fatal disease I had found out I had.

"What happened?" he asked.

Finally, I got myself under control enough to say, "Dude, I'm not a Christian!" That set off some more sobbing and another minute or two of regaining control. "Man, I ended up sleeping with a girl tonight. I'm doing the same old stupid things I did when I wasn't a Christian! I haven't changed. I am the same old Scott living for myself and doing what pleases me."

Jeff smirked and suppressed a laugh.

*You've gotta be kidding me,* I thought. *I'm in this very fragile and unflattering moment, and this jerk is laughing at me?* I wanted to jump up and punch his lights out. How dare he make fun of me in such a desperate situation?

I think he sensed that I didn't appreciate his response, and he quickly said, "Well, if you weren't a Christian, do you really think you'd be this upset about what you did?" Jeff was a man of few words, but when he did speak, you knew he had given it some careful thought.

It dawned on me that all the other times I had slept with a girl, I was high-fiving my friends, running my mouth off, and strutting around campus like I'd won a medal. This time was different. I had truly given my life to Jesus, and I believe that when I did, he sent his Spirit to live inside me to help me live the way Jesus did.

It made me think back to the Michael Jordan story. I was in that place where I hadn't fully given control over to God, so I was still fumbling around on the court. That night in Jeff's room, I asked God to forgive me for playing my old way. I was ready to get back to playing the game of life his way.

God is like the ultimate coach. When we fail as Christians, he always wants to give us another chance to succeed. God's focus is not on our failure, contrary to what many people might think. Instead, he's watching to see if we will get back up to fight again. We can become so focused on our current failures and waiting for an imminent, looming punishment that we miss out on the real picture. But I imagine God as the kind of coach who yells, "Get up, get up, get up! Quit your crying and get back in the game. Run the play I called. You can do this—you're the best I have!"

I love this quote from the movie *Evan Almighty*:

> If someone prays for patience, you think God gives them patience? Or does he give them the opportunity to be patient? If he prayed for courage, does God give him courage, or does he give him opportunities to be courageous? If someone prayed for the family to be closer, do you think God zaps them with warm fuzzy feelings, or does he give them opportunities to love each other?

The next week, I went to a friend's graduation. She was a beautiful high school senior whom I'd met when she attended an honors program at Valdosta State. We grabbed something to eat, and after the ceremony, her boyfriend left and went to a party. She and I went to a different party at someone's house. At one point, we were alone, and she leaned over and said, "I'd really like to sleep with you."

It was like finding a four-leaf clover. How often does a beautiful young lady look you in the eye and say that? My first thought was, *Where were you a month ago, before I became a Christian? This would have been a done deal!*

But immediately I remembered the conviction and the emptiness I had felt the last time I'd gone against my faith and chosen to please myself instead of truly looking after the other person's best interest.

I must have sounded stupid when I said, "I really appreciate what you're offering, and if this would have been a few weeks ago . . . But I've changed. My heart has changed, my life has changed—really, everything about me has changed. You may not see it right now, and I am still a huge work in progress, but I gave my life to Jesus and everything about me is different."

I shared with her that I had been searching for love and a relationship in all the wrong places and that I had found it. I had finally found peace. She listened to me tell her how I had become a Christian and passionately express what it meant to me.

Obviously, it wasn't the reaction she was looking for, and I think she was insulted. Why wouldn't she be? How many red-blooded college guys are going to turn down a chance to sleep with a beautiful young woman? She was greatly disappointed in my newfound morality at such an inconvenient time, but I felt that I was finally trying to live my life in a way that would honor God and move me closer down the road to his purpose for me.

It was a very difficult decision. I knew I had made the right choice, but it didn't feel good to a guy who loved the life of instant gratification. To follow Jesus, I knew I would be required to make sacrifices. At that moment, looking into those lovely brown eyes, it felt like a great sacrifice. But with great sacrifice comes great reward.

So, within just a few weeks of becoming a Christian, I had already felt the joy and peace of my new life, the emptiness of going back to my old life, and the struggle and temptation that would come my way if I was really going to follow Jesus. Being a Christian would be a life of daily decisions between allowing God to live and play through me or letting the old Scott make the calls.

There would still be times when the stresses of life would get to me or I would get caught up in a moment and lose my judgment. But maybe every now and then I'd get it right, as well. Whenever I fell back, I simply needed to remember to look up at my heavenly coach and hear him shouting, "Get back up and fight like I've been teaching you!"

One of the difficult things for me was that my mind and emotions were often unstable. The most challenging part of my accident wasn't losing my legs; it was my traumatic brain injury. You can see a missing leg, but you can't see TBI, so people didn't understand why my behavior might be way off; or why I would say things that were rude or inappropriate without thinking; or why I made decisions that were impulsive, unwise, and even illogical. Some women have a very difficult time with PMS, when their emotions get out of whack for a few days each month because of hormonal changes. My TBI acted in much the same way; it was like I had PMS all the time.

On some days, it wouldn't take much for me to lose control. One time when I was driving back to college in the middle of the afternoon, a guy was tailgating me and he flipped me off as we approached a stoplight. At the intersection, I got out of my car and walked back to his car. When he rolled down the window, I grabbed him by the throat and started choking him.

A few seconds later, I realized what I was doing. I didn't know how big this guy was, or if he had buddies right behind him or a gun in the glove compartment; I just popped my top without thinking about the consequences. When I came to my senses, I unclenched my hand and walked back to my car without saying a word.

There should have been an internal sensor in me saying, "You're getting too worked up. You should stop this." But there wasn't. For a long time, there simply wasn't.

My TBI manifested itself as anger sometimes, and as grandiose thoughts and behaviors at other times. I remember driving three of my female friends all the way to Atlanta, about sixty miles away, to eat at a fancy restaurant. That would have been fine if I were a millionaire. But I'm not a millionaire; I just acted like one a lot of the time. The internal sensor was missing when it came to spending sprees, too.

The TBI also meant that I had a very hard time with my classes. First, I had to overcome the problem of lost time from multiple surgeries, but then I also had to deal with the fact that I had the attention span of a five-year-old amped up on sugar cookies. Studying was a monumental task that I could do only in short spurts. If I tried to learn all the material, I'd just get overwhelmed and remember none of it. So I had to shoot for second best, which was to learn the highlights and hope that would be enough to enable me to pass.

Multiple times over the years, I would get so frustrated that I would drop my classes, or audit classes so I wouldn't have to take tests. I fell further and further behind, but I didn't see any other way to get by. Why did everything have to be so hard?

Truth be told, it got me down. In high school, I knew I could have worked harder and received better grades; but in college, I felt as if my potential had been cut short. I didn't understand why I wasn't able to concentrate or why everything seemed so out of my grasp. It would be years before I'd read more about TBI and learn that I was exhibiting classic symptoms. Meanwhile, I just thought that I was getting dumber and that I was a bit of a basket case.

I felt depressed a lot of the time. I had hoped that becoming a Christian would take that away from me, but it turned out that life was still life—faith or not, I was going to have some huge ups and downs. I could talk to God about it and try to make deals and bargains with him, but he wasn't going to take away every sadness or obstacle in my life. I was still going to have to learn how to get by, and that wasn't always easy. I kept looking for role models, for people who seemed happier than I was, so I could learn their secrets. God was giving me an opportunity to grow my faith, but at the time I didn't see it that way.

In the fall of 1990, I audited a French class taught by a professor named Moses. I didn't learn much of anything in class because I wasn't actually interested in learning French, but I was interested in knowing more about Moses. He wore this big Afro, and there was just something dynamic about him. He didn't need a sign around his neck proclaiming his faith; you could see there was something different and joyful about him. I wanted my life to emulate his, so I spent time after class with him and we became good friends. I told him I didn't really have a home church in Valdosta, so he took me to his. It was literally across the tracks, in a poor section of town.

I was the only white guy in the church. The worshipers were much louder than I was accustomed to and lacked the inhibition I had usually seen in church. If they felt like shouting something out in the middle of the sermon, they did it. But I loved their excitement about Jesus and the fact that they were not afraid to openly express their feelings. It was like going to a pep rally for Jesus.

I felt right at home because I was in a room full of people who loved God and loved me, and I was really excited about Jesus. In that church, no one cared about the color of your skin, if you were rich or poor, or what your title was in the world. We were simply people who once were lost but now were found, and by grace we would continue to encourage one another to walk in a way that honored God.

At school, however, I was starting to feel like I was drifting aimlessly. Valdosta State didn't have any particular program that I was excited about. When I thought about what I might want to do with my life, I kept thinking about the owner of H. Davis and Sons, upscale clothing stores in Albany and Macon, Georgia. When I was in high school, I couldn't afford anything there, but I really liked to look at the clothes. After I had some money from my settlement, I shopped there as much as I could. Most of the wealthy people in south Georgia went to see Mr. Davis to get their clothes tailored. He always looked well put together, and he was probably earning as much as the lawyers, doctors, and corporate executives he served.

People in the community respected Mr. Davis and came in to talk to him—and that's part of what was so appealing to me: the conversational aspect of the job. He knew what was going on in people's lives because they came in to get their suits for their kids' graduations and their nieces' weddings and their big business meetings. His job was to make people feel better about themselves by putting together outfits that made them look great.

*I'd like a job like his,* I decided. It combined two of my big interests: people and nice clothing. Valdosta didn't have a program in fashion merchandising, but the University of Georgia in Athens did. I talked to Moses about it.

"If the Lord is calling you there, then that's where you need to go," he said to me. I sent in my application and enrolled as a transfer student in January of 1991. There I would learn all about textiles, about buying and planning, and about how to open my own clothing shop.

A few months before I transferred to UGA, I had gone to a football game there, in which one of the Bulldogs, Chuck Carswell, made a great interception to seal a win for the team. After the game, I heard someone say that Carswell was a very outspoken Christian on the team. I said to myself, "I hope I get a chance to meet him when I transfer here. He probably knows where there's a really good African-American church."

My thinking was that if attending an African-American church in Valdosta was working for me, why couldn't I find one in Athens?

Sometime in February, I went to a Bible study group at UGA for the first time, and an athletic-looking young man sat down next to me.

"Hi, my name is Scott," I told him.

"Hi. I'm Chuck."

Could it be?

It was. In a school of more than thirty thousand people, the one person I had hoped to meet was sitting right next to me.

We were both still somewhat new Christians, and I asked him if he wanted to meet to talk about the Bible. He did, so we met up in his dorm. This became a weekly occurrence. We'd sit in his room and talk, and some other football players would come listen in. Before long, our talks were so popular that we had to move to a bigger room.

One night, I was leading the discussion with about twenty athletes, and it dawned on me that I was the only white guy in the room. There was something so humbling to me about the fact that here I was—the great-grandson of a Confederate soldier—helping to lead this fellowship. It was a profound realization that God can change anyone, regardless of his or her past or ancestral history.

One of my roommates at UGA was Ferrell Brown, a senior who loved to watch Georgia football and North Carolina basketball. At the last minute, a close friend of his who had signed a year's lease to share an apartment backed out and moved to Atlanta, so Ferrell had a room open. He and I met for the first time the day I moved into his apartment.

He found me in my room unpacking my things, and he wasn't quite sure what to think of me at first. Right off the bat, during our first conversation, I tried to tell him why the Christian group he had joined was weak and too conservative. Despite the questionable start, we became great friends within a couple of weeks, and he remains one of my closest friends today.

Ferrell and I were polar opposites in some ways. He was paying his own way through college and was very budget conscious, whereas I would bounce two or three checks before I'd realize I'd run out of money in my account. I frequented malls and department stores and could blow literally thousands of dollars on clothing at a time. As Ferrell liked to tell people, "No single man could possibly have more of an impact on Ralph Lauren's financial success than Scott Rigsby."

Lucky for him, though, we wore the same size. So we both dressed like kings.

Ferrell quickly noticed that I had some problems with boundaries. He didn't say anything to me about it right away, but he took note of some of the inappropriate things I did and the way I let my emotions run away with me, particularly when it came to women. It seemed as if I fell in love on a daily basis. It might be a waitress one day, a classmate another day, or really any cute girl who spent any significant amount of time speaking with me. That's the craziness of TBI.

One time, I took a trip to the Netherlands with my pastor, Mike Atkins, who was teaching over there at a Youth With A Mission base. When we went out to eat, I instantly fell in love with the waitress and was convinced that we should be together. How much can you really learn about a person in a few minutes while she is serving you food and drinks? I invited her to have dinner with us the next night us and fell even more deeply "in love." Fortunately, I didn't ask Mike to marry us, even though I thought I was ready. I came back to the States and professed my love for my newfound future mate.

My friends thought I was crazy—and I was. I didn't want

to be that way, but I just couldn't stop my brain from being so impulsive. And then it would progress to obsessive-compulsive.

This waitress didn't think anything about our dinner date. Months later, she moved to Curaçao to work, and I was somehow able to track her down and call her. This was before the Internet was readily available for Google searches. She was none too happy to hear from me.

"Who is this? How did you get this number? How did you find me?"

I thought, *Maybe this isn't going to work out after all.*

I know this may sound improbable, but erratic behavior is one of the really common effects of a traumatic brain injury. Lack of inhibition, impulsive decisions, mood swings, and depression are all normal symptoms, and they can last for years.

Even though I wasn't able to do much exercise to keep in shape, I tried to keep fit by weight training. Despite all the surgeries, I still couldn't run or do anything cardiovascular. I kept trying, but it was always a disappointment. I tried running around the track on a consistent schedule, until I came home one day and took off my shoes to find my sock was bloody. The man-made surgical seam on my reconstructed foot was split open again. I knew it wouldn't take much more of this before I would run the risk of infection.

It made me feel like a caged animal. All I wanted to do was run, and I felt as if my freedom had been stolen from me. This made me bitter, resentful, and depressed. As much as I wanted to be an athlete, I had to settle for watching others do what I wanted to do.

Ferrell and I traveled all over the Southeast together to see football games. We wanted to go to Mississippi for an Ole Miss game once, and I told Ferrell I knew someone we could crash with. We drove to Oxford, Mississippi, and when we arrived, I had to admit I could not remember the guy's name I had said we could stay with. There were no hotels or motels with vacancies within an hour of the town, and we didn't have any money.

This was before the Internet and cell phones, so we pulled over to a pay phone, and I called information three times with names I thought could be right. This was Mississippi, so the same operator answered all three times. She helped us find the right person—or at least, I hoped it was the right person.

We called the house and a roommate answered. I calmly asked for the guy. He was not there, so I explained the predicament to the roommate.

"See, he's a friend of mine, and we're in town for a football game, and I didn't get a chance to call him ahead of time to ask. . . . We can't get a hotel room. . . . Do you think maybe it would be okay if we came over and waited for him?"

The guy misunderstood and thought we were close friends of his roommate, so he invited us to stay over. He and his girlfriend greeted us when we arrived, and I could only hope we were in the right place. At about 2 a.m., after we had showered and were hanging out, I admitted that I didn't know if his roommate was my former friend. As they were freaking out, the roommate walked in.

I recognized him as a guy I had met a few years earlier when I worked on the beach in Destin, Florida. He had been an activities director for the resort, and I had worked with the lifeguards. I had talked to him only a few times during the course of the summer, but I remembered that he had told me his name and what school he went to. Luckily, he recognized me (the prosthetic leg helped) and was friendly, but he was awfully surprised to see me. I, on the other hand, would take it quite literally when people casually said things such as, "Look me up if you're ever in Mississippi." You have to be careful what you say to a guy who's fallen off a pickup truck and hit his head.

Whenever Ferrell and I got the chance, we would take

pretty girls from our Bible studies to the home football games with us. We dressed to impress in ties and button-down shirts, looking like modern Southern gentlemen. After the games, we would drop the girls off and head to Popeye's for chicken and biscuits and rice and beans. Then we'd go home and change into old, dirty shorts and T-shirts to watch more football on television.

Once, I caught myself yelling at the television and had a moment of self-realization. With chicken grease on my chin, I turned to Ferrell and said, "Two hours ago, we were with cute girls in sundresses, and look at us now!"

When all the college kids left campus in the summer of 1991, Athens was a ghost town. Ferrell and I went to the famous 40 Watt Club and paid three or four dollars to get in. There were maybe forty or fifty people there, and Michael Stipe and R.E.M. were playing. They weren't even listed on the schedule. That was the wonder of Athens; *Rolling Stone* said it has the "the best college music scene in the country." Sometimes I would even see Michael Stipe walking around town or eating at local restaurants.

In the fall, Jeff Falkowski and I moved into the basement of a house near campus. The landlady was a tiny, ninety-six-year-old woman named Miss Dixon, and she was mean as a rattlesnake. Wherever she went, she dragged around the smallest, hairiest dog I've ever seen. It was the size of a Chihuahua but looked more like Chewbacca from *Star Wars*, and it barked all day long. Her name was Precious.

The name should probably have clued me in to how Miss Dixon would feel about people making fun of her dog. I, however, told her how hilarious I thought this mini-Chewbacca creature was, and she shot laser beams at me from her eyes.

Rent was a hundred dollars a month, and it was almost worth that much! It was a good location, but it was a dump. Though the main house was in good shape, I don't suppose most women in their nineties spend much time renovating their basements. We had to enter through the back of the house, and there weren't any bedrooms, really—we just set up twin beds with a bamboo-curtain room divider. There wasn't a bathroom in the basement, so we had to go up a flight of stairs and through a closet to get to the bathroom. We also didn't have a television, so every now and then I'd venture upstairs to watch something on Miss Dixon's television.

Jeff got a big kick out of the fact that Miss Dixon liked him but hated me. It started with my gaffe about Precious, but it was solidified by "the car washing episode": One day I was washing my car in the driveway with Miss Dixon's hose, and I left the water running longer than I should have. She came over and screamed at me about how wasteful I was, with one hand on her hip and the other hand wagging her index finger in my face.

This tiny old woman looked like she wanted to take my head off. "I should charge you an extra fifty dollars for that!" she said. Did I mention she was thrifty? And mean? She also suffered from insomnia, so you'd hear her vacuuming at two o'clock in the morning, the yippy Precious at her heels.

When my friends would come over to visit, they'd sometimes fail to hide their horror about our living conditions. Many had a hard time understanding why we would choose to live in a place nicknamed the Dungeon. One hundred dollars a month. That's why.

In the fall of 1991, Ferrell and I managed to go to almost every University of Georgia football game, both home and away. He graduated in December and left the very next day to work for a ministry in Richmond, Virginia. But even after graduating, he came back often to visit; we took vacations together too.

By 1992, Worker's Compensation was tired of paying for my studies with no degree or end in sight. I imagined the thinking probably was, *He's been in college for five years. He should at least have an associate's degree by now! That's all we are required by law to pay for.*

So they quit paying, and my parents and I had to start paying my tuition. My dad said, "You need to graduate and get out of school now. Do what you have to do." The problem was that school at least gave me a goal and a structure, and I feared the unknown.

Even so, I knew I had to achieve my goal: just to get through college. I was beginning to feel like a failure because my high school friends had all graduated already. I had to keep making new friends to make up for the ones who had left. I hated change. It was depressing to see my friends moving on with their lives—getting married, having kids, and buying houses to start a future. I was happy for them, but I felt frozen in time.

My friend Jamie Vinson remembers the first time we met, in 1992, because I scared the daylights out of him. He was the friend of another friend, John, and he didn't have a car, so I picked him up to go watch the Georgia-Florida football game. We were both part of the Bulldog Christian Fellowship on-campus ministry, but we had never spent any time together.

I guess John hadn't prepped him about my missing right leg, because when Jamie got in the passenger seat of my car, he was shocked. You could see it all over his face. He was staring at my prosthetic leg—not a hard thing to do considering I always wear shorts unless I'm going to a wedding or a funeral. He didn't say anything, but it made him very uncomfortable that I was pressing the accelerator and the brake pedal with my prosthetic leg.

"I kept thinking maybe you should be using hand controls, or maybe you should just use your left leg. It worried me at first," he later told me.

We drove down a street with lots of sorority houses on

it, and I saw a sorority girl in her front yard with a beautiful chocolate Labrador. We were at a stoplight in front of this girl's house when her dog squatted to do his business. I rolled down my window and began yelling and cheering the dog on. The poor girl was not only frightened but so embarrassed that her face turned red. I didn't notice that, though. Jamie did. I thought it was hilarious. Just another time when my sense of social boundaries and social cues were way off kilter because of my TBI.

It's a wonder that Jamie wanted to hang out with me again, but what he ended up liking about me was very closely related to the thing that made him uncomfortable. My lack of inhibition meant that I had no qualms about asking and answering personal questions. While others might tiptoe around an issue, I'd just come right out and ask, "Why did you break up with your girlfriend?" or "How did your dad die?"

Part of that, I think, was that my leg made people feel bold about asking *me* personal questions. Every day, someone would say, "What happened?" and assume I knew they must be talking about my prosthesis.

For the most part, that was fine with me. I told my story again and again, and I never really got tired of telling it as long as people wanted to listen. Every now and then I wanted to say something smart alecky back, like, "I'm fine. What happened to *you*?"

Okay, a few times I *did* say that.

After the war in Iraq started, the questions sometimes changed. At a restaurant one time, a man came up to me, looked at my leg, and asked simply, "Iraq?"

I'm a very transparent person. I like being open and honest with people, and I think most people want to be open and honest too. They're just afraid of being judged for it.

Over time, I actually kind of enjoyed my prosthetic leg. I liked to do funny things with it, especially when people were just meeting me and didn't yet realize I had one. Sometimes, I'd sneeze and kick my leg off at the same time. One time, my current roommate Mark invited a few people over for dinner. I was reclined on a chair when they arrived, with my prosthesis partially detached and a blanket over it.

I hadn't noticed, but what looked weird to them was that my real foot was facing up, and the prosthetic foot was facing down toward the floor. When one of the girls noticed this, she looked shocked and didn't know what to make of it.

"Your feet are in opposite directions. How can you do that?" she asked.

So I took my leg off and handed it to her. Man, could that girl scream!

Another time, it was less intentional. After church, I challenged a friend to race me to the parking lot. As we took off running, my leg socket detached and the leg came loose. I tried hopping along on one foot, but as I hopped, my prosthetic leg began falling out of my pant leg. I was wearing khaki slacks at the time, and not everyone in church knew I had a prosthesis. A man saw my leg literally falling out of my pants, and he screamed like a victim in a horror movie as I finally fell over onto the grass.

Another year went by, and I still wasn't done with school. I didn't have much more to finish, but a few of my classes seemed impossibly hard. I got a D in my textiles chemistry class, which was one of my core classes. You couldn't get a D or an F in a core class and still graduate—it had to be a C or better.

Well, at least it was a way to postpone the inevitable. Someday, I was going to have to figure out what I was doing with my life. But not today.

# CHAPTER 6

During my last quarter of school, I got an internship in the fashion department of the Atlanta Apparel Mart; so in the fall of 1993, I moved to Atlanta and into another basement apartment. This time, it was in a house belonging to the mother of another friend. It was everything you'd expect from a basement apartment: dark and depressing. Just about all my friends had graduated by now, so I was virtually alone that year. My friend Jeff Falkowski and my landlady were the only people I saw with any regularity.

I had great visions of what a fantastic job this internship would be and how indispensable I would become. Instead, when I got there, they had me answering phones. It was a huge letdown.

Even worse, the managers sometimes loaned the other interns and me out to another company—which really made me angry. I had signed up to learn about fashion merchandising, not to do free work for another company.

The other company used us to stamp and label envelopes. Halfway through the day, I realized I had been labeling the envelopes upside down. I didn't care. *Serves them right,* I figured.

When a supervisor said something to me about it, I copped an attitude.

"I'm not even supposed to be down here," I said. "Not my problem!"

Again, my inability to control my emotions got the best of me. I was an intern, not the boss, and I should have just done the work graciously; but I was too easily set off. My brain injury interfered with so many things, from relationships to jobs.

Sometimes, the Apparel Mart would have fashion shows, and the interns were responsible for helping the models get dressed. I was not prepared for what this actually meant. As I walked through the door to the dressing room, a couple of dozen beautiful women were buzzing around buck naked. After the models sauntered up and down the catwalk, they would run backstage and change into their next outfits at a feverish pace. Along with the other interns, I would have to help these women take their clothes off and put their next outfits on.

This is quite hard to do when you're attempting to squeeze your eyes shut to block out temptation. I had been celibate for almost four years by this point, and this part of the job was just plain cruel. Eventually, I had to talk to my supervisor about it.

"Listen," I told her. "The thing is, I'm not gay. And these women are very naked. It's sensory overload. And I'm having flashbacks of these naked women when I'm driving home at night, which is causing a traffic hazard. I really can't do this anymore. It's making me sweaty."

She let me out of it. Years later, though, I was flabbergasted when a friend told me that her aunt used to work as a model for the Apparel Mart.

"Was she on the cover of a lot of bridal magazines?"

"Yes. How did you know?"

"Because I . . . I . . . oh, nothing. I just saw her around from time to time when I was . . . stamping envelopes."

It didn't seem polite to tell her that I'd helped her aunt undress.

After working all day as an intern, I would watch television for hours on end, sinking deeper into depression. One thing was becoming clear to me: I wasn't ready yet for a normal job. Working in my chosen industry meant standing on my feet for long periods of time, and I couldn't handle that. I felt unqualified to do any sort of work beyond the menial jobs anyone can do, and I felt wrong about seeking work in the fashion industry when I didn't believe I was actually capable of handling the physical demands it would require. What was I going to do?

I couldn't switch majors again. I was now in my seventh year of college, and my dad would have had a fit if I tried my luck at an eighth. There's a word for most people who go to college for seven years: *doctor*.

The fact that I graduated at all had more to do with the mercy of the professors than it did with my academic achievement. They had to stretch the definition of *passing* just a wee bit so I wouldn't haunt their halls for another semester. I worked closely with the Disability Resource Center at the University of Georgia, where they supplied me with note takers, more time for tests, and access to tutors. I would not have made it without their help and the support of my professors.

In the end, I didn't go to my graduation ceremony. My parents lived three and a half hours away and they had Tim to take care of, so they wouldn't have been able to make the trip. My friends had already graduated, and many had started families and careers. Nobody much cared about my graduation; it was more of an "it's about time" moment than it was a celebration.

Graduating from college, though, was as much of a curse for me as it was a blessing. At least in school, I had a goal and some structure in my life. My goal was to go to all my classes, study, and complete school. Now that I was done with school, I was missing a road map entirely. I knew I wasn't ready for the field I had chosen, so what exactly was I ready for? I had to do something—I couldn't just stay in the basement and watch television all the time. I was starting to make indentations in the couch cushions.

I had grown attached to the Bulldog Christian Fellowship, an on-campus ministry, so I tried to work there after I graduated. But the only way to do that was to ask people to support me financially. Basically, I would have been the Steve Singletary of the University of Georgia campus, trying to help young students find their way to faith in Jesus, but I would have to ask people to donate enough money to the ministry to cover my living expenses each month.

I hated asking people for money. It made me feel like a loser to go around begging like that. After about six months, I told the campus pastor, "I can't do this anymore."

My limitations were getting the best of me. I just wanted to feel normal again so I could have a normal life and a normal job and, with any luck, find a normal girl who would marry me. What I really wanted was to have my legs back—or at the very least, to have a normal, functioning left foot instead of the albatross I was dragging around day after miserable day. Even after multiple surgeries over several years, my "good" leg still didn't function properly. And every time I tried to exert myself to exercise, it would only get worse. I had started to wonder if maybe it wouldn't be best just to have it taken off and be done with it. And I couldn't help but think about how a few seconds and a few inches on that south Georgia highway had changed my life forever. If that stupid truck driver had just been a little less impatient . . . !

I lost count after my seventeenth surgery, and I also lost count of the number of pills the doctors had prescribed for me after all those surgeries. By 1995, I didn't need the painkillers much anymore, but pain wasn't the only side effect from the accident. Essentially, all my organs had been so jostled around that nothing worked quite right. Even today, I don't know which health issues stem from the accident and which would have occurred on their own.

Fighting every step of the way with the insurance company to pay for my medical costs also took an emotional toll on me. That's what brought me to a doctor. He prescribed Prozac for depression—and when that wasn't strong enough, an additional antidepressant on top of it.

Then I sat on the couch and watched television, just like I had before, only now I didn't care.

"These pills are great!" I told my friend, who had just come back from work. "I can sit here and watch the O. J. trial all day long and not feel bad or guilty about it!"

He stared at me for a second and then said, "Scott, if I watched O. J. Simpson coverage all day long, I *would* feel bad and guilty, because that's how you're supposed to feel when you waste your whole day. That's normal."

But I didn't get it. I thought it was the coolest thing that I could numb my conscience so completely. I could also stay awake for days at a time—which was fun for about a week. Then I realized that I couldn't keep staring at the ceiling all night for much longer. So I headed back to the doctor.

"This stuff is giving me insomnia," I told him, and he gave me a pill to help me sleep. But then I was groggy in the mornings, so he gave me another pill to wake up. Then there was a pill for the ringing in my ears, a pill for my appetite, and pills for panic attacks.

Looking back on it now, I think a lot of the secondary problems were side effects from the antidepressants. But rather than change my medication, the doctor would give me additional medications for each new symptom as it popped up. Maybe he was quick with his prescription pad because he was about to retire, but I was too drugged to argue with him. I wasn't entirely sane *before* the drugs, but after three years, they made me want to check myself into a treatment center to get help.

More and more, my focus was inward. I thought obsessively about the things that bothered me, and it was harder to function normally in groups. People would be talking about their little tiffs with their boyfriends and girlfriends, their bosses who skipped over them for promotions, their broken washing machines, and their bad haircuts. I wanted to say to them, "You don't even know what problems are!"

I felt supremely entitled to my anger and my depression, and no one else's problems quite measured up to mine. But by the same token, I didn't want people to see me as a guy with a problem. I still wanted them to see the gregarious old Scott—but that was increasingly harder to pull off. I achieved it sometimes, but other times I failed miserably.

The insurance company was one of the major targets of my wrath. What they represented disgusted me. I had lost my livelihood, and yet their entire goal was to get away with reimbursing me as little as possible for the costs involved in trying to gain some semblance of a normal life. Some days, when I was drugged up and enraged, I would leave nasty, terrible messages on the insurance claims adjuster's answering machine.

"You don't want me to come up there!" I'd say. I probably could have been arrested for some of the messages I left, and had this occurred in more recent times, that might have happened. They certainly bordered on physical threats, even if I had no intention of carrying them out. (That would have involved leaving the couch.) But I was so fed up with the insurance company and with the whole process that I occasionally had to vent my spleen.

I began having panic attacks, which meant I felt like I

couldn't breathe and I thought I was having a heart attack. The walls were closing in on me, and my chest constricted like someone had wrapped a harness around me. I just wanted to scream, "I need air!"

There were times when I had to walk out of places, like church. I felt as if I was going crazy inside—and what made it even worse was that I was sane enough to know I was going crazy. I knew things weren't supposed to be like they were; I knew my reactions were wacky and irrational. But I couldn't stop them.

It's like seeing your hand about to touch a hot stove and telling your hand, "Hey! Don't do that!" But your hand just goes ahead and touches that stove anyway, and you get burned. I had no self-mastery. It felt like my brain was sending out faulty signals that I couldn't intercept, even though I knew better.

*Why am I doing this? I'm not supposed to be nuts.*

There were days when I was upset that I woke up in the morning. I wanted to sleep as much as possible because that was a lot easier than facing another day in my life. Waking up meant dealing with people, facing the world.

Being around people was an exercise in extreme stress as I tried to hide my panic attacks. The anxiety of waiting for one to hit and trying to cover it up brought the attacks on even more. I'd be out with friends and think to myself, *You don't even know that I feel like I'm going to spontaneously combust right now.*

It was a horrifying feeling, not being able to convince my own body that there was no need to freak out. Avoiding people sounded appealing because at least then I wouldn't have to use so much energy trying to pretend I was still sane.

*I hope they don't find out how I really feel. What would they think of me? Would they even talk to me anymore?*

At church, I met a retired army officer whom everyone

called the Colonel. He had been a presidential pilot at one point, and he was also a Vietnam veteran. He was one of the pillars of the congregation, always quoting Scripture and behaving like a father figure to the younger members. But he always had some kind of wild business scheme going on.

For example, he'd used his retirement money to buy some convenience stores. He ran a bunch of them, and at least at first, they were successful. He also was a real estate agent and got involved in a bunch of multilevel-marketing schemes. He was always looking for a great get-rich-quick idea. At the time, I saw him as a fatherly mentor, and I believed whatever he told me. Although I don't think he meant to prey on me, I was an easy target.

One of the first things he suggested was that I should buy a house and quit throwing away money on rent. After all, I had the money from my settlement—what else was I planning to do with it? The idea resonated with me. A new project! Just what I needed to give me some structure and a goal in my life. A new house is a big venture, and I thought it would be cool to work on decorating, furnishing, and remodeling it.

So, on a whim, I bought a house in Atlanta from the Colonel. It was an irrational, spur-of-the-moment idea that I'm pretty sure I wouldn't have followed through on if I hadn't been on so many pills; but it seemed smart at the time. My dad paid cash from my settlement money.

There was really nothing wrong with the house, but I thought I should redo it, fix it up my own way. Really, I was thinking of it as an extension of myself. If I could fix this house the way I wanted, maybe I could also fix me. Maybe I could be proud of something again. I began ripping out the crown moldings, the doors, and then the walls themselves.

"I don't like plaster walls," I told my friend Jeff.

"You don't . . . what?"

"These plaster walls. They're no good. Sheetrock is smoother."

And just like that, I decided to tear down the perfectly good plaster walls and Sheetrock everything. I was looking for peace, satisfaction, a sense of being whole. I wanted a place that was perfectly right in every detail, but before I could finish one project, something else would bother me and I'd turn my attention there. It all seemed very important, so I'd stop what I was doing with the walls and change the furniture instead.

I eventually sank about $100,000 into a house that was worth about $120,000, and still everything was in a half-finished state. One of my best friends tried to talk me out of putting more money into the house, telling me it was a bad move; but I went ahead with my plans anyway, which started a downward financial spiral.

Several of my college buddies became my roommates in that house. Their rent money paid most of my bills, and they gave me some kind of touchstone to reality. They were all good guys with my best interests at heart, but they couldn't stop me from the destructive path I was on.

Some people think that addiction to prescription drugs is no big deal. They're legal, right? And doctors wouldn't prescribe them if they were really bad for you, would they? But prescription drugs can be just as addictive and harmful as illegal drugs, especially when combined with each other, mixed with massive amounts of alcohol, and taken over long periods of time. For me, it was three solid years—from 1994 to 1997—of swimming in pills and booze. I now call this my "drug era."

The decisions I made during this time are about what you'd expect from a drug addict. I blew my settlement money on things that made no sense. Mostly clothing. The problem was that I'd buy the same items over and over again at different stores because I forgot I had already bought them. One morning I'd wake up and decide I needed a white polo shirt, so I'd go into a store and buy a white polo shirt. Then, an hour later, I'd go into another store and buy the same white polo shirt because I was so dazed that I forgot I had just bought one. The next day, I'd go out and buy another white polo shirt, forgetting entirely about the day before.

It was as if my brain were a damaged record. It would keep getting stuck in the same spot and repeating itself. Pretty soon, my whole closet was full of identical clothing.

My appearance was important to me, and I had always believed that having nice clothing made a big difference. I was trying my best to hide the emptiness and the ugliness I felt inside. After all, I had majored in fashion merchandising for a reason: People who dressed sharply impressed me. Now, I just wanted to look like I had my act together. It was as if I could bring order to my chaotic life if I could just make everything match. If I had the right pants to go with the right shirt, and if they matched my belt and shoes, maybe I'd feel more put together.

The more money I spent, the angrier my father got. Somewhere along the way, he stopped being my father and started being my money manager, which wrecked our already strained relationship. All he could see in me was irresponsibility. He wanted me back under his roof, following his rules, and letting him dole out my money like a child's allowance. I just wanted a dad.

As the money dwindled, I knew I needed to do something. The Colonel convinced me to work for him as a vacuum-cleaner salesman. That, too, was a multilevel-marketing scheme. You had to try to convince other people to become vacuum-cleaner salespeople, too, and then you'd earn commissions on whatever they sold. The vacuums were ridiculously expensive and hard to sell, but my mom bought one—on

Thanksgiving with a house full of kids—just to get me to stop my spiel. It didn't take long for me to realize that this job wasn't a good match for me, if I wanted to keep any dignity whatsoever. I quit and spent my time just working on the house again. And eating. And sitting on the couch.

When I was drugged, I could have entire conversations with people and forget that I'd even spoken with them. I was always waiting for one of my roommates to come home from work or wake up so I'd have some company. For a few months, I took a minimum wage job at Home Depot.

While I was working there, Ferrell, my former roommate, came in with his wife. After college, he had spent two and a half years in Russia as a missionary, and that's where he'd met Rita. She spoke broken English. I don't think Ferrell spoke Russian before he met her; but once he saw her, he became a really good student.

This was the first time I had met Rita. I'm not sure what I said or what I looked like, but she was not impressed.

"You told me all these great things about Scott," she said to him later in the car. "I don't understand."

"You didn't meet Scott just now. The body was him, but that's not him."

Work was a long drive away, and I soon realized I was spending half my checks just on gas and lunch. Then my pastor hired me to be his personal assistant for about six months. It was something to do, but it wasn't a direction. My college diploma seemed worthless. Neither my body nor my mind was in any shape for me to start a real career.

Every now and then I'd tell my friends, "I'm not taking the drugs anymore. I'm done with that." But it wasn't true. The truth was that occasionally I'd get glimpses into what I was becoming—moments of clarity, I guess—and I knew I was in trouble. But I also had no idea how I would ever break the cycle.

So I kept renovating and kept retreating a little further

into drug-land. Some days, I was pretty good; others, I was miserable. My highs got higher and the lows got lower. I moved into the laundry room because I thought I would fix up my bedroom, and when I was bored, I'd go into all my roommates' rooms and do their laundry for them. Even living with so many people, though, I was still lonely.

"Hey! What are you doing?" I'd say on the phone to a friend.

"Scott, it's two in the morning. I was sleeping."

"Oh, it is? Sorry. So . . . are you awake now?"

They put up with me out of pity more than anything, I think. I wasn't much fun to be around most days. Some days, I didn't even leave my room. I just sat there exuding negativity and tallying up my complaints against the world and against God.

The depression got so bad that I started questioning myself about what I had left to live for. The world seemed black and empty. I cried to my mother on the phone, telling her that I was thinking about killing myself.

"You promise me, Scott, . . . you promise me that if you ever decide to do it, you'll come home and say good-bye to me first."

I promised. Her thinking was that by the time I drove all the way back home, I would probably snap out of whatever darkness I was in. I did seem to cycle in and out, but now the "up" cycles weren't coming nearly as frequently or lasting nearly as long. The "downs" varied only by degree. Some days I was very down, other days I was extremely down, and the rest of the days I was dangerously down.

The more down I got, the more pills I took. Sometimes, that worked enough just to keep me stoned and numb. If I couldn't be happy, my goal was just to stay sedated. I have no memory of a lot of that time and only spotty memories of the rest. It seems almost like a bad dream.

I racked up massive credit card debt—again. The first time I'd done that, my parents had paid it with money from my settlement. The second time, a lawyer stepped in and told my parents, "You should have him declared legally incompetent."

So that's what they did—which meant that, from then on, my finances and major life decisions would have to be approved by my parents. I couldn't get another credit card, apply for a loan, buy a home, or even get married without my parents' permission. They tried to dole out just enough money for me to get by each month—or less than that—because they wanted to make sure I got a job and didn't rely on my settlement money forever.

A mother in a Bible study class heard that I had a room available and thought I might be a good influence on her son, so he came to live with me. Turned out he was a drug dealer who slept with two AK-47s under his bed. His mom had no idea I had lost my own way about two years earlier. Some good influence I turned out to be!

Any remaining social decorum I had left soon vanished. I had no sense of propiety. When my buddy Jeff got engaged, his new fiancée went out to dinner with a bunch of us guys at a pizza parlor in Athens. Before the food had even been served, I started making inappropriate comments about how they would spend their honeymoon.

My friends sort of laughed in that "You're such an idiot" uncomfortable way, and eventually, Jeff's fiancée walked out in embarrassment.

"What did I say?" I asked.

I have no idea how he talked her into letting me be the best man at their wedding.

"I don't even know why you hang out with that guy," she said to him. "He's so obnoxious!"

"If you knew the real Scott, you'd understand," he said.

I became *that guy* at my various friends' weddings. They still invited me, and some asked me to be a groomsman out of loyalty, because we were buddies, but more than once, I made an idiot of myself and needed to be escorted back to my hotel room or warned to get off the dance floor and stop trying to molest the bridesmaids. I even passed out at the bridal party's table once. I woke up in the hotel shower, fully clothed, with the water running. I later got sick in my room. And in the rental car. And at the rental car return office. And on the plane ride home. The flight attendants bypassed the standard-issue barf bag and just gave me a full-sized trash bag.

My friends' new wives and girlfriends never liked me much. Later, one of my close friends admitted to me that he took his girlfriend aside after he introduced us and told her that the person she had just met was not the Scott Rigsby he knew. I was so far gone at that point that he couldn't see the old me in there anymore.

I didn't even look like me. I had always been very careful about maintaining my physique and my appearance; now I had let myself go completely. I gained weight, I didn't bother grooming myself, and my friends said I looked "dazed and confused." It was as if someone had turned off the light inside me.

It wasn't easy to see my friends get married, either, and to still be the single one.

"Who's going to want a guy like this?" I asked Jeff, pointing to my prosthesis. There were some realities even the pills couldn't erase.

In *Walden*, Henry David Thoreau writes, "The mass of men lead lives of quiet desperation." That was me. I wasn't living; I was just barely existing. There didn't seem to be any reason for me in the world. There was nothing I was especially good at or that made my life worthwhile. I was still consumed by the problems with my left leg, and I felt like I was dying inside. Something had to change.

Friends of mine had spoken to me before about all the pills. They told me they were worried about me, but I was pretty good at blowing them off about it. My pastor finally cornered me and gave me a real wake-up call.

"Look at what's happening to you, Scott," he said. "God has a better plan for you. You can't live like this anymore. You have to get clean, right now."

He was right, of course, and something about the way he looked right through me made me know I couldn't duck out of this one. I was angry that it had come to this—angry with myself and angry with God. Why had he let this happen to me? My life was in shambles and completely out of control. Wasn't God supposed to step in at some point and stop me from self-destructing?

At home, I stared at those pill bottles, all those white pills. Knowing what I had to do didn't make it any easier. As I cursed at God with everything I had, I heard a response—not audibly, but just as clearly. For one of the few times I can ever remember, I heard God say, "I'm glad you're finally being honest with me."

It was as if he were saying that it was okay for me to be mad—he wanted the real me, not just the me who tried to talk politely in church and prayed for world peace. He still wanted me even though I was broken and angry and feeling ugly inside. True friendship is for good and bad.

I took the pills I had left and flushed them down the toilet. Then I slept for about a week straight, coming off everything all at once. Doctors will advise you to wean yourself off each medication slowly. I didn't have the patience for that. When I was done, I was done. All the dizziness, nausea, and disorientation I went through during withdrawal felt like a rite of passage.

When I had straightened out my mind, I made the first clearheaded decision I had made in a very long time: I wanted that left leg gone.

I walked into Dr. Gillogly's office with the vocational

rehabilitation nurse who had been assigned to me by Worker's Compensation.

"What can I do for you?" the doctor asked.

"Can you cut this leg off?"

He said I hadn't been clean long enough for him to feel certain that I was making a smart decision. He wanted to make sure that I was off all the medications for at least a few months before I made up my mind. I agreed to wait exactly as long as necessary for him to feel okay about it, but no longer than that. The more my brain straightened out, the more eager I was to get the procedure done.

The insurance company thought I was crazy. Before they would consent to the procedure, they spent thousands of dollars to send me to a forensic psychiatrist for his expert opinion. Who voluntarily gets a leg chopped off? Didn't I know of the possible complications? Even though they had spent obscene amounts of money for my multiple surgeries over the years to try to keep the leg, they must have seen the second amputation as an even riskier financial gamble.

The psychiatrist spent some time with me and issued his report: "This should have been done twelve years ago." His expert opinion was that I was perfectly sane.

Worker's Compensation, however, wouldn't let me get the surgery until we had settled my claim. They had been sending me $89.33 a week since soon after my accident, and they wanted to stop doing that. According to the lawyer I spoke with, they could have kept me tied up in court for years, postponing my surgery and causing me to spend a lot of money on legal bills. He advised me to go ahead and settle with them, which I did, for about $250,000. As part of the settlement, they would allow me to have the surgery and then would pay for my medical bills for two years. After that, I was on my own. When the check came, my dad put the money in the bank, and I was finally through my last roadblock. There was no longer anything stopping me from having the operation.

The doctors told me I had to go in for physical therapy to build up my calf, which at first seemed kind of silly. They had put in a calf implant at some point to make my leg look as if I had a normal calf, but now that my leg was coming off below the knee, why did I need to worry about my calf at all? They said it would make my residual limb in better shape for the operation. So I did physical therapy to build it up, just to take it off.

Even after all the years of thinking about having my second leg removed, and the months of fighting to get it approved, the date sneaked up on me too quickly. Suddenly it was June 21, and I was one day away from surgery. After twelve years of infections and pain and embarrassment and aggravation, I was finally making the choice to do what my parents had thought would be too much to cope with when I was just a kid. I was making the choice to become a double amputee.

Was I crazy? The thought did cross my mind as I stayed at the home of a friend's parents before the procedure. I had asked my parents not to come. They had enough to deal with at home, and I just didn't need all the fuss this time. My friend's mother offered to take me to the hospital.

The night before the operation, I soaked in their bathtub and prayed.

*God, tell me I'm doing the right thing. If this isn't your will, then make something happen so I can't get the operation done tomorrow. But if this is your will, please let it go smoothly.*

I stared at my leg under the bathwater and thought, *This is the last time I'm ever going to see this leg. It's never going to be on my body again.*

How surreal, and how conflicted I felt about the surgery, even after fighting so hard to get it done. What if it was worse to have two prostheses? What if I was making a huge mistake?

There's no mulligan with an amputation. You don't get to take your leg back if you decide this double-amputee thing just isn't for you.

There was no other option the first time around. But now, I was the one taking control of my destiny. I didn't know what was coming, but I did know I was finished with this chapter—like throwing all your cards back in a hand of poker and hoping that whatever you get next is going to be something better than what you had. Whether tomorrow turned out good or bad, it was going to change my life, but that was a risk I was now willing to take.

# CHAPTER 7

On June 22, 1998, I waited nervously at the West Paces Medical Center in Atlanta. One floor above me was the office of the surgeon who had spent so much time reconstructing my left leg and ankle twelve years before. Just down the stairs, another surgeon was preparing to sever it. He was the team surgeon for the Atlanta Falcons and Atlanta Thrashers, which impressed me. If someone was going to chop off my leg, this was the guy I wanted to do it.

"Hey, are you ready to do this?" Dr. Gillogly asked as he walked into the operating room.

*No,* I thought. *You know, I could die right here on the table while you're chopping my leg off. You got a good night's sleep last night, right?*

"Yes," I told him.

Maybe—just maybe—I still had a shot at a decent life. I kept that hope in my heart as the anesthesiologist sedated me for my surgery. It felt as if a bad scene in my life was coming to a close, and all I wanted to do was leave that scene on the cutting room floor. My house in Athens was becoming a place of bad memories for me, and it felt like a dead end. I made the decision that I didn't want to return there after my surgery was over.

"Count backward from ten to one," the anesthesiologist said.

"Ten . . . nine . . . eight . . ."

Before I reached "seven," I had already drifted off.

It took about one hour for the surgeon to do the procedure. Twelve years to get here, and one hour to change the course of my life—about the same amount of time it might take to dry a load of laundry. I think he was even working on another patient at the same time. He was a very skilled surgeon, and doctors later told me it was a textbook-perfect job.

When I awoke, I wasn't in terrible pain. It was manageable. In fact, the worst pain I remember from this procedure was when a nurse who clearly had not attended the Florence Nightingale "How to Be Kind to Your Patients" seminars inserted a catheter because I wasn't able to empty my bladder by the established cutoff time after surgery.

Recovery was an entirely different experience from the first time around. Surgical procedures had come a long way, and there's a difference between recovering from the clean cuts of a planned surgery and the trauma of a leg ripped off on a highway. During this surgery, they had put a sort of plaster cast on my left residual limb and an adapter on the end of it to which I could attach a crude prosthetic foot. This allowed me to stand up during physical therapy and begin a little weight bearing. It also allowed the blood to flow to the end of my residual limb to make sure the tissue stayed healthy.

My brother-in-law Stanley had recently been laid off from work, so he and my sister Sue Ellen were able to come stay with me in the hospital. Stanley had one of those dynamic personalities that drew people to him—and I was crazy about him—so it was nice to spend time with him. He was the kind of guy who always knew how to adapt to pretty much any situation and not take life too seriously. When he was laid off from work, he didn't even ask why. He just accepted that it was time to move on.

I was in the hospital for only three days recovering from the operation, and then it was time for me to begin rehabilitation therapy. I was transferred to Shepherd Spinal Center in Panama City, Florida, which was also the location of the man who had made my prostheses for the past twelve years.

My vocational rehabilitation nurse, Jody, and her husband took me there, and on the way, we stopped in at my parents' home. The reality of my situation hit me as Jody talked to my mom. *I can't go back*, I thought. *This is forever. I hope it was the right decision.*

When I left for Florida to do my rehabilitation, my parents called a real estate company and asked them to take care of selling my house. They explained the condition it was in and asked the agent to hire a contractor to get the house fixed up and sold.

I had to pay the contractor $25,000 on top of everything I had already spent to fix up the jobs I had started. The investment was a terrible one; I sold the house at a major loss because of all the money I had put into it, and went back to living in rented apartments. That did wonders for my sense of failure. Not only had I barely made it through college in seven years, but I couldn't hold down a job and I couldn't even function as a homeowner, even though I had nothing better to do.

The insurance company didn't want to pay for an apartment for me in Panama City while I was recuperating, so I moved into a hotel room at a Hilton resort for about ten weeks. I was in a wheelchair during this time, and had no means of transportation. Jody negotiated a deal for a reduced rate. Mrs. Hilton lived in a penthouse suite and was an avid runner. She would see me wheeling around the hotel and often stopped me to find out how I was progressing.

In my time there, I ran up a $10,000 bill on the room, meals, cab rides, and laundry. Though the insurance company agreed to pay for some things, they were constantly nickeling-and-diming me and didn't make life easy. In fact, initially, they didn't want to reimburse me for any of the hotel bill.

*Fine,* I thought. *I'm just going to stay here and do my rehab, and when I come home, I'll have a sit-down with the judge, and we'll see what you are and aren't going to pay.*

On the other hand, the hotel management was wonderful to me. They could have kicked me out many times because I ran out of money, but they were as generous as they could possibly have been.

While living in the hotel, I'd go out for physical therapy. For the first week and a half, I didn't have a prosthetic leg, though, so there wasn't much else I could do other than wheel myself around the hotel and talk to the staff members. Luckily, there was also a movie theater across the street, so sometimes I wheeled myself there to watch a movie. Once I got my prosthetic leg, I started going to Gold's Gym to work out.

It was a lonely and uncertain time in a place where I didn't really know anyone. There was a hurricane while I was down there, and I didn't even evacuate the hotel with the rest of the guests. I just decided to ride it out with the staff members who had to stay. I felt I had little left to lose.

During my second week there, my prosthetics technician made me a temporary set of walking legs. I had just one request for him: "Can you make me taller?"

If there's a benefit to losing both your legs, it's this: You can adjust your height with prosthetics. I had always hated being short, and now I could be any height I wanted. Well, almost. The height I wanted to be was six feet one, and my reason was very simple: I didn't want my brother Jim to be the tallest person in the family anymore. He was six feet even, and now I was going to be an inch taller. Oh, the power!

The prosthetist agreed to give me a few extra inches. I thought it would be cool to have a variety of different leg lengths to match my mood for the day. Plus, I could ask potential dates, "Do you want a short guy or a tall guy?"

Once I had my new legs, I was able to start my physical therapy in earnest. My physical therapist, Jennifer, was terrific. She's one of the reasons I walk as well as I do. In a matter of weeks, I went from a wheelchair to a walker to crutches, and then to just a cane. Then came the day when I could walk on my own, with no cane. We were outside, and I turned to Jennifer and said, "I think I can run."

She didn't stop me, so I began walking faster and faster, picking up my pace until I hit a running stride. It was just six weeks after my surgery.

Freedom!

I had been waiting twelve years for this moment. Finally, I was able to run again, and the world seemed alight with possibilities. Having my second leg removed was the right decision. *It was the right decision!*

In short order, I began driving all the geriatric patients crazy because I would run up and down the hallways, making click-click noises with my prosthetics. I was like Forrest Gump when he was a kid. After about ten weeks, they finally told me—in a nice way—that my time was up. "We really can't help you anymore."

When prisoners are released from incarceration, they often have a hard time adapting to the free world again. Psychologists explain that when people are institutionalized, they adjust to the new reality and lose track of the outside world. It's sort of like being frozen in time. Meanwhile, the world moves on and changes without them. When they get back to it, they no longer know where they fit on the spectrum.

I went through that same sort of discomforting sensation.

I felt as if I had been imprisoned by my left leg for so many years, and I had spent the last three years in a drug-induced haze. Once I came out of the haze, I was strictly focused on getting my left leg amputated and dealing with all the apprehension and excitement associated with the surgery. Now here I was, a new man, but I still had no idea where I was supposed to fit in the world.

Although I could run, I still couldn't stand on my prosthetics for long periods of time. I stayed with friends for the rest of that year, eventually staying with a friend who worked out of town as a consultant for about five days a week. He was home just two days a week and had to run errands for some of that time, so I had the house to myself a lot. We'd go to church together on Sundays, and then he'd have to fly out to work again that night.

I kept in touch with friends through phone calls. One day while speaking with Ferrell, I let him know how depressed and alone I was feeling. I didn't like living by myself so much of the time, and I was still drifting around aimlessly trying to find something I could do well.

The next time we spoke, he told me, "I'm going to fly to Atlanta. We will pack up your stuff, and you are coming back to Richmond with me. Rita and I want you to stay with us, and we will help you get back on your feet."

I did not object. Instead, I went off to Virginia to stay in a two-bedroom condo with Ferrell; his wife, Rita; and their dog, Jerry. They wanted to make sure I wasn't alone when I was as depressed as I was, and they wanted to create a safe environment in which I could find some sense of direction.

When I got there, it was snowing. I had a severe case of the flu, and Ferrell had to take me to the emergency room to get medical attention. I cried just about every day. I felt so embarrassed and hopeless about having to move in with my best friend from college and his wife. How could I start to rebuild my shattered life? Which direction should I take? I couldn't get moving. I had analysis paralysis.

Ferrell told me to put together a résumé so he could take me to a job fair. I had a poor attitude about it from the start. My résumé was pathetic. Seven years of college, then brief jobs at places such as Home Depot. What was I qualified for? For twelve years, I had been a professional patient. If anyone needed an extra surgical patient, I was the man for the job. I was also excellent at watching television and talking to friends on the phone, in case anyone had openings in those departments. Otherwise, my experience was pretty limited.

The only talent I had was the uncanny ability to balance on my new legs. When I wore pants, no one even knew I had prosthetics—I walked steadily, just like people without physical challenges. I could even run short distances. But what job, exactly, requires that skill set?

I was convinced that nothing about me would make an employer want to hire me. Nothing distinguished me—except my legs. They were a conversation starter, if nothing else. So I arrived at the job fair in a dress shirt and shorts, to show off my prosthetics.

I had the audacity to apply for a management position, which I obviously didn't get. I knew that Ferrell hadn't brought me to the fair to embarrass me; he just wanted to get me moving in some direction. As they say: You can't steer a parked car. Ferrell just wanted to get the wheels spinning so we could get some turning action going on.

In the spring of 1999, I had to get some work done on my prosthetics, so I went to a local prosthetics shop. The technician said, "What do you do?"

I said, "I moved here to get a job, but I can't find one. I have no clue what to do."

"Maybe I can help you," he said. "My wife has worked in

the telephone industry for thirty-five years, and they have a new start-up company selling Cavalier Telephone services."

As he explained the sales job to me, it sounded like something I might be able to do, so I applied and was granted an interview.

"I know my résumé stinks," I said when I met with the hiring manager, "but I'll outwork anybody. I really need the job."

"How much are you looking to make?"

"Ten dollars an hour."

"We don't even have jobs that pay that little," she said. "We start at twelve dollars an hour." When it was all said and done, she decided to take a chance and hire me.

I began work in June, selling Internet services to clients. As I had hoped, I was pretty good at it, and the boss liked me. It was a stressful position, though, and being a start-up company, we faced cutthroat competition from the well-established phone companies. But as far as I was concerned, it was a decent job. For the first time in a long time, I had at least a shred of self-confidence that I could succeed in a job. Around Christmas of 1999, my dad called and said, "Your mom is not in good health. You ought to think about moving back down this way."

My mom was fighting a lung and heart condition. Despite her fragile appearance, I had always thought of her as having almost superhuman strength, so I fully expected her to recover. Still, I knew her health problems were scary, and I understood that my dad wouldn't have called me home if he didn't think the situation was serious. I gave my notice to the owner of the company.

"Are you moving back to Atlanta?" he asked.

"Yes."

"I have a friend who's about to become a manager at a telecom company in Atlanta. I'll put in a call for you."

Before I moved, I spoke with his friend on the phone,

and basically had the job lined up before I even made it back home.

"My friend doesn't call me about just anybody," my new boss said. "So if he thinks enough of you to refer you to me, then I need to hire you."

I was hired to be an inside salesperson, which meant I was dealing with existing customers, trying to sell them additional services over the phone. I liked it because there was already a relationship between those customers and the company—which was different from cold-calling and trying to convince people to switch companies.

My chatty nature came in handy. I made President's Club, selling 140 percent of what was expected of me. The way this company worked was that salespeople earned all kinds of bonuses and awards for exceeding their quotas. I won a trip to the Bahamas and a $4,000 television set.

I used some of my newfound financial resources to hire a personal trainer to work out with me three times a week. His name was George Hyder, and he was a pioneer in physical fitness in Atlanta. He had been in the Army, and he ran combat-like boot camps for people who wanted to get in shape. Camps like this are popular now, but George was one of the first to use this style of training. He called his company Steel Ballet. Early each morning, he would take people through basic-training maneuvers and have them run laps with military cadence calls: "I don't know, but I've been told . . ."

Everybody loved George, and George loved everybody. He was about six feet two, weighed 240 pounds, and had played football for the University of South Carolina. He was a handsome guy, popular with the ladies. But guys liked him too—he had a boisterous, larger-than-life nature that was infectious. You would always hear George before you would see him.

Even though I could afford to pay for his services only three days a week, he would always tell me to come work out with him the other two days of the week for free. He was very generous and had a huge heart.

He had a phrase that he would repeat to himself every day on his way to work in the morning: "I have a profound, positive impact on everyone I meet." And he did. He made everyone around him feel like a winner, like we could all achieve whatever we wanted.

One day when I was working out, I got frustrated because I couldn't complete the exercise.

"Listen, man," he told me. "I want you to always remember this when you're working out: Do what you can, do the best you can, and don't ever quit."

Those words became my motto: *Do what you can, do the best you can, and don't ever quit.*

We all have our demons, and George had his. He'd had trouble with drugs and steroids earlier in his life but had been clean for several years. Then he started dating a younger girl who was very much into the hard-core party lifestyle, and she lured him back into the darkness. He was trying to keep up with her, relive his glory days, and feel young again. I worried about him and didn't like the influence his girlfriend had in his life.

I loved George like a brother and wanted to help him as he had helped me. I invited him to go to my Tuesday night Bible study group, and he accepted. On Monday night, I called him, and he told me his girlfriend had left him.

"I'm sorry," I said.

"It's okay. Don't worry about it. All that matters is being connected to God."

"Do you still want to come with me to the Bible study tomorrow?"

"Definitely."

But the next morning, a friend of his called to tell me that George hadn't been feeling well that morning at boot camp.

She thought he might have the flu. Whatever the cause, something had come on suddenly, and George had been rushed to the hospital. She didn't know any further details, just that he was in the hospital and wouldn't make it to the Bible study with me that night.

That afternoon, when I went to visit George at the hospital, I found out that his kidneys had shut down. Then an undetected aneurysm had burst, and George was essentially brain-dead. I saw a tiny breathing machine filling the huge lungs of my big, burly friend, but he wasn't there. He died later that night. I would never hear that deep, boisterous voice yelling at me again. He was just thirty-seven years old.

I met George's dad at the hospital, and he asked if I would help set up the funeral. I had been to only one other funeral in my life at that point. I'd been lucky. Now, at the second funeral I would ever attend, I would deliver a eulogy.

My last phone conversation with George gave me some comfort. I hoped that he had made his peace with God and that there was a reason he died so young. People say that God doesn't give you more than you can handle; maybe God knew that George couldn't handle any more and decided to take him home before he got into more trouble.

For the way he gave of himself so deeply, George is someone who will always stay in my heart. His life was about helping others feel better and do better, and it's sad that he wasn't able to save himself.

I had to keep myself busy and keep moving so I wouldn't be overwhelmed by George's death. When I was faced with new challenges, I repeated the motto he had taught me, and I tried to emulate the way he had dealt with people. It was hard to keep a smile on my face at work, but each day, it got a little better.

It was a mixed blessing that the pressures at work were so great. At least the stress of trying to make my quota would keep my mind off other things for a while.

In 2001, for the first time in my life, I made a huge leap forward and earned more than $100,000—a long way from the twelve dollars an hour I had started with less than two years earlier. It looked as if I was going to get to shop at stores like Mr. Davis's again after all.

Then something awful happened: The Internet bubble burst.

Cavalier Telephone went into Chapter 11 bankruptcy, but I kept working anyway. I made President's Club for the second year in a row for having the top sales percentage based on my quota, but this year there was no trip and no TV. There was only a $1,000 bonus check, and Uncle Sam helped himself to almost half of it.

By the start of the new year, I was taken away from the cushy world of inside sales and pushed out into the harsh world of cold-calling. I became a door-to-door salesman for voice, data, and Web search products for small- to medium-sized companies; my mission became one of trying to sweet-talk my way past the gatekeepers at as many businesses as I could in order to wrangle business away from our competitors. All this while, I was trying to downplay the fact that my company was in deep financial trouble.

My sales success rate plummeted. Although I was good at resolving customer issues and up-selling additional data services to pre-existing customers, I was terrible at cold-calling and the art of hunting for new business. I just couldn't do it. I hated hearing the word *no*, and I took every rejection personally.

After finally finding something I was really good at, it was hard to lose that. The bonuses dried up. I could forget about trips to tropical destinations. I got depressed again and went to see the doctor. He recommended that I go on medical disability leave in the summer of 2003.

During this time off, I went to go see a pulmonologist

because of a number of troubling symptoms. I often could not get out of bed because of overwhelming fatigue, I fell completely asleep at stoplights, I would doze off and not remember mile markers when I was on long trips, and I experienced brief but frightening episodes of total paralysis when I was in a state between sleep and awake. There were times when I felt like I was awake, but I couldn't move at all. The doctor conducted a sleep study, and the results were shocking to me.

"You have narcolepsy," he told me.

"I have what? What on earth is that? How did I get it?" I asked.

"Well, it's a chronic neurological disorder. Your brain can't regulate your sleep-wake cycles normally, and that causes your body to get mixed signals about when you are sleeping and when you're awake. We're really not sure at this time what causes it, but my medical opinion is that your traumatic brain injury is the cause. It has taken this long to become debilitating. It can be treated with medication."

This was seventeen years after my accident. The aftereffects just never seemed to let up, even almost two decades later. I felt like a car that was on its last few miles. What else was going to break on me?

Miserable and angry, I went out of town to a bachelor party for a friend who was getting married. I got monumentally drunk and started a fight. After a brief punching match, a bouncer threw me out of the bar and onto the ground. Then I got the brilliant idea that I needed to cross the street. I'm not sure why, but I took off my legs and crossed the street on my knees with both prostheses in my arms. Maybe I was thinking, *As drunk as I am, I'll have better balance if I lower my center of gravity.* A traumatic brain injury and massive amounts of alcohol are never a good recipe for logical reasoning.

Passersby must have been thinking, *This is a bad night for that guy. Don't serve me whatever he had.*

The strange sight of an elf-height creature cradling two artificial legs did not escape the watchful eye of the local police. Two officers were waiting to greet me on the other side of the street. As they were debating whether to drive me home or take me to the station, their domineering and unmerciful commander arrived on the scene.

"My civil rights are being violated!" I hollered at him. "You should know something about that!"

Did I mention that this was in Birmingham, Alabama? And that the commander was African-American? That had to be one of the dumbest things that has ever come out of my mouth.

The officers quickly placed my hands behind my back. I'm also relatively certain that my forehead hit the top of the door-frame—accidentally, of course—as they threw me in the back of the police cruiser and escorted me to jail. I did not pass "Go," and I did not collect $200.

Did you know they take away your prosthetic legs in jail? You can hide weapons in them, apparently, which is why I spent the night with no legs. They let me out the next day, once I had sobered up.

I tried working at two more telecom companies, but I was no more successful at either place. I went on medical disability leave again with one of the companies, and I got fired from the other one. When I wasn't looking for a job, I spent my time just working out and trying to get my head together. I finally decided that maybe I needed to try a new industry.

I tried working for a company that made ink to refill printer cartridges, but I lasted only about a month before I was fired. I had been knocked down for the umpteenth time, but it was time to get back up again. This time, I worked as a salesman for Yellow Book USA, selling phone book ads door to door. I was horrible at that, too.

For the third consecutive summer, I went on medical leave, unable to work due to clinical depression. That meant I got up to ten weeks off at a fraction of my normal pay, and the company couldn't fire me until I either got better or the time was up. Each time, a doctor had to certify that I was clinically depressed and that I was not able to perform my normal work duties. This time, as my disability leave time ended, my mental health wasn't any better, and I didn't know what I was going to do. From 2002 to 2005, I had gone on disability three times, and I had been fired twice. How many times could I strike out before I was out of the game altogether?

I had even applied at three of the largest prosthetics companies, but none of them would hire me. The largest of the three had never hired an amputee as an outside salesperson. That seemed odd to me; it was as if they were saying that they wanted to sell to amputees, but they didn't want any amputees selling for them. Going back to work selling phone books was a major source of dread, yet I had no other source of employment.

Then, on my last day of leave, I got a phone call from a man named Doug Dershimer, a manager at Soliant Health, a medical staffing company. He had seen my résumé on one of the online job sites and was interested in interviewing me. It felt like a miracle in the making. We met in person, and he was very caring and sympathetic when he heard my story.

Like me, he was a rabid college football fan, and like me, he was a Christian who knew what it was like to be down on one's luck. He hired me on the spot as a medical staffing recruiter, even though I had no recruiting experience. I'm not sure if he thought I would last there or not, but Doug was a guy who always rooted for the underdog, and he wanted to give me a shot.

True to my history, I was an unsteady worker. It soon became apparent that I was not good at this job, and I knew my position there was tenuous. Doug was my manager, and that's the only thing I had going for me. He really wanted me to succeed, so he kept me around, even though my performance wasn't up to par. I wanted to be good at this line of work, but it was easy to see that my time was limited. Every day, I wondered if I'd be fired, but Doug kept sticking his neck out for me and buying me more time, hoping against all hope that I would get the hang of things. I never did.

So many times in my life I thought I had hit rock bottom. After my accident, obviously—I couldn't see past the belief that I was supposed to be an athlete but that my legs had been taken from me. Then I hit bottom again after college, when I realized that I was unable to hold a normal job and that my degree was useless. Then again as I flushed those pills down the toilet after years of prescription-drug addiction. But each time, there was at least the hope that things could improve—that my left leg would finally be fixed and that would solve my problems.

But now there was nothing else to be done. My left leg was gone; it was no longer holding me back, yet I still had no real purpose in my life. I was merely existing. My friends all had their acts together, and I was just biding my time at another job I wasn't good at, with no love in my life, no home of my own, little to no money, and no vision for the future. As Helen Keller once said, "It is a terrible thing to see and have no vision."

It turned out that rock bottom wasn't the accident, or the postgraduation blues, or the drug years. Rock bottom was Christmas Eve of 2005, when I found myself sobbing on my parents' living room floor.

Lots of people evaluate their lives during the holidays, and I was no exception. My conclusion was that I had wasted more talent, opportunities, resources, and finances than anyone I knew. I was broke in every area of my life and had nothing to show for my time here on earth—or so I thought.

Why had I been saved from a catastrophic event if there was still no reason for my existence? I had no plan, no purpose, and no destiny. Life, for me, was like staring into the abyss.

*Why should I continue living?* I asked myself. The only answer I could come up with was that I wanted to see what happened next.

Up to that point, I had lost most of the battles in my life, but if I ended my life, I would lose the war as well. That, to me, was unacceptable. I was not going to lose the game of life. I hate—I mean I *hate*—losing!

*Before I make a drastic and final decision, maybe there's one last option I haven't considered yet.*

I can't think of anyone closer to God than my mother. She's not perfect, of course; no human is. But I would put my mom's relationship with God up against anyone else's. With all due respect to the pope, if my mom beeps in on call-waiting while God is chatting with him, God is going to click over and take her call.

I decided that my mom was going to be my last hope, my secret weapon, and my advocate to get God's attention. For the past three years of my life, God's voice had either been silent or I had been unable to hear him. My prayers appeared to have been completely ignored. If anyone could get God's attention, surely it would be my mom. So I called her into the room and asked her to pray.

She sat in a chair next to where I was lying faceup on the floor, and she prayed as tears streamed down the sides of my face. As always, my mom's prayer was eloquent and respectful, but it also had a tone of urgency. What mother, seeing her son or daughter in serious pain, would not plead with a physician to heal her child? My mom pleaded with the Great Physician that night with all her faith.

I would love to say that as soon as she said "Amen," our house shook, the roof split open, and a bright light burst through the opening to engulf me with warm fuzzies, but that didn't happen. In fact, it seemed as if my mom's prayer had hit the ceiling and bounced back and was lying on the floor beside me. What was I to do now? My plan had failed. I would have to plead my own case.

I don't remember everything I said, but what I do remember saying is, "God, if you will open up a door for me, I will run through it!"

There was no earthshaking response or angelic choir, but at the very least I felt a peace that God knew I was listening and was ready to experience his purpose for my life. I went to bed and tried to trust that he had heard me and that things would improve.

A couple of weeks later, while browsing in a bookstore, I found out that God has impeccable timing.

At the magazine racks, one of the covers caught my eye. I noticed a woman with a prosthetic leg, so I picked up the issue. It was *Triathlete* magazine, and the woman on the cover was Sarah Reinertsen, a single amputee who had just completed the Ford Ironman World Championship triathlon in Hawaii. I excitedly read her story. She was born with a tissue defect and had had her left leg amputated above the knee when she was only seven years old. A few years later, she joined her school's track team just because no one thought she could do it and she wanted to prove them wrong. My kind of person.

Sarah became the youngest member of the United States Disabled Track Team and went on to set several world records for short-distance running. After a while, she decided to find out not just how fast she could run, but also how far; she started training for marathons, then triathlons. The article said she was the first female amputee ever to finish the Hawaiian Ironman.

I didn't really know what an Ironman was at the time, though I knew it was a triathlon. It turns out the race is regarded as the ultimate physical challenge—the world's toughest one-day endurance event. I thought about what a role model she was, for able-bodied and challenged athletes alike. But I particularly thought about little girls with artificial legs and how they must look at Sarah with awe. She represented such possibility.

As I finished reading the article about Sarah, my eyes settled on the magazine right next to it: *Men's Journal*. I picked it up and began to browse through it.

Flipping through the pages, I discovered an article about U.S. Army Major David Rozelle, a soldier who had lost part of his right leg in Iraq when a land mine exploded under his Humvee. Rather than go home and take a desk job, he had completed his rehabilitation and training and returned to active duty with his prosthetic leg—the only soldier known to have done such a thing. David wanted to be an inspiration for his fellow soldiers so he was now training for triathlons.

*How terrific*, I thought. So many times, I had wanted to be able to offer some kind of hope to the soldiers returning from Iraq with missing limbs and other disabilities. I wanted them to know they could still do something great with their lives—but the problem was I hadn't yet learned that lesson for myself.

*God, if you open a door for me, I promise I will run through it.*

Was he really taking me so literally?

As I looked at the picture of David Rozelle and thought about all the soldiers who had fought for my freedom only to return home with broken futures, I realized, *This is what I'm supposed to do. I believe God wants me to do an Ironman competition.*

# CHAPTER 8

There were a few small problems with my newfound plan—aside from the blatantly obvious fact that no one on two prosthetic legs had ever even come close to completing the Ironman distances in a triathlon.

The first problem was that I would need to swim 2.4 miles in the ocean, but I would have to learn how to swim all over again. As a young boy, I had learned to swim in a nearby pond inhabited by water moccasins, the dreaded serpents of the South. But that was when I had legs. I had no idea how to swim without legs. It would be a whole new experience. And somehow, I would have to learn to swim fast enough to make the swim segment cutoff time, which was 2 hours and 20 minutes.

If I made it through the swim portion of the race, I would have to ride a bike 112 miles, completing the swim and bike portions of the race in 10 hours and 30 minutes or be disqualified. My next problems: I hadn't ridden a bike since I'd gotten my prosthetics; I didn't own a fancy triathlon bike—or any bike, for that matter; and I couldn't afford even a cheap one. How in the world would I learn to ride a bike if I didn't have one?

If I could pull off those two unlikely feats—the swim and the bike ride—I would still have to run a full marathon: 26.2 miles. The problem there was that I had never even run the 0.2 of the 26.2 miles. It seemed like a long way to drive, much less run. The marathon was the last leg of the race, and it also had a cutoff time: midnight.

I would have only seventeen hours to make history. If the clock struck midnight and I had not crossed the finish line, I would not turn into a pumpkin—no, it would be much worse than that. I would turn into a guy with another shattered dream, going home to face my friends and their looks of pity.

Comparing myself to the triathletes in the magazines was sobering; I didn't look anything like them. My former athletic days were long gone, and I was now overweight, with a paunchy belly. I had played softball and flag football over the years, but you don't have to run very far in either of those recreational sports.

Then there was the fact that my sleep disorder left me fatigued before I even started exercising. And considering that I was falling asleep at stoplights, was I also going to fall asleep while biking?

To top it all off, I had no money to fund this endeavor. *This is crazy! I can't even pay my bills.* I was already borrowing money from friends to cover my rent and keep my lights on, while praying that there would be some money left over to buy something to eat. I needed a coach to give me direction and guidance, but I couldn't afford one. I would have to make do until my circumstances changed.

My family thought it was a ludicrous idea. My sweet mother pleaded with me to reconsider this absurd journey, which she was convinced would lead only to more heartache, frustration, and disappointment. Her fear was that failure at this last attempt to find meaning and purpose might be the straw that would finally push me over the edge to end my life.

Me in my senior year of high school—just two months before my accident in1986.

## *Growing up*

‹ Me on top of Henry, our Brahma bull.

My parents, Randy and Ruth Rigsby. ›

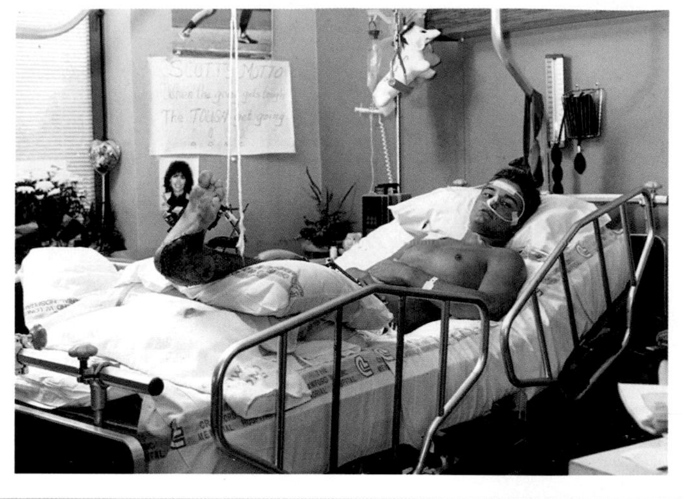

Recovering at Emory Crawford Long Memorial Hospital. My left thighbone was broken, my left ankle was totally mangled, and my left heel bone was missing.

## *9-second life change*

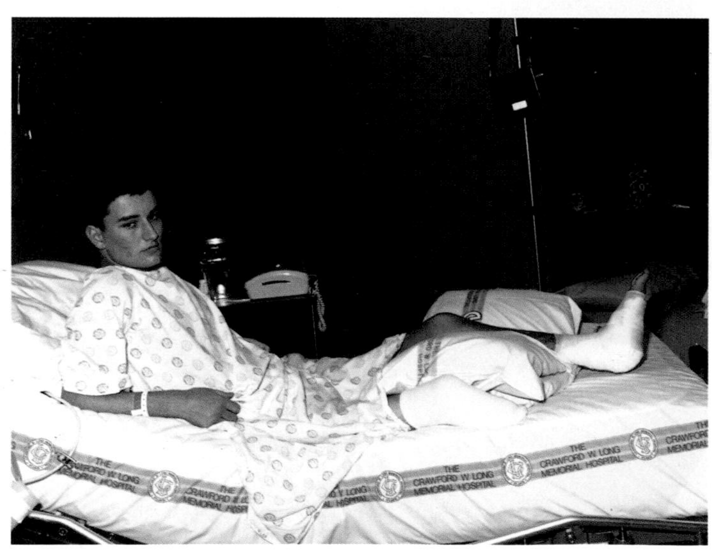


Within two days after the accident, my right leg was amputated below the knee.

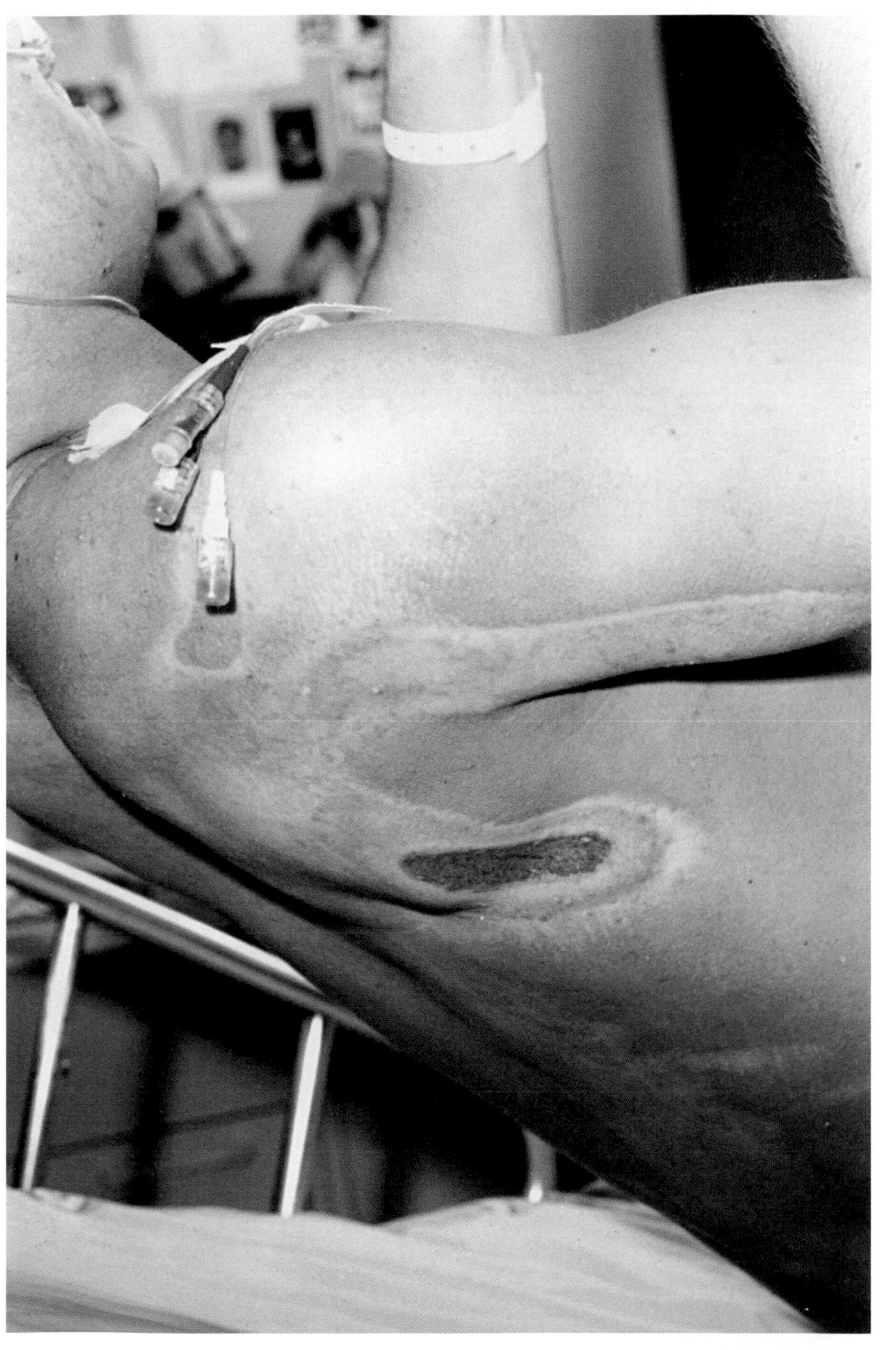

I suffered third-degree burns on my back from being dragged along the hot Georgia asphalt.

Two days before the Hawaiian Ironman competition in October 2007.

On the bike at the Coeur d'Alene Ironman in Idaho, 2007.

## *On a mission*

‹ Finishing up the running stage of a half Ironman in South Carolina in 2006.

Coming out of the water after the swimming portion of the Tri the Parks Triathlon in Georgia, 2006. ›

Race day at Kona (the Hawaiian Ironman), October 13, 2007. Here, one of my handlers, Marti Greer (right), helps me out of the water.

## *16 hours, 42 minutes, 46 seconds*

‹ Putting on my running legs for the final 26.2-mile push to the finish line.

Because I couldn't afford a bike of my own, I borrowed one for the competition—four sizes too small. ›

Crossing the world's most famous finish line in 16 hours, 42 minutes, and 46 seconds.

Kim Houx focuses on fine motor skill rehabilitation while visiting with Scott about the challenges of being a multiple amputee (April 2008).

## *Helping others*

Check out the looks on the children's faces as I show them how my prosthetics work. Priceless.

My dad would not even acknowledge the possibility that I could complete such a pipe dream.

"Son, you should have started this thing twenty years ago!" he said with a scowl.

He was right. I was thirty-seven years old; my best athletic years were behind me. I could not go back in time. But I believed God's timing was perfect. Throughout my life, it seemed he had been painfully slow, but never late.

I had never been an endurance athlete, but I believed God would make me into one. He had done that sort of thing throughout history—using the weak things of this world to confound the wise. And I certainly had enough weaknesses to fit the bill.

So, to recap: I was too old, too fat, too tired, and too broke. The more I thought about the unthinkable task that lay before me, the more that list of "Why I Should Not Even Start Down the Path" continued to grow. The odds weren't just stacked against me, they were towering over me and blocking out the sun.

I had no idea how I was going to make this dream come to fruition, but I was filled with hope—real hope, the kind I hadn't felt in years. All this time, I had been praying and waiting for God to show me that he had a special plan for me in this world, that he was going to use me for an extraordinary purpose. Deep inside, I was completely confident that training for a triathlon was the answer to my prayers. God would use every one of my weaknesses to bring about his ultimate plan.

After doing some research, I discovered that my hunch was right: No double amputee using prosthetics had ever completed an Ironman. My purpose was clear. I would complete the race just like the able-bodied triathletes. I would swim without my legs, I would use a regular bicycle with no modifications, and I would run on my running legs to cross the famous finish line of the Hawaiian Ironman.

*If I can do this, I could change the world!*

That was what mattered. If I could accomplish this, I could redefine the limits for amputees. My life—my crazy, sad, mixed-up life—could become an inspiration for the hundreds of thousands of amputees in the world.

The first day, I called all my close friends, along with some not-so-close friends and a few people I'd met while standing in line at the grocery store or something.

"I'm going to do an Ironman," I told them.

What's really amazing is that not one of them told me I was crazy. Mind you, it might have been that they didn't know what an Ironman was.

"Now, what is that?" they asked.

I would tell them about the distances, the time requirements, and the place and how I was going to be the first double amputee to do the race on prosthetics. For most of them, there was just an instant acceptance.

These were the people who'd watched me flounder for years. I had given them no reason to believe that I was ever going to get my act straight—yet somehow they all knew that this was the thing I would finally finish. I had so many people pulling for me, wanting to see me find some kind of inspiration and pull out of my depression, and they all seemed to accept just as readily as I did that this was the answer to their prayers.

On the second day, reality set in. God had given me a dream—now it was time to not just talk about it but do it. In the Bible, God told Noah to build an ark because it was going to rain and flood the earth. It had never rained, yet Noah was obedient and followed God's plans. I knew that God wanted me to complete an Ironman, and I wanted to be like Noah and be obedient to my calling. My problem was that God had given Noah detailed plans to build the boat. Where was my blueprint?

When faced with insurmountable odds, the most important thing to remember is to focus on what you know how to do, not all the things you don't know how to do. I didn't know how to swim and I didn't know how to ride a bike, but I did know how to run. Even though I didn't know how to run very far, it was still something to start with.

I lived in an apartment because that was all I could afford after having lost my life savings. The cool thing about the apartment complex was that it was next to my church, Buckhead Church, which had a good-sized parking lot because it used to be a Harris Teeter grocery store.

I decided to get up every morning before daylight and run in the church parking lot. I ran there because I didn't want anyone to see me slow to a walk when I ran out of steam. I wanted people to see something extraordinary when they saw me run, and that would take a while. Each morning before work, I would run until I couldn't run any more, and then I'd think, *Okay, that's enough for today.*

Every day, I tried to run longer than I had the day before. For two months, I ran in the parking lot every morning, until I felt comfortable enough to run on roads and running tracks without having to stop and walk. Each morning, I went to work happier than the day before.

Once I became comfortable with my running ability and endurance, I switched my focus to learning how to bike and swim. When I asked around to find out if anyone knew a good triathlon coach, the workers at a local bike shop spoke highly of a coach named Tony Myers. Tony was a top-notch cyclist himself, who also ran a local spinning studio. I called him and said, "I'm a double amputee, and I want to do an Ironman. No double amputee has ever come close to finishing an Ironman on prosthetics. I need your help. Will you meet with me?"

"Sure," he said. "Come on over."

Tony's business, Athletic Training Services, was located

in a little studio behind a strip mall. There wasn't even a sign to show it was there. There was one door to enter and leave. In many ways, the door was symbolic of the effect that Tony had on people's lives. Most people left in better shape, both mentally and physically, than when they entered. I was betting on him to do the same thing for me.

A friend from church went with me to meet Tony for the first time. Inside his studio, it was dark and warm, and the air was thick. Tony sized me up for a minute, with a Simon Cowell–type look of grave doubt on his face. I needed to do something to give him a glimmer of hope that he wouldn't be wasting his time and that I had the right stuff for this dream to become a reality.

"Do you want to see me run?" I asked. "Come on, I'll show you."

He followed me out into his parking lot, and I ran a few down-and-back, thirty-yard moderate sprints to show him what I could do. He later said that seeing me run was what convinced him that maybe I really could do the Ironman.

My next hurdle was convincing Tony to work with me without payment.

"I don't have any money for a bike," I said, "and I can't pay you for your help—at least not yet. But I'm hoping to get some sponsorships—and if I do, then I'll be able to pay you for your coaching time. Do you think you could help me?"

Tony had been in a bike wreck a few weeks earlier, and he was still recovering from a traumatic brain injury. It was severe enough that he had experienced some seizures, so he couldn't drive and was dependent on others at that time. Maybe that gave him some extra compassion for me.

"Sure," he said. "We'll do it."

The important thing was that he didn't laugh at me. He didn't discourage me or tell me about the insurmountable odds of the massive undertaking I was proposing. I think that's important. When people tell you about their big dreams, even if the dreams sound unrealistic or far-fetched, why pour water on their fire? The reality is that those dreams may or may not come to fruition, but the pathway to finding out is much more bearable if you have people supporting you along the way. And I did. If those around me had any doubts, they kept them to themselves.

Tony put me on a spinning bike immediately in one of his morning classes. There were about twenty-five of these state-of-the-art stationary bikes in the front of the room. The sound track for the session was Tony's own mix of mind-numbing, heart-pounding beats. Within minutes, he began yelling instructions at me, just like he did with everyone else in the class. That was his thing—he motivated by yelling and cursing. That's how we knew he cared about us.

Tony is a guy who takes no excuses, and I liked that because I knew he wasn't patronizing me. He wasn't about to go easy on me just because I had no legs. If I'd had no arms, either, he would have told me to hang onto the handlebars with my teeth and quit my bellyaching. This agonizing yet rewarding experience began every day promptly at 5 a.m., and the morning class could last for two hours if the participants were up for the challenge.

A couch and a few chairs provided a place for people to sit and discuss the oncoming storm of physical exertion or to brag about what they had just endured.

As I later learned, Tony fully understood what it took for people to transform their lives. He had once weighed 285 pounds, which was morbidly obese for his 5'8" frame. Cycling had saved his life, and now he was a sleek 150 pounds. He is a very intelligent man and could have had a successful career in the business world, but then he would have missed his true calling in life. His purpose was to help other people transform their lives in that small, tucked-away spinning studio.

When I got on a bike, I didn't worry about whether or not it fit, or how my prostheses were supposed to fit into the pedals. Tony found me a bike with toe cages to put my walking feet into, and I just rode. I think that's what he liked about me the most. I knew that the important thing at that point wasn't how efficient I was; the important thing was to get on the bike and ride, period.

So much of endurance training is just about showing up to the workout and putting in the hours. As you get more advanced in the sport, things such as intervals, hill repeats, strength training, and specific drills become important, but quality time in each discipline is paramount.

Equally important is the mental preparation that is needed in endurance training. It's about not letting anything interfere with your commitment so that you can get in whatever training you need to get done. Every day, I could have come up with a hundred reasons to sleep in or to skip training: I was too tired, too sore, too busy. Maybe I was getting a cold; maybe I had errands to run. But I had to keep reminding myself that, barring an emergency or serious injury, training was not optional. I also was grateful to have someone holding me accountable. Tony had his own endearing way of letting me know he didn't approve when I had a lame excuse for missing a workout.

"You have your priorities messed up!" he would scream.

Sometimes when I ran, my prosthetic feet would crack. While waiting for another pair to be made, I duct taped the cracked ones and kept running. I tried not to worry myself out of training. Instead, I'd try to think it through logically.

*Okay, so my feet aren't in great shape. I'm going to run anyway. I'll bring some tape in case they break, and I'll carry my phone with me so I can call someone if I get stuck. Someone will pick me up—I can figure out what to do then, if it happens.*

My last challenge was that I needed to learn how to swim.

Pete Higgins is the swim coach at an elite private school in Atlanta. He is also, hands down, the best high school swim coach in the state, having coached more than 150 high school and independent school All Americans. Pete had been a coach for about forty years, and his teams had won more than twenty-five state swimming championships.

He was the kind of man I would need in my corner. But would he take on a colossal challenge like me? There was one way to find out. I called Pete and told him what I wanted to do. He said, "Well, let's meet and see what happens."

Here's the part where I hope no one from that school is reading this book. I'll write it very quietly: Pete would sneak me into the pool almost every Sunday afternoon. You may have read the heartwarming book *Tuesdays with Morrie.* Well, I had Sundays with Pete. I not only learned how to swim but, through Pete's wisdom and guidance, I learned lessons that would help me stay afloat in the midst of life's most treacherous waters. Pete would sit at one end of the pool with a pencil and a tiny, handheld, spiral notepad. It was there he would watch me and work his magic.

At first, our time together was a journey of discovery for both of us. Pete wanted to know what would happen if I actually tried to kick with my partial legs fully extended while holding onto a kickboard with my hands. I had never used a kickboard, so I didn't know what would happen.

What happened was I started going backward. The USS *Rigsby* was like a steamboat, except I was in reverse.

*That didn't work out so well,* I thought.

In a grandfatherly way, Pete said, "Let's not do that again."

To some degree, I think Pete was more excited about the challenge of teaching me to swim than I was about learning. He was so used to working with elite athletes who needed only a little guidance and direction. On the other hand, I was like putty in a sculptor's hands. With me, he had the potential to mold a masterpiece.

In contrast to Tony's tough manner, Pete's way of teaching was to focus on my positives, even if they were few and far between. He never told me I was doing something wrong; he would only suggest a different way of doing it. What he did was build a confidence in me that I would carry throughout my Ironman journey.

I was pretty pathetic as a swimmer in the beginning, but he was patient with me and we made great improvement each week. Then, in the fall of 2006, Pete's son Bobby, who had been diagnosed with Lou Gehrig's disease, needed his full attention. Pete had to stop coaching me in order to be there for his son. Although our coaching relationship was coming to an end, our friendship remained. We kept in touch, catching up from time to time.

After that, I joined the master swim program, Tri-Master Swim, at Concourse Athletic Club in Atlanta. Twice a week, I swam in the mornings and evenings with two coaches who worked on my strength, speed, and endurance.

At the beginning of all this training, I still worked at Soliant Health. I worked there for about eight months before getting fired in April of 2006. Frankly, I deserved it. I was horrible at the job, and my heart wasn't in it. Doug, my manager, had stuck his neck out for me from time to time, and he arranged to get me some severance pay, which wasn't customary for my position. He told me he believed in me and what I was trying to accomplish with the Ironman. I don't know whether Doug thought I could complete the Ironman or not, but he always made me feel like nothing could stop me.

I knew that if I was really going to get in shape to do an Ironman, I would have to pump up my training routine even more—and that's extremely difficult to do while holding a day job. Athletes who compete at an elite or a professional level usually don't have day jobs—they just train, train, train. I needed not only more time to train but more time to experiment with different types of prosthetics and components. I had no frame of reference. I didn't know of another double amputee who was trying to do what I was attempting.

I had one final nest egg, and it was time to cash it in.

My grandparents had left me a small piece of land on the farm, behind my parents' house. I wanted to sell that land and use the money to tide me over so I could put all my energy into training, but I was not allowed to sell the land because I was still legally incompetent. I'd need my parents' permission to sell it.

I explained to my dad all about the Ironman, and how no double amputee had ever done it before. I told him I believed that this was God's purpose for me and that I wanted our soldiers coming home from Iraq to know that their sacrifice was not in vain—they could still live an active lifestyle. Then I told him I wanted to put my land up for sale.

"I don't want you selling that land," my dad said. "I want to keep it in the family."

"It's my land," I said. "And I want to sell it. Do you understand what I'm trying to do here, Dad? I'm trying to make history. I am trying to fulfill God's purpose for my life!"

No, he didn't understand what I was trying to do. He thought that my Ironman dream was really stupid and utterly pointless—that I should stop all the nonsense and get a real job and find someone willing to marry me and forget about the whole "trying to make history" thing.

*But God wants me to do an Ironman. I just know it,* I said to myself as I nursed the wounds from another losing battle with my dad.

It was painful and frustrating that he couldn't understand I had finally found a reason to live and something to be hopeful about, to be happy about. For the first time since I was seventeen years old, I felt as if I could see a bright future. All my dad saw was financial irresponsibility and foolish dreams. Even so, he offered a compromise.

"Tell you what. I'll reverse the paperwork so you can be legally competent again, and then I'll buy that land from you. I'll pay you $200,000 for it. I'll pay you some of that up front, and then $1,000 a month after that."

A thousand dollars a month was not enough to live on in Atlanta—or anywhere else, really—but I didn't have a choice. It was better than nothing, and I still had hopes that I'd pick up sponsorships and odd jobs along the way. My dad figured that by doling out the money so slowly, he'd force me to find a real job, but I had other plans. I was going to follow my calling, and I would scrape by one way or another. Nothing else seemed important anymore.

That month, I entered my first triathlon. There wasn't much forethought; I just needed to give it a shot to see if I could do it. On a whim, I entered a sprint-distance triathlon in Panama City, Florida. Sprint triathlons are the shortest-distance triathlons. People sometimes think that triathlons are long-distance events, but triathlons are just competitions that include swimming, biking, and running (in that order), with a time cutoff for each discipline and an overall time to complete each event. None of them have to be long races. Besides the sprint triathlon category, there are the Olympic-distance, the half-Ironman, and the Ironman triathlons.

The Emerald Coast Sprint Triathlon consisted of a one-third-mile swim in the Gulf of Mexico, a 15-mile bike ride, and a 3.1-mile run. Ironically, it was on the same beach as the world's largest nightclub, where I had spent countless hours destroying my body. It was odd to see the parking lot now filled with hundreds of bikes.

I borrowed a bike from a friend of a friend. It didn't fit me, so I adjusted my prosthetic legs to fit the bike. At that point, I'd never ridden a real bike using prosthetics—let alone outdoors on real terrain; I had used only the stationary spinning bikes inside Tony Myers's studio. Almost all triathletes have clips that lock their shoes into the pedals, but I couldn't afford those yet, so I just took off my shoes and rode barefoot. Well, not exactly barefoot; I rode with my prosthetic foot shells and no shoes.

I had also never swum in the ocean to that point, only in a pool. I really didn't know what it was going to be like, but I knew I had to start somewhere, and this seemed as good a time as any. I sort of suspected my coaches and physical therapist would think it was too soon, so I didn't tell them I was going until the day before I left for the event.

The normal progression probably would have been to try a couple of road races before tackling a full triathlon. I had never even done a 5K race before. But remember what I said about my problem with patience? I don't have any. I didn't want to run a road race. I wanted to do a triathlon to start my Ironman journey.

As I drove to Panama City the night before the race, the weather verged on tropical storm conditions. In the morning, it was still pouring, but there was a momentary break in the weather when I set up my bike and leg parts in the transition area. It was the first time I'd ever seen a "transition area"—the station the athletes go to in between the swimming and the biking portion of the race and between the biking and the running portion.

Usually, the transition area opens about an hour and a half before the race starts to give the competitors a chance to get their things in place. So, at about 5:30 a.m., I would have to have my brain together enough to make sure I'd set out everything I'd need. The problem for me was that I didn't have any idea what I needed, and there wasn't anyone to call to ask for advice. Are these the right prosthetic sleeves? liners? feet?

socks? My pain of discovery would one day be some other amputee's gain.

I had also never even attended a triathlon as a spectator before, which I really should have done. At least then I could have watched the athletes and taken notes about what they did. Instead, I took a guess. I had packed everything but the kitchen sink, and I left that out only because it wouldn't fit in my transition bag. I tried so hard to look like I knew what I was doing, like I did this all the time and my fellow athletes must just have failed to notice the legless guy before.

But I discovered just how little I knew about what I was doing when I took off my legs and toddled over to the swim area with all the other triathletes. As I kneeled on the beach to await the starting gun, I realized that everyone else had wet suits on. I didn't know that I could wear a wet suit. Not that it actually mattered, because I didn't own a wet suit and certainly could not have afforded one. The only other swimmers without wet suits were the Navy SEALs. Yep, it was just the SEALs and Scott Rigsby, hard-core and fearless. All I had on were my regular swim trunks, and let me tell you: That water was cold. April rainstorm cold.

Because of the weather, there was an hour and a half delay of the swim start. Sixty miles down the road, another triathlon had canceled the swim portion because of rough seas, turning its event into a duathlon instead. Our race didn't cancel the swim portion, but the officials warned us that the conditions would be bad.

Spotters on Sea-Doos fought the rough current to hold the marking buoys in place. Then the starting gun went off and I dived into the ocean. By the time I made it past the first buoy, rescuers had already pulled someone out of the water.

*Thank goodness that wasn't me*, I thought. *I'm still in this thing*.

I was the last person to finish the swim, but I finished it, and that was fine with me. I wasn't in it to win; I just wanted to get it done.

I swam with no prosthetics—just gel liners over my stumps. As I came out of the water, I had to walk on my knees. I looked like some kind of sea hobbit emerging onto the beach. There I was met by a volunteer, who had a towel and a bucket of fresh water. I poured the water over each prosthetic liner to wash away the sand and used the towel to dry my stumps as I placed them into the sleeves of my walking legs.

I had to walk about three hundred yards across the sand and through the beach club to the transition area. By the time I got there, prosthetic legs and parts were everywhere. My transition area looked like a mannequin store had blown up. The storm had soaked everything and scattered my stuff all over. I had no idea what to do. People offered to help, but I didn't know what to tell them to do.

I just wiped off everything with towels as best I could. Once I was finished, I headed off to the bike portion, where I put my feet into toe cages on a regular bike.

When I had about three miles left to go on the bike course, a police motorcycle got in front of me and a police cruiser got behind me, escorting me the rest of the way. I guess they decided I needed a little protection. With the police escort, at least no one was going to knock me off my bike. I felt like I was the mayor of Panama City. We were cruising through red lights as people's jaws dropped to the ground at the sight of a guy with no legs riding a regular bicycle.

It felt amazing to ride a real bicycle for the first time. I could understand now why Tony was so passionate about cycling. There was freedom from the cares of the world, even if only for a short time. This was the first and, to date, the longest bike ride of my life, and I hoped there would be many more like it.

After the bike portion, I put on my running legs and

completed the 3.1-mile course. I crossed the finish line dead last in the blistering hot sun of the Florida panhandle, but I crossed the finish line. For me, it was a huge accomplishment. It meant that I really could do this—that my Ironman dream wasn't just a crazy notion. It was something within my reach if I worked hard enough.

Over the course of the next seven weeks, I completed five more sprint triathlons and improved my time at each race. It's not normal to race that many times in succession, but then again, there was nothing normal about what I was doing. I had to find ways to try out new prosthetic components and ways to transition more quickly in a real race setting. These sprint triathlons were the laboratory in which I could conduct my experiments. If I failed on the shorter courses, the consequences were minimal. I was working out my issues now so I wouldn't have to figure things out later on a bigger stage when the stakes would be much higher. Also, I couldn't afford therapy so I ran the weekly races to help me cope with my inner demons.

In June, I ran my first road race with other amputees. The Achilles Track Club sponsored a 5K "Hope and Possibility" race in Minneapolis, in partnership with the Amputee Coalition of America. The Coalition was holding its annual conference that weekend, and the race was on the last day.

Dick Traum, the founder of the Achilles Track Club, was the first single-leg amputee ever to run a marathon. The club's chairperson, Trisha Meili, is best known as the "Central Park Jogger"—the woman who nearly died at the hands of an attacker in 1989. Part of what helped her rebuild her life was learning to run again with the club's help. She wrote a best-selling memoir titled, *I Am the Central Park Jogger: A Story of Hope and Possibility*. The race was named after the title of the book.

In both her book and her life, Trisha tries to be an

example of what's possible even after horrifying tragedy. Six years after her attack, she went back to Central Park and ran the New York City Marathon. She called that "reclaiming" her park.

When I looked at Trisha Meili, I saw someone further along on the same path I had recently started. Like her, I wanted to become a beacon of hope. If this woman, who had been so brutally attacked that she was comatose for nearly two weeks, could now appear before crowds with a big smile on her face to show others that life goes on, what might *I* be able to accomplish?

The Achilles Track Club is filled with inspirational people who have done unthinkable things—who recovered when doctors never expected them to recover, who walked when they were expected to remain permanently in a wheelchair, and who ran despite all odds. Many of them will tell you that before they were disabled they weren't as active as they are now. And they've learned that we don't just *go* through pain; we *grow* through pain.

The Achilles Freedom Team, one of the club's special divisions, is specifically for wounded soldiers returning from Iraq and Afghanistan. The program is meant to help these soldiers get rehabilitated and back into active lives through the sport of running. Several members of the Freedom Team had completed the New York City Marathon together the previous year.

"There's no hierarchy in suffering," Trisha Meili said in the *New York Post*. "Everyone has their own separate issues, but there's a common bond that we share." And she was right. Whether we came by our suffering at the hands of an attacker, a car accident, a land mine, or any other cause, there was something unifying all of us: We refused to roll over and accept a limited life. We were out to show ourselves, and maybe others, that we were still alive—really alive.

I felt good among this group, and I became friends with several members. Mary Bryant, vice president of Achilles, is a breast cancer survivor who ran her fourth marathon just days after her fifth round of chemotherapy. In addition to overcoming her own obstacles, though, she was also used to helping people with disabilities, including her brother, who was a quadriplegic. He was her inspiration to start running.

She started the Achilles Freedom Team for wounded veterans at the Walter Reed Army Medical Center, where many of the recent amputees gave her strange looks when she told them she wanted to train them to run marathons. However, after suspending their disbelief at least temporarily, many of them began training on hand-crank wheelchairs.

In 2002, Mary was officially the slowest runner in the New York City Marathon, finishing behind all 31,830 other racers—but with good reason. She was racing with her friend Bill Reilly, an athlete with cerebral palsy who pushed himself backward in his wheelchair the entire racecourse, more than nine hours.

Mary was the one who insisted that I had to try the 2006 New York City Triathlon, which was also the Physically Challenged National Championships. I told her it sounded like a great idea, but the race was closed and the registration for it had long passed. Mary's uniqueness is that she doesn't see obstacles; she sees only the way around, over, or through them. She got me registered in the race.

That race became my first record-setting accomplishment: I became the first known double amputee to finish an Olympic-distance triathlon on prosthetics. Also at that race, any physically challenged (PC) athlete finishing in less than four hours earned a spot on the 2006 USA Triathlon team. These athletes would compete at the 2006 International Triathlon Union (ITU) World Triathlon Championships in Lausanne, Switzerland. It was an Olympic-distance triathlon with the world's best short-course triathletes. I finished in less than four hours and earned my spot on the team.

At that point, the media started to pay a little attention to me. I got my first few pictures and articles in newspapers and magazines, which felt great.

*This is only the beginning,* I thought. *These people don't know it yet, but I'm going to do the unthinkable.*

I completed three Olympic-distance triathlons in six weeks, the last one being the ITU World Triathlon Championships. My physical therapist, Kate McDonald, told me in great frustration that I was overtraining and pushing my body too far too soon. I love Kate like a sister, so like any good brother, I decided not to listen to her advice.

The day before I left for Switzerland, I got an e-mail from another Atlanta triathlete, Mike Lenhart, who went to the same church I did. He and I had been introduced before and had met up at a previous race, but I didn't really know him. Little did I know that he had been eavesdropping on my conversation at church the previous week. By Mike's account—which, for the record, I believe is false and unfounded—I was bragging to a couple of young women about how I had won my category in all these triathlons. Mike grinned to himself and thought, *Well, of course he's winning his category. There's no one else* in *his category!*

Mike was partly right about my USA and ITU classification. There was no category for me, but I was competing against guys with legs in these PC races. At the time, there were no other double amputees running in these races, so the race officials put me in the same category as guys with muscular dystrophy, cerebral palsy, arthritis, spina bifida, nerve damage, retinitis pigmentosa, and multiple sclerosis.

Mike told me he wanted to figure out why there weren't more physically challenged athletes participating in triathlons in the United States. He liked seeing me out there, but I was basically the only PC athlete he knew; he was thinking about starting an organization to encourage other challenged athletes to join the sport. "Would you be willing to meet with me and talk about it?" he wanted to know.

"Sure. I'm leaving for Switzerland tomorrow, but I'll call you as soon as I get back."

Competing at the ITU World Triathlon Championships was life changing for me in many ways. For starters, I hadn't traveled very much. It was an amazing cultural experience meeting interesting, funny, inspirational people from all over the world who shared the same excitement and passion I have for triathlons. It made my love for triathlons and my desire to be a lifelong ambassador for the sport to the physically challenged community that much greater.

The race setting in Switzerland was breathtaking. I remember sitting on the top dock, right before the swim start, and gazing at the view of majestic, snow-covered mountains while the sun beamed off Lake Geneva. During the frigid swim, I was shocked that I could actually see the bottom of the lake—a most welcome change from swimming in the murky lakes of northern Georgia during my first few sprint triathlons, not to mention the Hudson River during the New York City Triathlon. I didn't think my swim went particularly well, but it ended up being a personal record.

The biking segment of the race was challenging, making me grateful for the hills in Georgia and for my bike coach, Tony, who would yell, "Increase your resistance!" during our spinning classes. Cresting the hills on the bike course and being greeted by a view of the Swiss Alps was surreal and worthy of any postcard.

Finally, there was the run. It was simultaneously one of the most encouraging and humbling experiences I have had. As I started the run, thousands of people were cheering wildly. I had heard large crowds yelling before, but never cheering in that many different languages.

The run went extremely well, and I set another personal record. I'm quite certain that my fastest run time had a lot to do with one particular turn in the race, where, every lap, I was cheered on by Carla Loureiro, one of the most beautiful triathletes I had ever seen. It was worth running another lap just to hear her say in her sweet South African accent, "Go, U.S.A.! Go, number 20!" One of the best things about that race was that Carla and I became good friends.

When I got back from Switzerland, an extensive feature story about me graced the front page of the sports section in the Sunday edition of *The Atlanta Journal-Constitution*. It was the first weekend of college football, so it was one of the paper's most widely read editions throughout the South.

Meanwhile, back at my apartment, I found out my power had been cut off. It was a humbling experience of a very different sort. There I was, becoming a minor celebrity traveling the world as a physically challenged triathlete, and Georgia Power had shut off the juice because I couldn't pay my bill. I stayed with my buddy John for the night and borrowed money from him to get the bill paid. Over the years, many of my friends had loaned me thousands of dollars to pay my bills. I've been lucky to always have people I can count on when I need help.

A reporter who had done a previous story on me called me to ask how things had gone in Switzerland. When I told him about coming home to no electricity, he was horrified. The news segment that night was very critical of the electric company for shutting my power off while I was out "representing my country." It wasn't the power company's fault that I hadn't paid my bill, of course, but the televised news report didn't do it any favors.

After being back a few days, I called Mike Lenhart and we

got together to have a serious talk about developing a strategy to get more PC athletes into the sport of triathlons. Mike, who had grown up with a father who was a retired colonel, told me that he originally got into triathlons as a hobby after finishing active duty as an Army captain. What he had noticed over the past few years was that the number of able-bodied triathletes joining the sport went way up each year, but the number of PC athletes had stayed pretty much the same.

Especially because of the conflicts in Iraq and Afghanistan, Mike didn't understand why there weren't more wounded soldiers joining the sport. He thought it would be a good way to get them integrated back into the community and back into an active way of life. Really, it could just as well have been basketball or Ping-Pong, but triathlons happened to be the sport Mike liked to do.

Mike decided to start a foundation that would match able-bodied athletes with PC athletes. He named it Getting2Tri and asked if I wanted to be a part of it. He offered to become my training partner, and we would be the pilot program in this not-yet-existent organization.

Mike was already making plans for the end of October, when he was going to attempt the Great Floridian Triathlon, which is an Ironman-distance race. I told him I was working toward an Ironman, too, and wanted to know if he'd help me get ready. He agreed, and it turned out great for me. Where I was scattered, Mike was organized; where I was a dreamer, he was a scheduler. He nicknamed me Big Rig and helped me work on my discipline and techniques.

No double amputee on prosthetics was known to have finished a half-Ironman—a 1.2-mile swim, a 56-mile bike ride, and a 13.1-mile run—which must be completed within eight hours. I was going to travel to Greenwood, South Carolina, to try to make history on October 1, 2006, by competing in the South Carolina Half Ironman Triathlon.

The weekend of the race, though, coincided with my twenty-year high school reunion. I had promised to speak to my high school's football team and to give the invocation at the homecoming game on Friday night. (We won big, by the way.) I also agreed to two media interviews and squeezed in visits with my parents and old friends. The next morning, I drove to South Carolina with Tony Myers and Mike Lenhart.

The finish line on the racecourse was something you'd expect to see in the movies—a perfect grassy knoll that provided an amphitheater-like setting for spectators to watch and cheer.

The night before the race, Mike told me, "I want you to imagine this grassy area filled with people watching you reach your goal. When you get tired out there tomorrow, remember that the finish line here will be worth the pain everywhere else."

That night I meant to go to bed early, but the University of Georgia football team was losing, and I couldn't go to sleep until they got the lead. Ugh! I ended up getting four and a half hours of sleep before the race.

Nevertheless, the triathlon went very well. Everything that day just seemed to fall into place. Despite the lack of sleep, I awoke feeling very strong. When I arrived at the transition area, race director Jeremey Davis and his crew had given me lots of extra space for all my stuff. (Some races can be logistical nightmares, and I've had to stack legs on top of one another to get all my things in the allotted area.)

At the swim start, I had the usual nerves, but I really felt the encouragement and prayers of so many people easing my anxiety. Just before we started, Jeremey made the announcement that I was about to make triathlon history.

He would later say, "The energy was electric as the athletes in the water gave him a 'wading ovation' unlike any I had heard. It really sank in just before he got into the water when

Scott handed his coach his legs. I thought, *This man is about to attempt what was once thought impossible and do it with a smile on his face*. When someone like Scott tackles a task like this, it makes us all realize how strong we . . . human beings can be. Any chance we get to witness this sort of courage, we will take."

The swim went even better than I had hoped. I had planned to finish in an hour, but I made it in forty-six minutes. Not bad for a guy who had learned to swim only six months earlier!

I was somewhat familiar with the bike course because Mike Lenhart and I had ridden a modified version of the course the previous Sunday. I say "somewhat" and "modified," because one would think that at West Point or Army Ranger School they would have taught Mike how to read a map. He had us completely lost when we were supposed to be practicing riding the course. It worked out great for me, however, because Mike's course was more difficult than the actual racecourse.

Mike had a strategy for me to go faster on the bike. He said he was going to tape a picture of Carla Loureiro—the beautiful South African triathlete who had cheered me on in Switzerland—onto the back of his bike jersey and ride ahead of me to motivate me to go faster. If that didn't work, he was going to get some long, fake French braids and hang them out both sides of his helmet. (Carla wears her hair in braids when she races.) Fortunately, he didn't have to resort to such drastic measures.

I finished the cycling stage in time, loaded up on food, and went out on the run—13.1 miles—which would be the longest distance I had ever run. My running legs were not set up to carry me that kind of distance consistently, but I wasn't going to let anything stand in my way of finishing, even if I had to walk on my knees or crawl to the finish line.

As I ran up the final hill to complete the race, people were lined up along the grassy knoll cheering wildly—just the way

Mike had asked me to picture it. As I came closer, Jeremey Davis began talking to the crowd.

"Some people have a setback and choose to fade away; others choose to stand up and face the obstacles. Scott Rigsby is one such person."

I crossed the line and hugged my coach and wept. I was thrilled to achieve my short-term goal and to move closer to my ultimate goal, the Ironman.

I had to keep increasing my distances to test myself and see if I had what it takes to do a full Ironman. On one particular training run with Mike in a local park, an elderly man on a bike came toward us. He had a spare bike tire around his neck, and he appeared homeless. You'd think that a homeless guy with a bike tire around his neck would win the "weirdness" contest, but no . . . apparently I was still the weird one.

He stared at me for a few seconds before exclaiming, "Where's yo feets?"

"I ain't got none!" I said and kept running. Sometimes those moments of amusement are just the distraction you need when running. Otherwise it could get boring.

My running feet, which I'd had since April, had now begun to show cracks, and the carbon fiber was delaminating, which meant it was time for a new pair. They were under warranty, so I knew I could get a new pair manufactured for free. I also needed lots of new sockets and new prosthetic cycling feet with cleats bolted into them, but my greatest need was a prosthetist who specialized in making prosthetics for active amputees.

My current prosthetist, John Fredrick of IPA Prosthetics and Orthotics, was six hours away in Panama City, Florida. John had not only been my prosthetist for the past twenty years but had always been a friend. Now I needed more advanced prosthetics, which would require a lot of trial and error on both our parts. The crisis I faced was that I didn't know how John could make better legs for the events, and he really didn't have the time or the resources for experimentation. It felt like the end of an era, but it was time to move on.

I did a little research to find out who had worked on the prosthetics for other amputees in the Ironman and came upon a company in New York. I called and asked if it would help make me new running and cycling legs. The prosthetist agreed, but he was very concerned with making sure I got his company a lot of good press. They had sponsored another athlete and didn't feel they'd received enough advertising in return.

Mary Bryant from Achilles Track Club was kind enough to pay for my flight to New York. As soon as I arrived and we had discussed the specifications for the legs he would provide, the prosthetist started pressuring me to sign an exclusive contract, making his company the sole supplier for my prosthetics and spelling out how I would advertise for them in return.

"I'm not going to sign anything until I get back home and meet with a lawyer," I said, which the prosthetist objected to. At that point, I should have seen that things here were not going to end well, but I spent ten days in New York having new legs made nonetheless.

When I got back to Atlanta, I had a race a few days later. It was a duathlon: a three-mile run, a twelve-mile bike ride, and another three-mile run. The run went fine, but on the bike course, one of my new cycling feet broke and I had to ride the last six miles with one leg. Well, really, it was half a leg. It was a very hilly course, too. Amazingly, I still beat about fifty other cyclists to the finish line.

I took the broken foot to a bike shop, and the owner said, "The screw in this cycling cleat is stripped. Whoever did this doesn't know anything about cycling, or the screw wouldn't have been positioned in this way. They also wouldn't have put this type of cleat on there, either."

When I called the prosthetist and relayed the information from this conversation to him, he was furious that I would believe the bike shop owner and was questioning his expertise. After he had yelled and cursed at me, he told me to mail back my cycling feet, saying that he would fix them. He also told me that my replacement running feet had come in and that I should send back the old ones.

I never saw any of them again.

For two months, I waited and called and waited some more. "I don't have any other running legs," I told him. "I need those feet in order to train. I have to keep running while you're working on my cycling feet."

"You'll get your running feet back when you send me the signed contract," he said.

"And what if I don't want to sign that contract?"

"Then you owe us thousands of dollars for those running feet."

I asked him to mail me back the cracked feet, but he said he couldn't—he had already sent them to the manufacturer. However, when I called the manufacturer, it couldn't track down my cracked feet. The representative confirmed that the prosthetist still had them, but he would not give them back. I told the prosthetist that I really needed some feet to run on because I couldn't afford to stop training; I had several races coming up.

He claimed he had "upgraded" my running feet and wanted more than $1,000 from me. I didn't have enough money for shipping, let alone a thousand bucks.

Next, he billed my insurance company $15,000 for his work, even after I had shipped him back the bad walking feet he'd put on me and while he was holding my running feet hostage. The manufacturer tried to step in and get him to send me the feet, but he still wouldn't.

What it taught me was that there is corruption in every

line of work. Somehow, you don't expect to come across such opportunists among people who make their living supposedly helping amputees. But, sad to say, he's not the only one like this. I have encountered several others who aren't in the prosthetics business because they actually have a desire to help challenged athletes. Instead, they see athletes with disabilities as expendable means to an end: We're the heartwarming stories that make them look good, thereby making them more money. Fortunately, my overall experience has been much more positive than that, and I have met some great people in the prosthetics industry.

The silver lining in this dark cloud was finding my current prosthetist, Stephen Schulte of ProCare-Prosthetic Care in Suwanee, Georgia. Stephen is one of those once-in-a-lifetime kinds of people who are completely genuine and ridiculously good to their clients. He would work all day, go home to his family, drive his daughters to their sports practices, eat dinner, and then come back to meet me at the prosthetics facility around ten after his family had gone to bed. Sometimes, he'd stay with me until one o'clock in the morning, working on my legs. And then he'd have to be back at work at eight the next morning. Who does that?

One time when I was having a problem with my legs and Steve and his family were on vacation, he agreed to meet me at a gas station along the way—in the pouring rain—to make an adjustment for me. While holding an umbrella in a torrential downpour, he watched me run around the parking lot and fixed my legs right there on the spot.

Stephen or his partner, Rusty, would show up at all my major events—even the ones out of town—to make sure my prosthetics were in good shape before the race. After checking out my equipment to see if it was functioning properly, whoever had come would then go back to work. Many times they never saw me complete the race; by the time I crossed the finish line, they had already flown home to work on the arms and legs of other amputees who had aspirations as important as mine. Stephen and his staff helped everyone: rich, poor, black, white, young, and old. Having people make that much of an investment in me, just because they cared, spurred me on. I wanted to make them proud.

Most people who work with challenged athletes, as well as those in the prosthetics field, are really good people. My trust was more fully restored when I contacted Freedom Innovations, a newer prosthetics manufacturer in Irvine, California, with a top-notch research and development team in an aerospace engineering plant in Utah. When Stephen and I contacted them about my problem, they sent me some new feet right away, free of charge. They believed in what I was doing. Stephen worked intensively with me to get the feet fitted and ready so I could get back to racing again.

That Christmas, I caught up with my parents and siblings and told them what I was up to—that I had set some world records; that I was in a bunch of magazines and on television shows; that I had my first major corporate sponsor; but more important, that I had helped people along the way.

My dad didn't say much of anything to me during my visit, and later I asked him, "How come you've never told me you're proud of me after all the things I've done this year?"

"Because I'm not proud of you," he said.

I wish I could tell you that I was secure enough in what I was doing that it didn't sting, but that would be a lie. It stung, badly. I don't care who you are or what you're doing in life; deep down, you want your parents to be proud of you.

My dad wasn't going to be proud of me even if I completed my ultimate goal—and he was determined not to be proud of me in advance. In his opinion, I was wasting my life. I could have let that get to me to the point where I gave up my dream, but I knew I had to live my life, not my father's life for me.

With or without his support, I was going to do something extraordinary.

Mike and I ran the ING Miami Half Marathon in January of 2007. The Freedom Team of the Achilles Track Club was there, so there were a number of athletes in wheelchairs and handcycles. All the PC athletes got a five-minute head start at 6:05 a.m., and the rest of the runners began at 6:10. It was pouring rain, but spirits were high.

Soon, the front of the pack—a group of world-class runners from Kenya—caught up with us. They were on one side of the road, and we PC athletes were on the other. The contrast struck the camera crew filming us—there we were, two extremes: some of the best distance runners in the world right next to a bunch of competitors with missing legs and other disabilities. The Kenyans were there to win the race; we were there for an entirely different type of "win." We were all there to cross our own personal finish lines.

An airline's marketing team had read my story in *Competitor* magazine and knew I was getting some good press for racing, so they called me up and offered to sponsor me for three road races. I would put their logo on my jersey and mention them in my interviews, and in return, they would give me free airline flight miles that I could use however I wanted.

My buddy Mike McClain tried to negotiate with them for me. He was trying to get some actual green money for me, because if I was going to keep up all this racing, I would have to find a way to pay my bills. Besides, there were travel expenses and entry fees for me to get into these races. But he reported back, "I think this is the best we're going to get."

It was better than nothing, and I proudly wore their logo across my shirt as proof that someone believed in me . . . at least a little. It topped the other logos I had all over my shirt—basically, if anyone gave me anything for free, I put their company name or logo on my shirt. I looked like a NASCAR driver. You probably could have bought me a cheeseburger after a race, and I would have put your logo on my shirt.

I had plenty of "in-kind" sponsorships, meaning that prosthetics companies and medical services knocked down their bills for me, but no sponsors paid me any outright money. I pushed that all to the back of my mind and kept going, however, figuring I'd eventually find a way to earn money for racing.

On March 25, 2007, I ran my first full marathon, the ING Georgia Marathon. The news media were there in force, and a loudspeaker blared the news that Scott Rigsby was there trying to set a national record as the first American double amputee to complete a full marathon on prosthetics. News helicopters whirred overhead. No pressure or anything.

Friends of mine came to cheer me on, as well as several people who had worked with me to get me ready for this—my coach, my chiropractor, my massage therapist, and my physical therapist. My training partner, Mike, ran the race with me. It meant he had to slow his usual pace to stay on track with me, which is harder than you might think. Runners like him, who are used to being out on the road for three and a half hours for a marathon, have a hard time purposely slowing themselves down. Mike had never run that slowly before, and it was hard on him.

It was eighty-seven degrees, the hottest day on record for March 25 in Georgia. I was worried before the race started. It wasn't because of the heat, though that certainly didn't help; it was because my legs were not fitting properly. At mile 6, it felt like sweat was accumulating in my prosthetic socket, so I turned to Mike and said, "Hey, I need to stop and dump the sweat out of my legs."

Mike had seen me do that before, so it wasn't a big deal. We ran over to a park bench and sat down so I could take care of it. I took off the leg and liner, and what splattered all over the pavement wasn't sweat—it was blood. About a cup of it.

I hadn't realized my residual limbs were bleeding so badly. I had lost body fat and a considerable amount of weight while I was training, so my prosthetic sockets were looser than they should have been. That meant that they were rubbing the skin off of my stumps as I ran.

Mike looked horrified, but he said, "It's going to be okay." I wasn't sure if he was reassuring me or himself. "It's going to be okay. Don't think about it!"

As I repeated the process with the other leg, he kept calling out these pseudo-encouraging phrases.

I finally had to tell him, "Okay, calm down, Mike. You're freaking me out."

I had known my sockets were getting loose before the race, but there just hadn't been time to have Stephen make me new prosthetics. I had simply put on extra prosthetic socks to make up for the volume loss inside the sockets, but that worked only for so long. It's kind of like wearing shoes that are two sizes too big for you. You can get away with wearing thick socks for a little while, but not if you're going to run a long distance in them. Even though my prosthetist was there with me at the marathon, there wasn't anything he could do on the spot to help.

"Well, what do you want to do? Should we call it a day?" Mike asked.

"No, we came out here to do something, and we're going to do it."

We kept on going, and every four or five miles on average, I had to stop and dump cups of blood out. One of those times, a television cameraman from Comcast Sports South had just approached me to get a quick shot, and as he saw the blood, he whipped that camera away so fast you'd have thought he had seen . . . well, an amputee tossing cups of blood out of his legs. I suppose it wasn't the most pleasant sight for a television viewing audience.

Another time, I had just sat down under a big oak tree when a woman noticed me and thought I must be overheated, so she brought me a bottle of water. I took off my leg and poured the water on my stump, making the blood turn bright red and run all the way down the sidewalk. Mike says the poor woman looked like she was going to pass out.

We lost about forty-five minutes of time stopping and dumping the blood, not to mention that it's hard to get back to your pace when you have to keep stopping cold like that and detaching and reattaching prosthetic legs. Even though I'm used to doing it, there's still a process that needs to be followed, and it isn't as simple as just putting on shoes.

First, I had to take off my prosthetics by pushing a button to release a pin that was attached to the gel liners that were rolled up over my residual limbs to form the prosthetic sockets. Then I would take off my socks to clean everything out. I'd dry my stump with a towel—and by the way, you can call it a stump, a residual limb, a nub; it's all the same to me. Then I'd turn the gel liner inside out and place it against the end of my stump and roll it up to midthigh, making sure it was a smooth fit. The liner, which is similar to a gel insole you might have inside your shoe, is meant to cushion the residual limb from the hard carbon fiber of the running leg, a custom-fitted prosthetic socket with a curved running foot attached to it.

Then I'd put thin prosthetic socks over the pin liner. If I lost weight, I'd add more socks; if I gained weight, I'd take the socks off to make sure my leg was always fitting properly into the socket. Finally, I'd put the pin liner into the hole in the socket and listen for a click to know that I was securely locked into the leg. Then I would repeat with the other leg. Once I had tucked the little towel I used to dry my stump back into my race belt, we were ready to go again.

Mike must have adjusted to seeing me bleed all over the street because he said, "We can do it. We can break five hours."

I laughed at him. My race time was the last thing on my mind at that moment, and I couldn't believe he still cared.

"I just want to finish this thing," I said. "My pain tolerance is greater than anyone I know, but at this point it's maxed out."

The race director, who is a friend of mine and apparently sadistic, had routed miles 22 through 26 to be all uphill. Along the path, spectators would call out, "I saw you on TV!" or cheer me on. I smiled and waved at them and thought how nice it would be to go lie down with my bloody stumps in a bucket of ice water after this crazy race was over.

And then we were at the finish line.

It took us just a few minutes more than five hours to complete the 26.2-mile marathon. I think my physical therapist, Kate, had watched the whole race with one eye closed. She said that seeing what happened after I crossed the finish line was "atrocious."

Cameras were in my face, clamoring to capture history as I did what no American double amputee had done before. I celebrated by sitting down and dumping a full load of blood out of my legs. A couple of people knelt down and picked me up and carried me to the medical tent. My stumps were like they had been in a cheese grater—just giant blood blisters and ripped-away skin—and blood was everywhere.

Any other runners who saw me at that moment must have been thinking, "Holy cow, that guy just ran 26.2 miles on bloody stumps." I felt like such a tough guy. If you ever want to earn street cred with triathletes, bleeding is a good way to do it.

My friends were allowed to come into the medical tent. All the guys were jealous because my beautiful physical therapist was doting over me and my beautiful massage therapist was massaging me. Twenty-six point two miles seems far less harrowing when you get pampered from beauties like these at the end.

A doctor came over and looked at my legs and said, "That's going to take a long time to heal."

But I didn't have a long time. In less than three months, in June, I was going to attempt to complete the Coeur d'Alene Ironman, and I needed time to train for it. I couldn't afford to take much time off to let my stumps get back to normal. I knew, however, that the open sores ran a high risk of infection, and that could sideline me altogether.

It was far too painful to put my walking legs on, so Mike and I permanently "borrowed" a wheelchair from the medical tent. It was one of those clunky, hospital-style wheelchairs. After we did a few brief media interviews, Kate joined us on the way back to my apartment.

She and Mike had never been to my place before, so they were surprised when I told them I lived on the second floor. Mike looked up the steps and down at me in the wheelchair, and then turned to Kate.

"Why would a guy with no legs live on the second floor?" he asked her.

Mike put the wheelchair into my truck and came back to help me up the stairs. Then it turned into a *Seinfeld* episode. There we were, two guys in blue running shorts, and he had to lift me and carry me up to my apartment. I didn't have my legs on. We tried piggyback style at first, but Mike has neck problems and was still in pain from running the marathon, so I slid around to his front, and we were chest-to-chest all the way up the stairs.

"How 'bout them Bears?" The conversation was beyond awkward, and he made me promise not to tell anyone about this "close encounter." Sorry, Mike.

The next day, I put on really thick, old prosthetic liners and walked on my knees down the steps to my truck. The last thing the insurance company had taken care of before they settled with me was to install hand controls on my truck, so I was still able to drive without my prostheses.

I was scheduled to do an in-studio interview with Comcast Sports South, and I had to be in my wheelchair. I walked to the set's chair on my knees and sat down. Then I placed my prosthetic legs up to my stumps to make it look like they were attached, but they weren't. They were just propped there, and could have fallen off at any time, so I had to keep still to avoid freaking anyone out. It was too painful and dangerous to put the prostheses back on.

After the interview, I drove myself to a doctor's office, where I would spend two hours a day in a hyperbaric chamber for seven consecutive days of treatment.

Most people think of hyperbaric chambers only in terms of divers who need to recover from decompression sickness ("the bends"), but hyperbaric oxygen therapy is actually great for a lot of conditions, from strokes to carbon monoxide poisoning. It can be very helpful for sports injuries and any sort of infection, because it helps to increase white blood cell counts.

The summer before, I had spent time in this doctor's hyperbaric chamber when I had ripped a quarter-size hole in my leg from a bad friction burn I got during a practice run. That had healed quickly, so I decided to try the treatment again this time. I got out of the truck on my knees and got into the wheelchair, rolled into the office, and a staff member rolled me—chair and all—into a large dive chamber, which has a maximum capacity of about ten or twelve people. Patients would sit on both sides with their backs up against the chamber walls and put oxygen masks over their heads, attached around the neck with an airtight seal. It's a claustrophobic person's nightmare.

The idea is to raise the pressure in the chamber to simulate conditions below sea level, and allow each person to breathe pure oxygen for a couple of hours while watching a movie on a television screen. At the end of those seven days, my stumps were healed, and all the skin on my body looked healthier than it ever had. I was able to put on my prostheses and walk again.

Stephen decided to switch me from a prosthetic pin suspension system, which was traumatizing my residual limb, to an elevated-vacuum prosthetic system that would actually heal my leg after grueling workouts. The primary benefit of this system is that it gives better linkage between the prosthetic socket and the residual limb; but more importantly, it also provides volume management, which means that my residual limb does not fluctuate in size from morning to night. Even slight variations can make a big difference with something as precisely fitted as a prosthetic liner and socket.

My doctors, my cycling coach, and my physical therapist all told me to slow down. They worried that I was doing too much too soon and that I'd have to pace myself if I wanted to avoid doing permanent damage to my body. It was hard, though—I loved competing, and the more I did, the better I felt about myself. I wanted to do marathons and triathlons every week.

My biggest hope came true when I found out I had won one of the five coveted lottery spots reserved for physically challenged athletes to compete in the Ford Ironman World Championship in Kailua-Kona, Hawaii.

Hawaii is where it all began in 1978—the result of a debate that had raged among some Navy SEALs about who were the best athletes: runners, swimmers, or bikers. Then one of the competitors came up with the idea to combine all three sports in grueling succession. The winner would be called an Ironman.

Every year since then, more and more crazy people have made the journey to Hawaii to prove something to the world, or to themselves, by giving everything they've got—and then some—in the hopes of being named an Ironman, too. There are thousands of triathlons around the world each year, but the Hawaiian Ironman is the triathletes' Super Bowl. The terrain is tough, the competition is fierce, and the publicity is great. Every year, NBC televises a special based on the event.

Because the Ironman is supposed to showcase the very best triathletes in the world, the organizers don't make extra allowances for challenged athletes—we get the same amount of time as everyone else to finish our events.

Before I went to Hawaii, though, I would attempt to complete my first full Ironman race in Coeur d'Alene, Idaho. I had called the race director and told him what I was trying to do, and he welcomed me to compete. At the time, it sounded like a lot of fun. Now? I was scared. It was what I had been working up to for a year and a half, yet I had no idea if I was actually ready for it. And like a gambler betting all his chips on one hand, I knew that this gamble could end only one of two ways: victory or defeat.

I decided to aim for victory.

# CHAPTER 9

There was so much riding on this race—which my friends told me pretty honestly. Mike McClain was still working diligently to find companies who would sponsor me, but it seemed that every door of opportunity was slammed in his face. Although I had made a little media splash at the ING Georgia Marathon and at shorter-distance triathlons around the state, there was no proof that I could finish an Ironman—and I was not such a media darling that sponsors would line up to throw money at my fake feet.

Instead, Mike had to work hard at his sales pitch. "You'll regret it later if you don't sponsor him now," he'd say. "He's going to get a lot more expensive after he finishes this Ironman."

But the reverse was also true, and we all knew it: It would be a lot harder for me to ever get sponsored again if I attempted this race and failed. Then what? There was no backup plan. "Ironman or Bust" was invisibly tattooed on my chest. My credibility would be sunk if I didn't achieve my ultimate goal.

At the end of April, I read that there was going to be an Ironman training camp in Coeur d'Alene, Idaho, hosted by

Multisports.com. The Web site said that the camp had coached many Ironman champions. Between the long weekend lectures and workouts, I could ask any questions that came up during my training and get advice. I really wanted to go, but it cost more than $700. I knew I could use my airline miles to get there, and I had someone I could stay with, but I still couldn't afford the fee. I called the phone number and explained my plight to the woman who answered.

"I'm trying to be the first double amputee to finish an Ironman, and I'd really love to come out there to your training camp and practice on the course, but I don't have the money to attend. Do you think you could help me with my goal?"

The woman was very kind and understanding. She listened patiently while I pleaded my case, and then she told me I could come out to the camp at no cost. It was like Christmas in April. When I told Tony Myers, my coach, the great news, he asked me whom I had spoken with.

"Paula somebody. Her last name was hyphenated. Maybe Newby-Fraser, I think?"

"You were talking to Paula Newby-Fraser?"

"Yeah, why?"

"Do you have any idea who she is?"

"No."

I think Tony developed a twitch right then.

"She's the greatest female athlete ever. She's won twenty-four Ironman races, and she also was the winner of the Ironman World Championship eight times. What's wrong with you?"

"Oh. I hope I didn't say anything stupid."

It was like wanting to be a baseball player and not knowing who Babe Ruth was. I was hopelessly clueless about the world of triathlons and its legends; as usual, I had just dived in head-first and learned things along the way.

Before the training camp, I spent a week in Coeur d'Alene

with my friend Lindsay Janke and her family. I had met her on MySpace—she was also going to compete at the Ironman. She introduced me to her friend Scott Burkhardt, a multiple Ironman finisher. The three of us, along with local pastor Mike Terry, an Ironman hopeful like me, rode the course together just about every day. We rode in some of the worst kinds of weather that week: rain, sleet, more rain, and an occasional ray of sunshine. Lindsay loved to say on those dreary, cold, rainy days, "We're ridin' dirty!" That became our crew's catchphrase. My friends helped me learn every inch of that Ironman course before I started the camp.

The camp was helpful, and it gave me the chance to hang around with some world triathlete champions who had already finished an Ironman on this course. Paula Newby-Fraser and her life partner, Paul Huddle, ran the camp, along with several other coaches. They worked with us one-on-one and lectured on various topics, from nutrition to how to change a flat bike tire on the course. They also covered the most important topic: how to mentally prepare ourselves before the race and stay focused during it. We did workouts both on and off the course. It was too cold to do any open-water swimming, however, so we stuck to practicing in the pool.

One of the most important things I took away from that weekend was some advice that Paula gave us: "You're going to be out there a long time, and you're going to want to say some bad things to yourself. Don't. Be kind to yourself, and stay in the present. Don't think about things that went wrong at the start of the race. All you have to do that day is swim, bike, and run. When you're on the bike, don't think about the swim behind you or the miles ahead; just think about right now. Be in the moment." I carried those words with me in every race.

Before I went home, Scott Burkhardt handed me a personal check for $1,000. He told me he believed in what I was doing and wanted to help me out. He also said he wanted to help me find sponsors. I was astonished. I'm not sure if Scott knew that I was struggling financially, but he was always a guy who was sensitive to God's prompting to help people. He is one of the most generous people I have ever met.

When I got back to Georgia, another event was shaping up to change the landscape for physically challenged athletes. Oscar Pistorius, a double-amputee sprinter from South Africa, was trying to make it into the 2008 Olympic Games. However, the International Association of Athletics Federations had decided that his prosthetic legs gave him an *advantage* over able-bodied athletes. Having actually run on prosthetic legs, I found that unbelievable.

Oscar's managers needed some kind of proof that the prosthetics didn't give him an advantage—that was the only way he could win an appeal and get a chance to compete. Where exactly was he going to find such a study to prove his case?

It turned out he found it at Georgia Tech, where I had worked with researcher Mary Beth Brown a year earlier to complete the world's only study of amputee athletes using prosthetics versus equally matched able-bodied athletes.

Georgia Tech offered the first masters program in the country in prosthetics and orthotics, and I often volunteered there as a patient-model to help the students learn about amputees. I became involved after I had wandered into the exercise physiology lab in 2005 to ask a question.

"Can I use a heart rate monitor in my training? Is it accurate for amputees?"

Researcher Mary Beth Brown said she'd look it up for me, but she was surprised to find that there was nothing in the literature about heart rate response and energy expenditure for amputees on prosthetics. She decided that would be a neat thing to study, so she created an experiment—she matched amputee athletes with able-bodied athletes who were alike in all other ways (weight, height, age, body fat, and so on).

Her goal was to find any information that might help amputee athletes; after completing her research, she presented her findings at a couple of medical conferences. Oscar Pistorius's defense team heard about it and was specifically interested in my data because I was also a double below-the-knee amputee—the only double amputee in the study. So, essentially, I found myself at the heart of a controversy that would determine whether or not someone like me could ever compete in the Olympics.

I had had no idea that letting Mary Beth do some tests and attach some monitors to my body while I ran on a treadmill for a couple of days was going to be so important, just as she had had no way of guessing that her study was going to lead to a landmark decision by the Court of Arbitration for Sport. The court overturned the Olympic committee's decision and ruled that Oscar had no unfair advantage because of his prosthetic legs. Therefore, he was eligible to compete in the Olympics. It felt like a victory for both of us, and I was honored to know that I could help this way.

As for my own endeavors, I had more of an outpouring of help and kindness from the Coeur d'Alene community than I knew what do with. A University of Georgia alumnus named Tom Greene was now a reporter at the *Coeur d'Alene Press*, and he wrote a story about me. My picture graced the front cover; inside was a four-page feature article detailing my Ironman journey up to that point. Tom's article included my e-mail address and cell phone number.

The day the article ran, Rick Gunther, a successful real estate agent in Coeur d'Alene, called me and said, "I read the article and it's great. My wife and I want you to stay at our house when you get out here for the race."

"Awesome. I'll take you up on that offer," I said.

Later that morning, I received a call from Jenni Gaertner. She and her husband, Mike, were owners of a local bike shop called Vertical Earth, and they wanted to sponsor me. Jenni and Mike invited me to come to their shop, where they hooked me up with hundreds of dollars' worth of free merchandise and offered to take care of any bike repairs I needed while I was in town. I headed home with a terrific feeling about how the world was rallying to help me reach my dream.

I didn't know then that the Gunthers wouldn't be the only ones to offer free accommodations. Thanks to the generosity of the many people who responded to the article, every one of my twelve friends who flew out to Idaho to support me had a free place to stay for the event. Luckily, I was also able to fly several of them out for free with the miles I had received from the airline. After all they had done for me, I was finally able to do something good for them in return.

I arrived in Coeur d'Alene ten days before the race, excited and nervous. Had I trained enough? Was I really ready?

The *Coeur d'Alene Press* article won an AP sports award. Because of that article, everywhere I went, people knew exactly who I was and what I was doing there. John Robideaux, a multiple Ironman finisher, was so inspired by my story that he offered me a car whenever I was in town, courtesy of his successful car dealership, Robideaux Motors. Having that kind of local support was phenomenal.

The Gunthers treated me like family. Their house is a local landmark. It's a big, beautiful house with an American flag on a pole in the front yard. Every year on race day, they would have a giant inflatable animal, such as a dinosaur, in their yard. People would actually use that in giving directions: "Turn left after the giant inflatable dinosaur." In time for the Ironman, that dinosaur was wearing a big sign that said, "We love you, Scott Rigsby!"

My coach, Tony Myers, wasn't able to make it for the event, but my close friend Carole Sharpless, a professional triathlete, was there coaching several of her athletes in preparation for the race. She had coached many people through Ironman races so I asked her if she would give me some advice based on her previous Ironman experiences. In typical Carole fashion, she enthusiastically agreed to offer some tips that she was giving her other athletes.

Most Ironman events have a pasta dinner two days before the race, at which the organizers can talk about the history of the event and any rules and last-minute instructions they may want to give, and the athletes can meet one another and talk through their preparations. On Wednesday, I found out I was going to be honored with the Ford Ironman Everyday Hero Award at the dinner the next night.

Ford honors one athlete with this award at every full Ironman event on the North America Sports Community Foundation race calendar. It's meant to recognize athletes who have done something significant to benefit others while training for the Ironman, which is true of so many people who do this event. Ironman is chock-full of people with honorable intentions and interesting stories, yet out of thousands of athletes, they chose me for the award. Ironworks Productions filmed a segment about my story and the circumstances that had led me to the Ironman, which they edited into a five-minute video to be shown at the award presentation.

Many athletes had brought friends or loved ones to the dinner, so there were probably more than three thousand people under the tent watching the video presentation. I sat in the VIP area while they brought out a vehicle with a giant television screen. On it, the words *Ford Everyday Hero* lit up the screen, followed by my name typed out one letter at a time. The crowd erupted in applause. After the video, they gave me a standing ovation, and I stood at the podium to say a quick acceptance speech and thank all the people who deserved thanking. (Well, as many as I could reasonably thank in a limited amount of time.)

"I'm out here to get this race done, just like you guys are," I said. "I wish everybody the best of luck and hope we all cross that finish line." Another standing ovation.

They also gave me some cool prizes: a triathlon bag; an iPod, which I never could have afforded on my own; a helmet; and other assorted, race-related gear.

What I was thinking was, *This is so great. What an honor. Could the pressure get any worse? All these people are going to be watching me out there; I had better not fall on my face. Smile and be gracious. Don't crack now.*

The day before the race, the city turns from bustling to quiet as the athletes try to stay off their feet and rest in preparation for the intense day ahead.

On June 24, 2007, I woke up extremely early, feeling nervous but good. *Today, my dream is going to come true,* I told myself. No matter what happened out there, I would just keep going. There were only two ways I was going to leave the course early: in an ambulance or in a hearse. Otherwise, I was going to find a way to finish.

I didn't know what kind of breakfast would be appropriate before an Ironman, so I asked Carole, "What do you think I should eat?" She brought out all this stuff—a banana, yogurt, granola, and who knows what else—and I started stuffing my face at 4:30 in the morning. I didn't look at half of it; I just threw it in my mouth and ate it. It was a much bigger breakfast than I normally ate.

The weather was in the forties, and my whole crew and I made our way to the transition area at about 5:45 a.m. At least by now I actually did have a better handle on what supplies I needed to pack in my special needs bags for each transition. And I now owned a wetsuit. I put the wetsuit on halfway and applied suntan lotion all over the parts of my body that would be exposed.

A guy with a Magic Marker gave us the participant body

markings: our race number on each arm, our age on the back of our left calf. Since I didn't have a calf, they put my age on my forearm.

By this point, my nerves mixed with my giant breakfast, causing an ugly ruckus. My stomach was rebelling, and I headed to the Porta Potties, which were teeming with other nervous people. I promptly got very, very sick. It isn't all that unusual for people to be sick during the race, but before the race even started? Not exactly a great sign.

Thank goodness I started to feel better a few minutes later, because I had to get over to the swim start right away. I put on my liners and sockets and walked over to the beach. Without my prosthetic feet and with just my prosthetic sockets on, I'm about four feet tall. From what I hear, it's an amusing sight to see me among the other athletes.

The water conditions were rough on the day of the race. For reasons that relate to race insurance, the harbor patrol told us that we could skip the swim portion of the race and not be disqualified. It could be dangerous for those who were not strong swimmers. We wouldn't be an Ironman at the end of the race, and we couldn't win any awards if we skipped the swim, but we could still complete the other two parts of the competition and call it a duathlon. About seventy-five people accepted that offer and left the beach, but I hadn't come that far to skip anything. I wanted to complete a full Ironman.

As the cannon fired to start the race, a jailbreak of men in their white swim caps and women in their blue ones dove frantically into the icy lake. Mass race starts are scary things, with more than two thousand people occupying a small area of water, kicking and flailing their way into position. Mike Lenhart had suggested that we wait a minute until the crowd had thinned a bit, but my heart rate was speeding and I was jacked up and ready to go. I hurled myself right into the middle of this mass of humanity and got kicked, pulled, punched, and smacked all over the place.

The wind was against us, and the waves were up to four feet high. Some people lost their way because they couldn't see the buoys over the waves, and many didn't finish the swim—kayakers paddled around to pick up anyone who was in trouble. Sometimes, as I was swimming along, people in front of me would stop dead or get hurled backward into me—not because that's what they meant to do but because the waves were so strong that swimmers couldn't control where they got tossed. Not only did we have to contend with the extra exertion of fighting the waves and the disorientation of not being able to see the markers, but seasickness was a problem too. A lot of the athletes would later say it was the toughest swim they'd ever done.

I made it through the two-loop swim portion in little over an hour and a half—a respectable time, especially considering the conditions. As I pulled myself out of the water and walked on my sockets toward the transition area, Carole Sharpless caught up with me and called out, "Hobbit coming through! Hobbit coming through!"

Then it was on to my weakest discipline: the bike. The course was breathtakingly beautiful and very hilly. Pretty much every time I got to the bottom of a hill, I had to start right up the next one. I was cutting it close timewise, but things were fine until I got to about mile 60. As I headed down a hill near Higgins Point at about twenty-five miles per hour, my bike chain came off and lodged itself between the large and small rings of the bike crank. This caused my pedals to lock and the back tire to go airborne, throwing the back of the bike forward and propelling me over the handlebars. I landed on my back on the pavement like a WWE wrestler had body-slammed me. My bike landed on top of me. My first thought was, *Is my bike okay?*

I got up, fixed the chain, wiped the blood off myself, and got back on the bike. The adrenaline and shock got me through for a while; you don't tend to feel the pain right away from an injury like that. But when I stopped to go to the bathroom at the next aid station, I ended up sitting down for a full twenty minutes because it hurt too much to stand. Then I knew I had to get going again. I rode out the rest of the 112-mile bike portion, finishing just ten minutes under the cutoff. What a relief!

I knew that Tony Myers would be checking in from home. There's a microchip system that keeps track of each competitor, and people can check the status of any athlete online at the Ironman.com Web site. The chip is supposed to record the athletes' timing at several checkpoints as we pass over timing mats, but unbeknownst to me, my chip wasn't working. So while I thought Tony would be thrilled to see I had made the bike cutoff, he was actually upset because my chip never registered that I made it to the finish line. He thought I had been too slow.

I made the transition to my running legs and began the marathon, but my shoulder, lower back, and neck were badly bruised and hurting. After a few miles, the pain was excruciating and my pace was barely faster than a walk. Carole was riding the run course on a mountain bike to check on her athletes. She had been nervously watching and checking on me, as well. Finally, at about mile 11, she pulled up beside me on the run course.

"Scott, you might be able to finish this race, but at what cost? We don't know the extent of your injuries. You have a slot at the Hawaiian Ironman in October. If you do more damage to yourself here, you might not be able to make that."

I didn't want to listen to her. I wanted to keep going. This was supposed to be the day my dream came true, not the day it *almost* came true. But after almost another mile of walking in excruciating pain, I reluctantly dropped out of the race, my heart as shattered as my back.

I left in an ambulance. At least it wasn't a hearse.

When I got to the hospital, they X-rayed me from head to toe and found that I had cracked a vertebra in my back from the impact of the crash. There were bone fragments floating around my spine. It meant that the decision to end the race had been the right one, which was only slightly easier to take. I could have made things much worse if I'd tried to run another fourteen miles, but I still felt absolutely devastated that I hadn't finished the race.

My friends and team members were either there watching the race live or calling in to get updates from other friends. So many people had been pulling for me and expecting me to finish the race, and I felt as if I had let them down. Jamie, my old college roommate, came into the room and hugged me. I lost it, tears of disappointment streaming down my cheeks. After all that buildup and the groundswell of local support, it was hard to climb down from that high.

At the awards banquet, which I had to attend in a wheelchair and in excruciating pain, I listened as they presented awards to the pros and age-groupers who had won or placed in the top ten in their categories. Even though I was sad for myself, I really was happy for them.

After the speeches, announcer Mike Reilly said, "There was also one person out there who gave it his all. He didn't quite make it, but we want to honor his efforts. We know one day he'll be an Ironman. That's our Ford Ironman Everyday Hero, Scott Rigsby."

Carole wheeled me up to the front of the stage, and my fellow athletes stood and applauded wildly for me once again. It showed me that even if I hadn't finished, just my presence there had been inspirational to them.

After the awards banquet, I stumbled across a Theodore Roosevelt speech that I have remembered ever since:

> It is not the critic who counts: not the man who points out how the strong man stumbles or where the doer of deeds could have done them better. The credit belongs to the man who is actually in the arena; whose face is marred by dust and sweat and blood; who strives valiantly; who errs and comes up short again and again; because there is no effort without error and shortcoming, but who knows the great enthusiasms, the great devotions, who spends himself for a worthy cause; who, at the best, knows, in the end, the triumph of high achievement, and who, at the worst, if he fails, at least he fails while daring greatly, so that his place shall never be with those cold and timid souls who knew neither victory nor defeat.[1]

I knew defeat. Now it was time to turn my focus to knowing victory.

This dream was bigger than just me. What I was trying to accomplish meant so much to so many people. Mike Lenhart told me that this Ironman had had one of the highest completion rates ever. Maybe when some people normally would have given up, they didn't because they thought about me clicking along on my prosthetics and figured, *If he's still out there in this race, I'm going to finish this thing.*

The mood among my friends was somber, though. Many of them were worried about my injured back. I wasn't all that excited about it myself, but I figured I was going to heal as quickly as my body could and get back into training. The healing was the hardest part. It was almost unbearable to know that I had a ticket to the Super Bowl of the triathlon world, yet I was supposed to sit on my backside for a month and not do anything to get ready for it.

But even though that's what I was supposed to do, I couldn't. I had a contract with the airline that had sponsored me to run the Peachtree 10K Road Race on the Fourth of July, just ten days after I had broken my back in Coeur d'Alene. It was then the largest 10K race in the world, with about fifty-five thousand participants, so the airline definitely wanted me to be there to represent it. I ran those ten kilometers hunched over in agony, with Mike Lenhart by my side. In the middle of the course there's a long uphill stretch nicknamed "Cardiac Hill," with Piedmont Hospital appropriately next to it. In case the hill proves too treacherous, runners can take a side trip to the emergency room—which sounded like a very good idea to me by then. After the race, I did nothing for the next three weeks.

Mike thought maybe that wasn't such a bad thing. Maybe the bike accident had been God's way of getting me to listen to my physical therapist and coaches and slow down for a while.

But I had one final race to run to fulfill my contract with the airline: the New York City Triathlon, which I completed on July 22.

At that point, the airline dropped the sponsorship and didn't renew my contract. I still had no paying sponsors and no income, except for the money my dad paid me—$1,000 a month—for the land he had bought from me.

It began to look doubtful that I would be able to afford to make it to the Ironman competition in Hawaii. Could this really all have been for nothing? Was this the way my dream was going to end?

*Just keep going*, I told myself. *Control the things you can control, and hand the rest over to God*.

I could control my preparations, so I decided to keep training. One problem I faced was that doing interviews, getting my picture taken, and speaking in front of groups of people about my journey turned out to be a lot more fun for me than hitting the pavement for training. Whereas before I would get on a bike four sizes too big for me and pedal with my elbows if need be, I was getting a bit spoiled now. I wanted the conditions to be right, I wanted my equipment to be right, and I wanted to feel good before practices.

There was, of course, some measure of self-defeat in all this. I didn't know if I was actually going to be able to afford to get to Hawaii, first of all, and second, I didn't know if I could handle failing twice. If, after all this, I didn't cross the finish line in Kona, did that mean I had been wrong about God's purpose for me?

That's when I met Scott Johnson. Scott is a fellow triathlete who first spoke to me at an open-water swim practice in July 2007 in Atlanta. He recognized me from the local media coverage and had seen me once before in a road race. At the race, I had been wearing my prosthetics with a skull-and-crossbones design, and his first thought at the time was, *This guy has some serious issues. He must be angry with the world because he lost his legs*. But after swim practice that summer morning, something told him to approach me anyway. Once he started talking to me, he realized appearance isn't everything.

"Are you Scott Rigsby?" he asked. "Strange thing, but I just read an article about you last night."

We talked about Coeur d'Alene and the races we had coming up, and then he asked, "Are you going to do Hawaii?"

"I have a spot in the race and I'd love to go," I said, "but there's a problem. I don't have a penny to my name. I can't afford to get myself there, let alone my team."

I explained to him that I had hoped to attract sponsors, but even though my buddy Mike McClain had worked so hard to promote me, I probably seemed like too much of a long shot for companies to want to take a chance backing me.

Scott told me, "I've been a corporate executive in sales and marketing for a long time, and I just did sponsorships for the local marathon. I think I can help you get sponsorships. Tell me your story."

I e-mailed him my accident photos and my story, with a note: "I'd really appreciate it if you can help."

Scott volunteered to be my manager, and in two months, he raised $20,000 in sponsorship money. Not only would I get to go to Hawaii, but this meant that I could bring my whole team out there too.

I only thought I knew what pressure was! This was a whole different ball game. This was an internationally televised event, and I was one of only five physically challenged athletes who had been fortunate enough to win a spot. The world was going to be watching me as I got my second chance at fulfilling my goal, and I'd probably never get this chance again.

It made me want to . . . eat.

My lovely and talented nutritionist, Ilana Katz, made up a regimen for me that included all the healthy things she expected me to eat, but what was somehow omitted from this list were all the foods I actually liked to eat. Nowhere to be found on her list were Doritos, foot-long Italian subs, burgers, fries, or Snickers. I felt sure she had accidentally overlooked them, however, so I filled them in for her.

I also didn't quite follow the training schedule Carole Sharpless had made up for me. Oftentimes, I "rolled over" my workouts—if she had written up a specific workout for me to do on a Monday, I'd get busy and figure I could do it on Tuesday, along with whatever else was planned for that day.

Mike Lenhart is the one who finally set me straight about that. He gave me what amounted to a "tough love" lecture, and followed it up with an e-mail telling me it was time to get serious or get out of the race. In the letter was a list of orders, including (among other things) that I was to follow every word of what Ilana and Carole had planned for me, to shut off my cell phone at 9 p.m. to make sure I got a good night's sleep, to buy an alarm clock to make sure I got up early for training, to take care of my equipment better to make sure it was always in good shape for training, and to quit using my iPod and other things that wouldn't be allowed in the race. I loved that darn iPod.

"We are all behind you, Scott," he wrote, "but there are no trophies for 'almost an Ironman.' Mike Reilly will not announce, 'Here comes Scott Rigsby . . . nearly an Ironman' at Kona."

It wasn't easy to hear, but I knew that Mike loved me and wanted me to be successful. He was absolutely right. I wrote back and apologized to my team members for letting them down and promised to do better. I made a commitment to get on track with Carole's schedule again and to make the adjustments necessary so I would be ready when the big day arrived. Mike's lecture was the kick in the pants I needed.

*I can do this. Bring it on.*

Many days, I trained with my friend Karen O'Riordan, or K.O. for short. She's a flight-attendant-turned-lawyer in her midfifties. She had her own special reason for doing the Ironman: She had watched the NBC coverage of the 2005 event and saw Jon Blais, a man who had finished the Hawaiian Ironman despite having ALS (Lou Gehrig's disease) and almost no use of his hands at the time. Jon had said that the Ironman was important to him because "when I'm sitting in a wheelchair down the road, I'll know that I fought the great fight." In keeping with a comment he made before the race, he log-rolled across the finish line at Kona, but it was his last race.[2] He died in 2007.

Karen's mother and grandfather had both died of ALS. Even though, like me, she didn't own a bike and wasn't a swimmer, she had decided then and there to train for an

Ironman to support Jon and to help raise money for ALS research.

She competed in Ironman Brazil in the spring of 2007 with the hopes of qualifying for the Hawaiian Ironman, and she did it. At every Ironman event, Jon's race number, 179, is reserved for a "Blazeman Warrior," one of the athletes from his foundation to fight ALS. In Hawaii, Karen would wear his number and would log-roll across the finish line in his memory. She also raised $50,000 for his foundation.

We were happy to train together, and in spite of the fact that both of us were serious about our missions, we had a blast. Karen is a lot of fun to be around. It was crazy hot in Atlanta at that time, though, with several days in a row over 100 degrees.

"I can't take it here anymore," she said. "It's killing my asthma. I'm going to Kona early."

So, thirty-three days before the race, she flew to Hawaii and found a nice place to stay, Puako Bed and Breakfast. It was a popular place; even locals who lived on the other side of the island would come and stay there. After her arrival, she told me about it: When she got there, a former professional bodybuilder, wearing only a Speedo—not even shoes—welcomed her from the garden. That was the owner, Puna, short for Punahele. He had shared his native home's beauty, history, flora, and fauna with visitors from all over the world. Karen enjoyed getting to know Puna and was eager for me to meet him.

Karen soon told me, "You have to get out here, dude. There's nothing like training on the course."

But how? As much as I wanted to get there early to practice, where was I supposed to come up with the money for accommodations and food?

Karen solved that problem by convincing Puna to sponsor me and let me stay there for free. He even agreed to provide free food for me—which he probably wished he hadn't once I got there and he found out how much I could eat.

Having the funds to get the team to Kona was a huge relief. Many friends, and friends of friends, responded to a donation site that Scott Johnson had set up as part of his overall fund-raising effort. I have kept that list of donors to remind me of how wonderful people are when it comes to helping someone achieve his or her dream. Some names I don't even recognize, but I know that they will be blessed for their commitment to helping others.

*This is just what I need,* I thought. *Getting there early will help me relax and focus and escape the pressure of the local Atlanta media.*

I was barely ten thousand feet above the ground en route to Hawaii when I realized that things were not going to happen as planned.

Sitting in an aisle seat and unable to get comfortable enough to quickly fall asleep in preparation for my ten-hour flight, I reached over to browse the *Delta Sky* magazine. My mouth dropped open when I saw my name on the cover and opened up the October issue to see a four-page article about my quest in Kona. I looked up and saw aisles of people with the magazine opened, reading about me. Being somewhat paranoid at that moment, I tried to shake off the feeling that the guy sitting next to me was staring at me. That's when I turned my head and saw that he had the article open and was smiling at me and staring at my prosthetic legs.

"Is that you?"

"Yes, that's me. The guy with no legs."

"You going to make it?"

"I hope so." We exchanged a few more awkward moments before I found my headphones and tried to drift off to sleep. Ten hours nonstop to Hawaii. *Come to think of it, that's the amount of time it's going to take me to do just the swim and bike portions of the race.* So much for relaxing.

Twenty-three days before the race, I settled in among the other eight or so guests, of all different nationalities and cultures, at the bed and breakfast. Karen is neat; I'm a slob. I ate the very nonhealthy local cuisine, which included lots of fried things and juice loaded up with sugar; K.O. always had a watchful eye on her girlish waistline. We were the Odd Couple, Hawaiian-style.

"You're fat," Puna told me one day, apparently oblivious to his own round belly. "How are you going to run this race?"

"It's your fault. Quit feeding me so much." He was a great cook and an even better host.

Between my carbon fiber foot and my foot shell, I wear a thin sock to keep the two from rubbing together and squeaking, but that's not always effective. Sometimes it rubs through anyway and squeaks whenever I walk. Puna nicknamed me "Squeaky."

His place was in a perfect location, just a mile off the highway and a mile away from Hapuna Beach State Park, where Karen and I could practice our open-water swims. We were roughly four miles away from the beginning of the toughest part of the Ironman course, the climb to Hawi. It's a fifteen- or sixteen-mile stretch uphill, fighting strong winds and the unrelenting sun the whole way. I didn't want it to shock me on the day of the race; I wanted to know what to expect, so Karen and I headed up that climb to Hawi many times and experienced those harsh winds on the toughest days.

Unfortunately, I had broken out in a rash the second day I was there, which I at first assumed was heat rash. I used the "ignore it and it'll go away" tactic until it became pitifully obvious that it was not going to go away. By the fifth day, I was covered with red spots from head to toe and had resorted to putting paper towels under my arms and walking like a robot to avoid irritating the rash further by sweating.

Training that day was impossible. Karen suggested that we instead take a day off to drive around and see the island. We went to the top of the volcano and did the touristy things. When we got back that night, I decided to do a little laundry—and that's when I saw the bottle of Tide, my evil nemesis.

I'm allergic to Tide.

It wasn't a heat rash. Everything from the sheets to the towels had been washed in Tide, and I was having a terrible allergic reaction. My mom had discovered this allergy when I broke out in a rash as a child after she switched laundry detergents, and it's something I've never really had to think about since then. It never occurred to me to check the detergent.

After a quick walk to a nearby general store, I swallowed some Benadryl tablets and covered myself top to bottom in Benadryl cream. My arms and sides were actually blistered, and I felt like someone had doused me in boiling oil.

Puna was kind enough to switch detergents, and my rash gradually went away, but an uncomfortable feeling lingered both in my body and in my psyche. The conditions in Kona, which I had expected to be tough, were even worse than what I had anticipated.

My "bring it on" attitude shriveled up in the tropical sun, turning from a grape to a raisin. Every practice ended with my being drenched in sweat and doubting my ability to finish the race.

*Is it too late to revise my prayer? I really shot my mouth off this time. Maybe I should have prayed for God to open some doors for me to walk through at a leisurely pace instead. Or crawl through. Can we check the statute of limitations on heavenly promises?*

# CHAPTER 10

My team made their way to Kona in stages—some more than a week before the race, others the day before. Scott Burkhardt was the first to arrive, and I was to pick him up at the airport. He text-messaged me from the plane: "I prayed for God to send me a hot woman to sit next to on this flight," he wrote. "You'll never guess who I'm sitting next to: Sister Madonna Buder."

Whoever said God didn't have a sense of humor! Sister Madonna is legendary in the triathlon world. She's a seventy-eight-year-old nun who has completed more than three hundred triathlons, including thirty-five Ironman races. She has set records for her age-group numerous times, and is the oldest female ever to complete an Ironman—a record she set at age seventy-five. She then topped herself at age seventy-six.

An HBO crew was in Kona to film her, and she and Scott got to talk on the plane.

"Are you in the race, too?" she asked.

"No, I'm going to support my friend," he said.

"Who's your friend?"

"Scott Rigsby."

"Oh! I know Scott. He's the double amputee!"

When I picked Scott up at the airport, Sister Madonna was right next to him, and she gave me a big hug. That is one hot woman . . . just not exactly in the way Scott had anticipated.

The rest of my team came as they could. Mike Lenhart tried to keep me on track and out of trouble. Stephen Schulte, my amazing prosthetist, could not attend the race because of a prior commitment, so Rusty Walker, another excellent ProCare prosthetist, flew to Hawaii to ensure that my prosthetics were ready for the big day. Rusty thoroughly checked out everything and then flew home. He had other commitments and patients, so he couldn't even stay to watch the race.

When Scott Johnson showed up, he stole my Doritos. What kind of man steals another man's Doritos?

We were on a sixty-mile road trip to a photo shoot for *Runner's World* at the time. It was publishing a story about my Ironman journey. Three days before the big race, I was supposed to be relaxing and concentrating on my game plan, but someone forgot to tell the media. On this particular day of "rest," the clock had barely struck noon and I had already done a mile practice swim in Kailua Bay, met with a reporter from a local newspaper, and then raced over to another hotel to do a one-hour interview with NBC Sports. I wasn't prepared for all the media attention, and it became one of the biggest challenges leading up to the race. It was very difficult to fit in everything I needed to do: training on the course, calibrating my prosthetics, greeting sponsors at prerace events, and accommodating all the media requests. There was almost no downtime in which to focus and rest.

Before we arrived at the photo shoot, we stopped at a convenience store for food. I came out with a few soft drinks, a couple of ham and cheese sandwiches, and another "secret" bag hiding Doritos. Scott has X-ray vision, I think. He gave me "the look," like when a parent catches a kid with a hand in the cookie jar. He had been on my case since he arrived in Kona about my dietary habits before the race. When he first arrived, we had met for lunch at a not-so-healthy hamburger joint, famous for its big, greasy burgers and onion rings. It was four days before the big race, and his antenna was up after he saw me devouring two thousand calories' worth of junk food.

I guess Ironmen are supposed to eat salad and protein shakes all day long.

The *Runner's World* photo shoot took almost three hours in the midday sun, amid valleys of lava rocks and miles of desolate roads. Mike McGill, a Hawaiian local and a world-class photographer; his wife, Lindsay; and their cool surfer-boy son, Finn, were walking around with Scott Johnson dreaming up crazy action photo opportunities. Everyone was pretty excited about the location and scenery, so I agreed to try a few risky moves to get some incredible shots for the magazine. Mike's energy got me jacked up, and before I knew it, I was doing all types of poses, running hill "repeats," leaping in the air—the first time I had ever tried that—and climbing up on razor-sharp lava rocks. After a few hours, I felt I'd been cooked on a grill over burning briquettes. I didn't realize at the time that I was expending a lot of energy, taking big injury risks, roasting my skin, and getting extremely dehydrated. I also didn't see the conspiracy taking place back at the car.

While I was posing for the pictures, my secret goodie bag disappeared. I assumed something dastardly had happened to it, but I was too tired to play detective. All I wanted to do was get back to my room and zone out. There was still more busy work to do in the next few days and a game plan to prepare. Constantly buzzing in the back of my mind was the reminder that I would have to finish this race. Otherwise, all this media hype and last-minute preparation weregoing to be a colossal waste of time.

On Thursday night, Team Rigsby attended the traditional

outdoor prerace pasta dinner on the grounds of King Kamehameha's Kona Beach Hotel. The event is really first class—the race organizers spare no expense. Thousands of attendees sit at enough tables to fill two football fields, entertained by Hawaiian fire dancers and all kinds of special guests.

It was there that Ford again honored me with its Ford Everyday Hero award. This time however, there was an arena full of people in attendance, and the video presentation was so big that it was shown on three massive JumboTron screens. The screens were three times the size of the Ford SUV that was suspended in the air next to the stage. It was like going to a drive-in movie, except with my face filling up the screens. I was truly larger than life.

What was reassuring to me was that Ford and the World Triathlon Corporation hadn't given up on me when I didn't finish the race at the Coeur d'Alene Ironman. They were willing to stick their necks out and bet on me again, even though Kona was a harder race and the pressure to finish was even greater. I felt the same sensations of exhilaration and self-doubt as the crowd stood and applauded.

*I'm getting all this attention, and I still haven't finished an Ironman,* I thought. *I don't deserve all this. If I don't make it to that finish line, I'm going to be the boy who cried wolf.*

Back in 1978, the first fifteen Ironman competitors received a set of rules and instructions that ended with this handwritten note: "Swim 2.4 miles! Bike 112 miles! Run 26.2 miles! Brag for the rest of your life!" That was still the plan.

You have to finish the whole thing in less than seventeen hours, and there are individual cutoff times for each portion of the race—so if you don't finish your swim in time, you don't get to go on to the biking or running parts of the race.

My main worry was the bike. That's the biggest challenge for most amputees because it's impossible to get prosthetics that can pedal the way real feet can. You can't grip and flex around a pedal with a prosthetic foot. If I could just make the bike cutoff, maybe I'd have a chance. Maybe.

On October 13, 2007, the Ironman would begin at 6:45 a.m. for the professional athletes, and 7 a.m. for the "age-groupers," the term for people who had finished well for their age-groups in Ironman-qualifying races. Those of us who were there by lottery would also start at 7 a.m.

When I got my "golden ticket" to compete in the Ironman World Championships, I felt like I had won the *other* kind of lottery. What a score! But as the big day drew near, my worries began to outpace my enthusiasm.

Hoping to get some encouraging words, I e-mailed my friends about my experience preparing for the race:

> I rode 100 miles total the past two days on the hardest part of the course. There is a seven-mile stretch that has unbearable wind. I haven't faced anything like it. It never lets up. If that isn't bad enough, I have never ridden in this intense of a heat—ever. The sun is unforgivable. There is no shade from it, and even with SPF 50 sunblock, my skin still got fried. I look like a lobster and have that sun-drained weakness that people get if they've been on the beach way too long. The air is dry and salty. It gets on your skin and you feel prickly.
>
> I cannot get enough fluids. I drank over 200 ounces riding thirty-seven miles, and I couldn't carry enough fluids unless I use a hydration backpack, which I do not have. I am struggling. It looks like a daunting task. The bottom line is if we have bad weather, i.e., unrelenting winds and scorching heat, well . . . I'm toast. I will give everything I absolutely have, but I am a realist.
>
> Anyway, I'm sunburned, dripping with sweat 24/7 (we are not running the A/C), and so tired most of the time. Hopefully, things will get better.

The other thing that was bothering me was that my team had seen me fail once before. I had been in a funk ever since my failure at Coeur d'Alene. Even though it was an injury that stopped me from finishing, I still felt like I had disappointed so many people. What if I failed again?

It would be all but impossible to find sponsors to fund my trips if I didn't finish this time. And all these people who had worked so hard on my behalf—getting me trained, fixing my equipment, drumming up support, flying out to cheer me on—how would I be able to look them in the eye if I didn't finish this race?

I knew my dad was just itching to see me drop out or fail. He didn't want me here and thought it was about time for me to give up this irresponsible dream. I was starting to think he was going to get his wish. I wouldn't give up of my own accord, but if I couldn't finish this time, I might not have a choice. I couldn't afford to come back on my own.

My friends wrote back encouraging things like this: "Focus on the event and visualize your approach for the race. Erase all the extra stuff in your head about the sponsors, media, team, and friends. You have a purpose, and in order to take the next step, you must prepare for battle. Detach from people for a while, take in your tropical paradise, and concentrate on why you are there."

That's just what I tried to do. I tried to get centered again, to remember my mission. I was there to do something great, something no one else in the world had ever done. If I could pull this off, I might really inspire people.

A few days before the race, after I had completed a practice swim in Kailua Bay, a man came up to me and said, "You have to finish this race, Rigsby. Our military men and women are counting on you to give them hope." I don't know if he was in the military, but as he turned to walk away, the huge scar I saw on his back stayed etched in my mind.

I thought about all those soldiers coming home disabled, and how lost they must feel.

The thing about hope is that you can't inspire it with platitudes. When I was eighteen, people could have told me that my life would be even more worthwhile without legs and that I could still do great things. But I didn't have any role models who could actually show me the evidence. I didn't know any double amputees who were pushing the boundaries of what was possible.

I would much rather attempt a race where I might fail because the course was so tough than finish a race that everyone knows isn't that challenging and receiving patronizing pats on my back. If I could finish this world-famous race with its well-respected course, I'd have evidence that might inspire hope in someone else. I would have credibility when I went into hospitals. I could talk to other physically challenged people and give them proof that they really can do unthinkable things.

*Get back out there. Get in the game.*

Swimming in the ocean was still a novel experience for me because almost all of my training had been done in pools. The water here was crystal clear and beautiful—you could see all the way to the bottom as you swam. You could see bright red and orange coral, turtles, schools of fish, jellyfish . . . jellyfish? No!

I got stung during a practice swim.

Did you know they actually sell sunscreen with jellyfish repellant included? I didn't know it until then, but you can bet I stocked up on it in time for the big day.

One of the coolest things about triathlons is that regular guys like me get to train and race right alongside the superstars. An average Joe who plays basketball at his local YMCA with his buddies might never get the chance to shoot hoops with Kobe Bryant, but in Kailua Bay, I was practicing my swimming right next to the top triathletes in the world: Chris McCormack, Chrissie Wellington, Kate Major, and Normann Stadler. These names are not famous outside the world of triathlons, but they are our all-stars. And I got to hang out with all of them.

The Saturday before the race, the official Ironman program came out, and my story was featured in it. I was the only athlete of 1,800 who was included in the program alongside the top title contenders. Six former Ironman champions—and me. They labeled me "The Miracle." It was a great honor, but it really freaked me out. That kind of exposure made me feel like I had an eight-hundred-pound gorilla on my back that was gaining weight each day. Because of the article, people began recognizing me and talking about me when they saw me around town. "Hey, that's the guy with no legs."

I've really never minded the stares and the talk. My prostheses have given me the opportunity to talk to people who might never have paid attention to me otherwise. Sometimes I think it was God's way of giving me a great conversation starter. People have no qualms about coming up to me and asking, "What happened?"

They don't mean any harm. Sometimes, I know I'm their worst fear. Athletes look at me with pity in their eyes and want to know how it happened so they can make sure it never happens to them. They can't imagine going on living without their legs.

There are other people who see me and believe that somehow I can relate to their pain. I can't begin to count the number of times I have been sitting in a restaurant alone, and total strangers have sat down next to me and shared the most intimate details of their lives—details they would normally confide only in their spouses or therapists. I simply listen and nod occasionally to assure them that I'm following along with what they are sharing. I don't ever ask why they are revealing such personal and painful experiences to me. Maybe it's that, to them, my legs signify a person who has endured and overcome an enormous amount of emotional and physical pain, and we are a band of brothers and sisters. After a time of personal reflection and confession, they usually say, "Thanks for listening" and walk away.

Out here in Kona, though, the locals looked at me with respect, and maybe a little curiosity: Could this guy with no legs really do this, when most able-bodied people can't?

Well, I wasn't sure, but I was going to try. I had just a little more faith than I had fear.

Physically challenged athletes competing in the Ironman get to have two "handlers," rather than one, to assist them with whatever equipment they may need in the transition areas and on the racecourse. One handler is a person of their choosing, and the other is someone who is randomly assigned by race officials from a pool of volunteers in Kona. I chose Mike Lenhart for my handler, and the Ironman people assigned me a woman named Marti Greer. She was a former national-champion gymnast at the University of Alabama and also a triathlete. She and her husband were the race directors of the Buffalo Springs 70.3 Half Ironman in Lubbock, Texas. Marti was so focused on taking care of me that she never got around to telling me about her own achievement: that she had finished the Hawaiian Ironman in 2000. In every area of my life in which I was weak, God was faithfully surrounding me with people who were experienced and strong to help me fulfill his purpose.

The day before the race, my team took both my cell phone and my legs away from me. They were only looking out for my best interests. They wanted me to relax, focus on the race, and stay off my feet. That night, they imposed a 7:00 curfew. I lay awake and stared at the ceiling. I had run the race a thousand times in my mind, but that was with a body that was not out of shape, broken, and battered. I needed peace about tomorrow.

I lay on the floor of my hotel room by myself and prayed, just as I had prayed with my mom back in 2005. But I didn't have any tears this time.

"Lord, I want to thank you for this day and all these people you've brought into my life to get me to this moment in this place. Like Esther in the Bible, I believe you made me for 'such a time as this.' I believe that you created me specifically to finish this race. I really need your help. Father, I'm tired and my body hurts. I'm not in shape, I'm overweight, I've never swum this far . . ." I listed all the reasons I was afraid that I could not finish the race. Then I said, "But Lord, if your Spirit swims, bikes, and runs through me, I will finish this race. With every breath in my lungs and all the strength in my muscles, I will keep going, only I can't do it without you. There's only one way to find out if I can finish this race, and that's to put my body out there and my unwavering faith in you, Lord. I have to know that you are with me. Show me that you are with me."

I didn't hear anything from God. I just said what I needed to say, and then I went to bed. As I fell asleep, I had one thought on my mind: "No matter what, I will not stop."

It's usually hard to sleep the night before a big race, but I actually had a peaceful sleep. I awoke about 3:30 in the morning and took a shower. I never worried about logistical planning for the race because my training partner, Mike Lenhart, the former Army Ranger commander, was the ultimate strategic planner and organizer, and I had faith that Mike had everything under control. The night before, he had already packed my bags for me—my swimming sockets, biking legs, running legs, liners for each leg, A+D ointment, a towel to dry the sweat from my legs, dry race uniforms for each discipline, extra goggles, wet suit, cycling gloves, helmet, sunglasses, waistpacks for the bike and run, extra prosthetic socks, prosthetic sleeves, arm coolers, leg coolers, race belt, running shorts, sleeveless shirt. Everything we could think of was in place, and a few of my friends were assembled in my room.

"Let's say a prayer," said Scott Burkhardt, my friend from Idaho. He led us in a prayer that God would see me through this race and let me fulfill my dream so I could inspire others to have faith in God to achieve their dreams.

Then, in the darkness, we piled out of my room and joined the other members of Team Rigsby who were waiting for us. It was "go" time! First, I headed to the body-marking tent and got my timing chip activated so my family, friends, and race officials could track me during the race. Then I lined up to get marked with a huge permanent-ink pen. All the athletes get their legs and arms marked with their division and race number. Those numbers get checked and double-checked to make sure you are who you say you are.

When the markers, who are volunteers, got to me, they marked my arms, and then seemed totally perplexed when they looked at my legs. I made them sweat it out for a few seconds and then said, "You don't have to mark my legs. You can put my division on my forearms and my number on my biceps." You could almost hear them think, *Phew!*

Once I was properly inked up, I headed to my transition area to set things up. Physically challenged athletes share a tent for all their supplies. The tent was small and humid and cramped with bikes, hand cranks, and racing chairs. There, I made sure I had enough air in my bike tires—but not too much—and that I had plenty of water and ice. I filled my bike bottles with Gatorade Endurance Formula and stuffed thirty-two Powerbar Gels in my bike food box.

The commotion and excitement were mounting all around me. People spoke all different languages and were of all ages and colors. Morning light crept in slowly, illuminating the ocean with shining silver flecks.

Walking down the steps that would lead me to the swim start, I met Dave Orlowski, one of the original fifteen athletes who had participated in the very first Ironman. He was planning to do the race again in 2008, thirty years after first making history. He wished me luck and told me he'd see me when I finished the swim.

To kick off the race, Navy SEALs flew over the water to the sounds of the national anthem, then jumped out of the plane and parachuted into the ocean. While the age-groupers and lottery winners were making their way down to the water, the cannon for the professionals went off so they could get their head start.

Then the rest of us were herded into the water all at once. Imagine that. Nearly 1,800 athletes jumping into the ocean and corralled into a starting area. It was a giant people soup, with body parts kicking and chopping and bobbing everywhere. I had to tread water for about five minutes at the starting gate, which is harder than it sounds, especially when your adrenaline and nerves are ready to burst. It was a claustrophobic feeling, being in the middle of this throng of humanity. Competitors often refer to it as a human washing machine.

I looked back and could see the Ali'i Drive finish line, all lit up in the distance like a Hollywood movie set towering over the local shops and restaurants. There it was, my destiny awaiting my arrival—but then it suddenly dawned on me that it might be almost midnight before I would see that sight again. I felt a knot form in the pit of my stomach. My fellow racers began to fill in the open space of water around me. I felt them bumping into me as we became more and more packed like sardines. I thought about that question my sweet eighty-two-year-old mother had asked me over and over again: "Son, now why are you doing this?"

I wondered the same thing as my arms churned back and forth frantically to keep my head above water. I turned to my left and stared at the beautiful steeple on the Moku'aikaua Church and was reminded exactly why I was . . . *BOOM!*

The starting cannon exploded like thunder piercing the sky, unexpected and louder than you'd ever expect it to be. The sound turned this gathering of beautiful bodies into mass chaos. Elbows and knees came out of nowhere, and people punched and kicked with fury to swim past one another. Everyone jockeyed for dominance over the others.

An Ironman swim start is nothing more than a glorified prizefight in the water. If you are brave or foolish enough, as I was, to venture to the front of the pack, you are asking for a beating. The problem was that, with 1,800 people all clamoring to get into a natural swimming rhythm at once, there was a distinct lack of "excuse me" and "oh, you go first." No, these people were classic type-A personalities, and they didn't mind creating a little blood on the way to their destination. They weren't swimming around one another—they were swimming on top of one another. I think if they could have swum through one another, they would have.

Maybe, under other circumstances, they were all a bunch of great humanitarians, but on this day, in this situation, it was all about getting ahead. They would actually grab other swimmers and yank them backward to propel themselves forward.

About three hundred meters in, someone kicked me—I got a sharp heel right to the goggles, which made my right eye swell shut.

Perfect. The race had barely started, and now I was swimming with no legs and one eye.

Every ten strokes or so, I would lift my head to make sure I was on track to the first buoy, but I soon got a crick in my neck that made it very difficult to keep looking up. So I decided to follow other people's feet. My strategy was to look for Ironman tattoos.

Lots of people who've finished the Ironman get tattoos

on their ankles to commemorate their accomplishment. I figured that anyone with a tattoo would be a good person to tail, because he or she had finished at least once before. My top preference was for big people with those tattoos because bigger people create bigger drafts that can pull those behind them along.

The strategy apparently worked. When I neared the boat that marked the halfway point, I checked my watch and saw that thirty-five minutes had elapsed. *Pretty good*, I thought. I had gone about a mile at that point. Just 139.6 miles left to go before I could go out wearing my Ironman medal and get a cheeseburger.

If you aren't careful, it's easy to get distracted by the beauty of the water. Yellow tang fish, sea turtles, parrot fish, moray eels, schools of akule—these were my underwater companions, enjoying their leisurely daily pace just a few feet below the frenzied activity of the swimmers. I had to force myself to pay attention to the feet in front of me instead of to the magnificence below me.

As I swam, other competitors tried to shove me out of the way by swimming into me. I'm a big guy, and I made a decision early on: I'm not going anywhere. You go right ahead and swim over me if you have to, but that's going to take a lot of effort. I ain't movin'. People really did swim over me from time to time.

I came out of the water feeling good, with the exception of being able to see out of only one eye. I ripped off my swim cap and goggles and headed up the swim exit steps with Marti grabbing one arm and Mike grabbing the other to help me up. On my way to the transition tent, there was an outdoor shower where I could use one of several overhanging freshwater hoses. I washed off the saltwater and tried to soothe my post-prizefight-damaged eye. Just before I left, Carole, my friend and coach, kissed me on the cheek and told me she was proud of me. She had to lean down to do so because I stood only four feet tall without my prostheses.

On a training ride earlier in the week, Carole had had a horrible bike wreck in which she bruised a kidney and broke both wrists, two vertebrae, and three ribs. But she showed up at the Ironman anyway to support me and see me finish. It meant the world for me to see Carole at that moment.

As I left the showers, I knew I was on track when Carole yelled her favorite phrase, "There goes my hobbit!"

My true test was just beginning, however; now it was time for the bike. Marti slathered my face with sunscreen. Mike handed me my bike legs, and I put them on as quickly as I could. I put on my arm coolers—special clothing that reflects the sunshine. They had worked so well in training that I got a local seamstress to sew two of the arm coolers together to cover my legs because my carbon legs get almost unimaginably hot in the blistering sun and the reflection from the lava fields. I put on my sunglasses and helmet and walked my bike across the timing mat, where I was allowed to begin the bike race.

Maybe it was a good thing I couldn't understand the languages many of the other competitors were speaking. I wanted to believe they were saying, "Nice going!" and "Keep it up!" as we passed one another, but it was just as likely that they were cursing at me. Nobody really wants to get passed by a legless guy.

The first part of the bike course was actually lots of fun. It's through the city of Kona, and there were thousands of adoring fans lining the streets to greet loved ones as they rode by. My favorite part was seeing people's heads turn as I rode past them. You could tell they had never seen a guy with two prosthetic legs riding a regular bike, let alone a triathlon bike.

After a few miles in town, the course works its way onto

the Queen K Highway and then to a town called Hawi, the turnaround point before heading back toward Kona.

Heading out onto the Queen K Highway is a nerve-wracking and breathtaking experience for a triathlete. It is all you hear about from previous Hawaiian Ironman participants, and the stories of its many victims are endless. You can train for an entire year, through all types of weather conditions and mountainous terrain, and have your hopes come crashing down on this unpredictable and legendary track of burning pavement.

There are numerous Ironman courses that have hot and humid weather, with extremely windy conditions, and some can boast of hillier terrain, but the Queen K combines them in ways that most athletes have never encountered. This part of the course is something to be respected and feared. Despite the deceptive beauty of picturesque oceanside views on one side and a mountainous, green backdrop on the other, invisible headwinds blowing through the valleys of endless lava rocks can suddenly bring a bike to a screeching halt. Crosswinds have literally blown people—even world champions—across the freeway and off their bikes.

A few days before the race, I had sought advice from the pros about how to tackle the illustrious Queen, trying to make it appear to be part of my "strategic plan," as opposed to muddling around in outright fear. All I remembered their telling me was that, as I approached mile 30, if I saw the whitecaps picking up along the shoreline and very few clouds hovering over the distant mountaintops, then I'd better prepare myself for a nasty climb to Hawi and a worse trip back home. That thought triggered the dreaded "triathlete calculator game," the one that plagues all endurance athletes: It tempts them to spend mindless minutes in endless loops of math equations figuring "miles per hour vs. distance to go" forecasts.

*Fifteen miles per hour with eighty-two miles to go. If I slow down to twelve miles per hour for three miles because of the winds, then I will need to go sixteen miles per hour for . . .*

If only I had worked this hard at math in school.

It was 94 degrees, probably about 110 with the heat index. Not a cloud in the sky, and the sun was pounding down on us—but around mile 30 on the bike, I realized something weird: I wasn't hot. Normally, I would have been drenched in sweat by this point. I had been riding for just under two hours and was exerting myself plenty, so why wasn't I breaking a sweat?

*Something must be wrong*, I thought. Fear crept in. Was my body malfunctioning? I actually asked the question out loud: "Why am I not hot?"

I heard a voice come back to me—not an audible voice, exactly, but more dreamlike.

"Because you are wrapped in the shadows of my love."

In that instant, I was above my body, and I saw two angelic wings covering me. The only thing I could see beyond the wings was a partial shadow of half my wheels turning. I know what you might be thinking, but for the record, I gave up drugs a long time ago, and I had not had a sudden relapse.

NBC cameramen had been tracking me all day, but this was one of the few times they'd gone up ahead—thank goodness for that because this was an experience I didn't want interrupted. I felt the presence of God on me, and it was amazing.

The tears came fast and plentifully. I was trying to ride on, but I was sobbing with joy. I couldn't believe the amount of love that filled me at that moment, as if every prayer that anyone had ever said on my behalf had gathered together on that spot and was echoing back at me. I felt them. I felt that there were people praying for me to reach my dream. God was answering all of us at once, protecting me, urging me onward. I felt like Peter from the Bible when Jesus asked him in the middle of a storm to trust him, to step out of the boat, and to walk on the water. God wanted me to finish this race.

"Okay, Lord, I'm going to finish this thing!" I said. "I'm going to make you so proud of me."

That was mile 30. It was a feeling I wanted to hold forever.

# CHAPTER 11

I made it about twenty more miles coasting along on this beautiful high before things got really unpleasant. I was reduced to about ten miles per hour at my best effort, and the wind whistled through my helmet so loudly that I couldn't hear anything else. What made the bike stage in Hawaii so challenging at times was not just the intense, constant heat but also the headwinds that could instantly stop you in your tracks and the crosswinds that had blown people off their bikes in prior years.

The bike I had borrowed for the race didn't fit me, and I imagined I looked like one of those giant guys on a tiny tricycle in the circus. The improper fit was making my backside rub against the seat until I was raw. Just past the turnaround point at mile 60 was a place along the side of the road that was called the "special needs" area. Before the race, athletes were given a special needs bag in which they could put comfort food, specific supplies, or small equipment, then race officials delivered the bags to this area. You were not required to stop, but many age-groupers did. Although I had comfort food, including a peanut butter and jelly sandwich and a soda, what I really wanted was some Vaseline—which apparently hadn't been packed.

"Excuse me, can I get some Vaseline?" I asked the volunteers. No one seemed to know where to find any, or why I'd need such a thing.

"Help! My butt is on fire!" I said.

What I said didn't seem to register with anyone, so I repeated myself with a little more authority and volume. People have said stranger things to these volunteers, I assure you.

Still, no one could find Vaseline, and I had to somehow get back on the bike and prepare for another fifty-two miles on a blistering backside. I had wasted almost thirty crucial minutes seeking aid, without relief, and dumping the sweat out of my legs. I gingerly mounted my small steel pony of a ride and off I valiantly sped, going about twenty-five miles an hour down the seven-mile stretch of road I had just climbed. After a few miles, a van sped up and pulled beside me.

"What the heck do these guys want?" I said under my breath. I was in no mood to deal with people.

"Hey! Do you need some Vaseline?"

*Did he just say what I think that he said? Could it really be true?*

I slammed on the brakes and stopped.

Out came the biggest jar of Vaseline I had ever seen, glistening in the sun as if it were a healing balm sent from the heavens. I'm relatively certain I heard angels sing. I was so happy to see it that I popped open the lid and took an entire handful, then stuck it down the back of my pants.

"Ahh, that's amazing! Thanks, guys! You saved my butt!" I called out.

There was so much Vaseline that it managed to escape through my shorts and get all over my bike—in the chain, on the pedals, all over the tires, everywhere. Later, my bike mechanic wanted to know what in the world had happened to my bike, but for now, I didn't care. Relief was all that mattered, and what sweet relief it was.

At this point, I was ahead of schedule and feeling pretty good about it. Then I hit the sobering reality of the legendary crosswinds. What makes them even worse than their sheer might is their unpredictability. They show up in gusts, like shoves from a big bully just hiding around a corner waiting to topple someone over. My biking legs were very light, making me a top-heavy, unstable bull's-eye. As soon as I thought I had figured out where the wind was coming from—surprise! It would take a whack at me from a completely different direction.

More than once, it sent me hurtling toward a guardrail. Fighting the constant changes was as mentally exhausting as the headwinds were physically punishing. Just beyond the guardrail was a rough hillside leading straight down to the ocean. I was determined, however, that I was through with swimming for the day, thank you.

Around mile 78, the small trees along the roadside bent over from the wind gusts, and the bushes around the lava field were almost parallel to the ground. I mashed and mashed on the pedals with all my might while my knuckles turned white from my death grip on the handlebars. If I was going anywhere, it felt like backward.

I buried my head down closer to my handlebars, but my bike was so small that I could never get into the aero position all the cool triathletes use. My bike and I had been tested for aerodynamics at a famous wind tunnel in North Carolina. After the test, the researcher said, "We have good news for you. You probably can't get any more *un*aerodynamic than you are now."

Competitors say that the real race of any Ironman starts at mile 80 of the bike stage. If this was the real start, I was in deep trouble. My body wanted to quit. I told it to keep going, but it told me to get in a cab and order room service at the hotel. I needed a mediator.

So I began talking to God again, seeing as he had so obviously been on my side before.

"Lord, could you help me out here with the wind? This kind of stinks on a universal level. I don't know if you heard me, oh, ten miles ago praying to you about no wind, but I just wanted to remind you of that prayer, in case you forgot."

Nothing happened. If fact, the wind seemed to pick up. My legs were on fire, and the sun had baked the rest of my body. I waited a little while longer so as not to seem too impatient. Then I tried again. "Would you please stop this wind? Oh yeah, in Jesus' name. Thank you. I'll get back with you in a minute."

Nope.

I was trying to drop hints politely, wasn't I? I was doing my part. Why wasn't God stopping the wind for me?

"Hel-lo! Your guy is attempting to do the unthinkable here! You parted the Red Sea for Moses. You shut the mouths of lions to save Daniel. All I am asking for is a tiny bit of help with this blasted wind!"

A photographer came up beside me in a car and called out, "How are you doing?" My frustration came out all over this poor photographer. I was furious with God, and anyone in my path was going to hear it.

My tirade to God continued. "I cannot believe you brought me out here to desert me! I'm going to be so stinking tired that when I complete this bike course—let me rephrase that, *if* I finish this bike course in time—I'm not going to be able to run! I am so exhausted. My legs are trashed. And you won't even help me out with the wind."

God needed to take me and put me in a time-out. I was having a full-blown, two-year-old's tantrum.

Just then, Scott Johnson drove up alongside me with a few photographers. He was driving a media car and came by as often as he could, usually to call out words of support, get some photos, and make sure I was doing okay. This time, though, he decided to be funny.

There were my Doritos, on the end of a stick, poking out of the passenger window. Just out of my reach.

I looked at the chips, I looked at my grinning friend, and I might have growled. He had no idea that I was in no mood for jokes at the moment.

"I haven't peed all day," I said.

"Thanks for the newsflash."

"No, seriously, I drank gallons of Cokes and Gatorades and water, but I can't pee! What does that mean? Maybe my kidneys are shutting down!"

He called my team members to find out what they thought, and the conflicting advice came from all angles.

"Maybe you're dehydrated. I think you need to drink more."

"You're probably just sweating it all out."

"It's the heat. It's making all the liquid evaporate."

"You need more salt tablets!"

As I fought the headwinds and my own fears, I couldn't stand the sideline commentary. At first, I just gave Scott that look you give people when they have pressed too many of your buttons. Then I let him have it. "You know what? Screw you!"

Having done triathlons himself, he forgave me because he knew I was in a bad mental place and hurting physically. To ease my fears, he called Carole Sharpless—who was continuing her bike wreck recovery in a hotel room.

"Scott hasn't peed," my friend said. "Should we be worried?"

"No, don't worry," she said. "He's drinking enough. He's just evaporating it faster than what his body can absorb to go to the bathroom."

Once I had the official diagnosis from Coach Carole, I felt better about it, and Scott decided that it was probably best to leave me alone. Struggling like I was, it wasn't fun to have people watch me. So he took off with the photographers, and I went back to yelling at God to obey me and fix the conditions.

I waited for a voice, a sign, something. But there was nothing but the howling of the wind and my own heavy breathing.

And there I was, like Lieutenant Dan, the double-amputee character from *Forrest Gump*, in the scene where he's caught in hurricane-like conditions out at sea with Forrest. Lieutenant Dan climbs the mast of the large shrimp boat, and as he sits precariously atop this structure without his legs on, all full of crazy, he raises his fists and lets the rain and winds pummel him, all the while screaming at God, "Come on. You call this a storm?!"

That was me. Lieutenant Dan. Calling for a showdown with God. And just as I was getting worked up to fever pitch, I looked across the highway and realized I was directly across from the spot where I'd had the angelic vision on my way up the mountain. What a jerk I was to forget so quickly.

*Get a grip*, I told myself. *You're losing it. Calm yourself down.*

"Excuse me, God? Um, sorry about that stuff back there. Are we cool?"

But again, I heard nothing.

*God is not talking to me. I have ticked him off*, I thought. *Woe is me. I'm abandoned out here.*

I totally deserved it, but what was I going to do now—aside from actively panicking? For ten miles, I had been battling this relentless wind, thrashing and flailing and hurting all over. Competitors aren't allowed to have headphones on, so I didn't even have the solace of music to keep me going. Triathlon is a lonely, individual sport, especially at a low point like this. And now I didn't even have God to keep me company. Without his help, I was going to fail.

In my mind's eye, I saw the face of the prosthetist who

had stolen my legs. He would be dancing a jig to celebrate my downfall.

I could hear him saying, "Serves him right! If only I had made his legs, he would have finished!"

The thought of never crossing that finish line made me ache. There had to be a way; there had to be some hope. What else could I do?

*Well, if God* were *talking to me, what would he tell me? He would tell me that when life is spinning out of control, control the things I can control, and leave the rest up to him.*

*I can control my heart rate. I can ease up the tension on my bike pedals and switch to an easier gear, and my heart rate will go down.* As the gears turned, I watched my heart rate monitor, and I started to tune out the thirty-mile-an-hour wind that was whistling through my helmet and trying to blow me off the bike. I ignored the craziness that was going on around me. I focused less on how tired my legs were. I forgot my concerns about not having the strength left to run the marathon, and I put aside the fear of not finishing.

*As long as I keep pedaling, I have a chance. Keep pedaling.*

My friend and fellow competitor Andy Baldwin spotted me as he was nearing the end of his marathon. "Go, Scott!" he called out to me. "You are the man! You can do it!"

I waved back to him. *I am the man. I am* so *the man.*

Amazingly, the wind died down and I picked up speed. In fact, I went faster than I had gone when I started the race. And finally, almost eight and a half hours after I started, I actually got to the end of the course, at the pier, and handed my bike to one of the "bike catcher" volunteers with just forty minutes to spare before the bike cutoff time.

*I made it! I did it!*

Mike handed me an ice-cold bottle of water, and I dumped it over the back of my neck. To this day I claim that was the sweetest, coldest water ever, far beyond anything at the polar caps. Before I could savor it, Mike handed me my equipment and my running legs and cut me off when I started telling him about the insane biking conditions.

"Just focus on the present. Let's get you out on the run course," he said.

As I fastened on my running legs, Marti dished out loads of encouragement in a motherly, comforting way.

Now all I had to do was run 26.2 miles. Which would be . . . really . . . easy?

LED headlamps were strapped to the top of my prosthetic running sockets, an acknowledgment that I knew in advance I'd be running in the dark. Whereas the professional athletes typically finish in the eight- to ten-hour range, I knew I was in for at least a fifteen-hour day, and the sun would set around 6:30 p.m. The idea of it didn't thrill me. Running alone in total darkness for hours could get eerie.

As the sun set along the shoreline of Kailua Bay, volunteers passed out glo-sticks. Athletes would wear them as necklaces and bracelets so they could be seen and not run into one another in the dark. The route was almost cavernous: a black asphalt highway surrounded on both sides by dark lava rocks.

The humidity hovered somewhere around 70 or 80 percent, making the air heavy with the feeling of a crowded locker room. Every few miles, I had to stop and take my legs off, dump sweat out of my prosthetic liners, wipe my stump down with a towel, put on some Vaseline, and reattach my prosthetics. Aside from the fact that it was really painful to run with the open blisters I was nursing, it was also very frustrating to have to stop and go so often, where my heart rate couldn't stay steady and I had to build back up to my stride each time I stopped. My anxiety mounted—*how much time am I losing doing this?*

Then there was another problem: I can't stand ignoring

people. Along the path, volunteers and race fans would ask me how I was doing, or give me souvenirs, or want to talk to me about the weather or my legs or whatever. I'm really bad at saying, "Sorry, I'm in this race and I have to get back to running now." So whenever I stopped, I'd have conversations that delayed me longer than anticipated. Then I'd try to make up for the bonding and informational sessions by running like a madman as soon as I got going again.

Trouble was, I could not anticipate the tremendous obstacles that were about to plague my marathon run. This race was getting more difficult than I could have expected, and as the sun slowly set, my encouragers began to leave the course to round up their friends and families to discuss the day's events over dinner. That was a great revelation: It was dinnertime, and I still had to run twenty more miles. Twenty more miles in the dark.

As I approached the next mile marker, I had to stop and dump sweat out of my legs. It was then I noticed that my sockets were fitting loosely, which was to be expected at some point in the race. The tissue on my stumps shrink when there is a significant loss of body fluid. To compensate for this volume loss, I was supposed to roll a small, five-inch prosthetic sock over my liners, place my legs back in their sockets, roll up the sleeves over my thighs, and be back on my way. If I didn't, then I'd be right back to the bad situation from the earlier ING Georgia Marathon in which my stumps had blistered and bled through the whole race.

I opened my Fuel Belt waistpack to get my prosthetic socks and found that I had the wrong supply pack with me—it was my bike pack instead of my running pack, so it didn't have any socks in it. It was my fault for having packed both events in the same color waistpacks. However, I thought I had made it clear enough by writing "bike" on one with a Sharpie marker and "run" on the other. Still, someone had given me the wrong pack when I was leaving the transition area.

I had to call for help. The World Triathlon Corporation allowed physically challenged athletes' handlers to bring them equipment on the course, just like the able-bodied athletes were allowed a bike technician's assistance on that course. The guys on the NBC motorcycle radioed back to the transition tent, where they attempted to find Mike Lenhart for me. However, Mike was away from the transition tent getting some food, so a woman tried to locate the right pack for me. The woman was Sarah Reinertsen, the amputee who had been on the cover of *Triathlete* magazine and had first inspired me to do this race. Marti also tried to locate the prosthetic socks.

Mike got back to the tent and noticed people rifling through my bags.

"Um . . . what's going on?"

"Scott needs prosthetic socks!" they told him.

"I have them here," he said, pointing to the forty-pound backpack he was lugging around. His backpack contained everything he could imagine I might need on the course.

There was supposed to be a motorcycle available for the handlers to find their athletes on the course, but when Mike and Marti got to the spot where the motorcycle was supposed to be, it wasn't there.

"Okay, we'd better just run and find him," he said.

Mike was in sandals and Marti was in flip-flops. Neither of them had expected to be doing any running that day. They took off together, but Marti eventually had to hang back—do you know how hard it is to run in flip-flops?

I had been at mile 7 when the call came in, so Mike figured I'd be at about mile 9 by the time he made it there. Unfortunately, I wasn't there yet. Scott Johnson met Mike and Marti there and gave the news that I hadn't been spotted, which was bad news. They backtracked along Ali'i Drive in the thick of darkness looking for me. I had already lost about twenty-five minutes while I waited for relief, and had just made the decision that I'd better start moving again, even if my legs didn't fit right. I still hadn't made it to mile 8 when they finally caught up with me. They spotted me only by the light of my leg lamplights.

People had crowded around to watch me. It was an atmosphere almost like Mardi Gras—the locals were drunk and silly. My appearance in the dark was a definite conversation piece; they could hear my feet clicking along, and they could see these little headlights on my legs and the glo-sticks around my neck and arms. Who was this guy clicking down the street with an NBC cameraman driving along next to him with a giant video camera?

As Scott, Mike, and Marti drew near, they asked some of the spectators to turn on their car headlights and point them at me so we could see what we were doing. Then they asked for a flashlight, and the whole crowd started screaming urgently and drunkenly, "Flashlight! Anyone have a flashlight?" "You have a flashlight?" "He needs a flashlight!"

My friends had joked with me in the past that I was like Will Ferrell's character in *Talladega Nights*: the Ricky Bobby of triathlons. The moniker certainly fit me that night. I always needed major pit stops and it took lots of people to get me around the track.

The process of switching out my legs cost me another thirty, irreplaceable minutes, only to find at the end of it that Mike had brought the wrong prosthetic socks. They were too thin.

"I can make it on these for a while, but I'm going to need at least another pair by the end of the race. These are going to compress and I'll need to add more in a few miles."

Poor Mike. Off he went in his sandals again, running all the way back to our hotel to find more socks in my suitcase. While there, he noticed his running shoes and thought, "Hmm. Maybe it's time to put these on." Before the day was through,

Mike would run about thirteen miles—a half marathon—to bring me equipment.

Meanwhile, I had to keep moving. At mile 14, a little local girl was playing on the side of the road. She was maybe seven years old, and was kicking around a ball with some other young kids. Her mom was a volunteer at the water stations. She shouted, "Look! That's the man with no legs who's going to finish this race."

Then she ran up alongside me and said, "You can do it! Even if you have no legs!"

I needed that little girl to say that at that moment. It felt as if she were an angel sent by the Lord himself to encourage me and give me a sign that he was still with me.

As the evening wore on, there were fewer and fewer people on the road, and it got quieter and more lonely. Even the sky appeared to me like a black hole, with very few stars illuminating above. At times, it was just me and the NBC camera people and lines of cars with drivers staring at me as they drove by. I watched the double takes as people looked and looked again to confirm what they had seen.

Some people honked, some cheered, and some just gazed in amazement, but they seemed to acknowledge that something special was happening. All you could see were camera lights, and all you could hear was the rhythmic clicking of my prosthetic feet.

Even the volunteers were tiring by then and were less excited about runners coming through their stations. Who could blame them? Those stations had been set up in the wee hours of the morning. By now, it was almost time to clean up and call it a night. The pros had finished several hours ago, yet I still had many miles to go.

One of the milestones at the Hawaiian Ironman is the Natural Energy Lab facility on the Queen K Highway. When you make the turn into the lab, you're at mile 16, and on the way out, you're at mile 19. I have never been in a cave, but I can only imagine that it's not much different from running on the Energy lab grounds at night. It's pitch-black and closed to spectators during the race.

*Please, Mike, make it back before I have to go in there.*

And he did—just in time. He had run all the way back to about mile 15, where he spotted the run course director on a motorcycle.

"Do you know where Scott Rigsby is?" Mike asked. "I'm his handler, and I have to bring him some prosthetic gear."

"He passed here a little while ago. Come on, I'll take you to him."

The director gave him a ride on his motorcycle along the course until they spotted me just before the turn to the Energy Lab. I stopped and dumped the sweat out of my prosthetics and added the right socks.

Scott Johnson had gone ahead in the media car and was waiting at the top of the Energy Lab entrance to encourage me before I ran down into the abyss. I could sense by his careful use of words and the concerned expression on his face that real doubt was creeping into his consciousness.

I was starting to wonder myself. Why on earth would they call this place the Energy Lab? I was feeling no energy from the experience and thinking, *I can't believe they actually take people on tours of this place.*

My time was fleeting and my pace was too slow. At this rate, I was not going to make it. Not only that, but my balance had begun to falter, as well, and I started to weave on the road. A few times, I almost ran into the NBC car. Several times, I stumbled and had to quickly regain my balance.

As I entered into three miles of solitary confinement, the run racecourse director reminded me that I was cutting it very close. It's never a good sign when a race official is concerned enough to mention your current pace to you. I knew I had to pick up my pace if I wanted to make it by the midnight cutoff time, but what strength did I have left? There was no extra fuel tank strapped to my back; I was running on sheer guts, willpower, and stubbornness.

"I'm doing the best I can! I know what I'm doing!" I yelled that out to no one in particular.

But I didn't know what I was doing, except for putting one foot in front of the other. By now, I was disoriented and fatigued, slowly stumbling forward. At the other side of the Energy Lab, Scott Johnson and the photographer waited in a media car for me to reappear, expecting that it would take me about forty minutes to complete it, based on the run racecourse director's estimations.

"If he takes longer than that, he won't make it," the director said.

But after almost an hour, I still wasn't out, and those awaiting my exit were calling Scott Johnson on his mobile and getting worried. They had reason to worry, too. At that moment, I was picking up my prosthetics supplies that had scattered all over the road when my waistpack ripped.

I gathered it all together and carried it under my arm like a football as I kept going. My spare prosthetic sleeves were in the waistpack, along with other supplies that included a small jar of Vaseline and some extra socks. The supplies made the waistpack weigh three or four pounds.

The NBC car that had been following me sped up and found my friend.

"Are you Scott Johnson?" they asked. When he answered yes, they said, "You'd better get to the bottom of that hill. Rigsby's in trouble."

He ran down about a mile and found me only by the headlights on my legs.

"My waistpack ripped!" I said.

"Scott, just forget it. You were supposed to be out of this

place by now. Man, you have to get going and pick up the pace!" he said.

"I need to get these new liners on. I have to dump out my legs."

"You can't. There's no more time for you to be fixing your legs. You have to run up this hill and keep running without stopping until you get to the finish line, or this dream is all over."

I paced around a little, trying to rationalize a way to stop and dump out my prosthetics like I needed to do.

"Listen to me," Scott said. "You have seven miles to go, and you've got to do it in an hour and a half or we don't get this thing done."

"Well . . . I need to do something with this pack," I said like a fighter who was punch drunk.

"No, you don't. Just throw it down. Someone will pick it up later."

No one was allowed to touch me while I was racing, or I would have been disqualified. So I had to toss my lifesaving waistpack contents off the race path and hope that I wouldn't regret it later.

As I made the throw, though, my balance faltered and I fell forward, face-first. There I was, in the darkness of a valley in the Energy Lab doing a plank on my elbows, looking at the ground just four inches from my head. That should have been the end of my race.

Every time I fell during a practice run, my prosthetic sleeves tore and broke the vacuum seal that holds my legs in place. Every time.

So I unsteadily held my body up with my eyes closed. I was terrified to tilt my head to look under my body and see if my sleeves were torn from the fall. If they were, there was no way I'd have enough time to put on a new pair and still make the cutoff time. I peeked with one eye, then the other. *Please God, not now after all this time and excruciating effort.*

With both eyes, I surveyed, and saw . . . no rip? No rip!

In amazement, I noticed that one of my tiny headlamps was cracked, and realized what had happened: Those two-inch LED headlamps had saved me. If my legs had hit the road, the seal would have broken, and the prosthetics would have been rendered useless. The headlamps stuck out just enough so that I had landed on them instead of on the prosthetics. The unbroken headlamp still shone, ready to lead me out of the darkness. My arms shook and sweat poured like a waterfall off my forehead as I stood up. I felt like the angels had saved me.

"Are you all right? That was inches from disaster," Scott said.

"Yeah, I'm all right," I said.

I tried to stop my body from shaking, but it didn't obey me. The song "From the Inside Out" by Hillsong United played in my mind:

> A thousand times I've failed
> Still your mercy remains
> And should I stumble again
> Still I'm caught in your grace
> Everlasting, your light will shine when all else fades
> Never ending, your glory goes beyond all fame.[3]

Scott tried to get my attention. "This isn't going to sound right, but please, just shake it off. There's no time left to stop. Maybe it will help to keep it simple: Focus on the fact that all you have to do is one mile, seven times. Okay? It's not seven miles. It's one mile, seven times."

I nodded and started to run again.

"Don't stop," he said. "All you have to do is one mile, seven times. Okay? It's not seven miles. It's one mile, seven times."

I nodded.

"One mile, seven times."

*Yeah, okay.*

He repeated, "It's just one mile, seven times. One mile, seven times."

I glared at him. "Don't you ever say those words to me again!"

Steam may or may not have come out of my ears. But he had succeeded in what he was trying to do: He had ticked me off enough that all I wanted to do was get running again just to shut him up!

It was time to fight like never before. With everything I had in me and every drop of faith I could find, I had to keep going.

*As long as I keep putting one foot in front of the other, I have a chance. If I can do this, I can change the world. No one has ever done what I'm about to do.*

As I left the zero-Energy Lab and made it onto the Queen K for the last stretch to the Emerald City of Kailua-Kona, it was now after 10:30 p.m. The highway was almost vacant of human life. My world included a few passing vehicles, distant lights from the surrounding streets, the die-hard remaining volunteers at the water stations, and those two people from NBC Sports following me in a convertible.

Their headlights were like the beam of light you see from a lighthouse. One misguided step on a rock or a broken bottle, and I might fall again. I thought of the verse in the Bible about being a light in the darkness. I don't think I ever had an image become so real to me as now, in this time of desperation and need.

The mile markers were one big blur. I simply repeated the process that had brought me this far: I quoted verses from the Bible over and over to myself; I thought about the songs played at the Buckhead Church back in Atlanta; and I envisioned the climactic scenes from *Chariots of Fire*, *Rudy*, and *Hoosiers*.

My regimen became a fast and steady pace to the water stations, then a very fast walk through each aid station while drinking one Coke, one Gatorade, and one cup of ice. Mile 21, mile 22, mile 23. One of the volunteers told me they were out of soup, which was irrelevant to me but another gentle reminder that most of the participants had passed through already and that the race clock was ticking much closer toward the midnight hour.

*Lord, please speak to me again. I've come so far. I'm too tired and the pain is starting to get inside my head.*

The last three miles were the most difficult ones I had ever run in my life. I had run seven miles without dumping the sweat out of my legs. I was about three miles overdue. Pools of sweat had accumulated inside my liners, so much so that it had separated the Vaseline coating from my urethane liners. My bare skin stuck to the urethane and was creating contact burns all around the tops of my knees. It was as if someone had placed hands around my knee and twisted in opposite directions.

With each step, the flesh was being ripped off my legs. It felt like all the skin under my prostheses had been peeled off and then set on fire. Sheer torture.

I fantasized about falling onto a stretcher at the finish line. *Please, just let me make it to the end.* I wasn't sure I could because the pain was becoming unbearable. People have asked me how I was able to push through that kind of pain.

Lance Armstrong once said, "Pain is temporary. It may last a minute, or an hour, or a day, or a year, but eventually, it will subside and something else will take its place. If I quit, however, it lasts forever."

I had to find that place in my mind where I could go and stay there just long enough to get me to the finish line.

Those who trust in the Lord will find new strength.
They will soar high on wings like eagles.
They will run and not grow weary.
They will walk and not faint. *Isaiah 40:31, NLT*

A guy pulled up on a scooter, and I ran alongside him.

"Hey dude, how am I doing with time? Am I going to make it?" I asked.

"Absolutely! You're almost there."

As I took a right turn off the Queen K Highway and ran down the hill on Palani Road, I saw the lights of the finish line area and heard vague sounds of a screaming crowd.

Those last couple of miles, when you have nothing left in you, it's the crowd that gets you to that finish line. Their screams, their applause, their kind words: "You're almost there! You can do it!"

Running on the familiar streets leading into the city, I was excited to see the faces of all my friends waiting for me. I wasn't even mad at them about the Doritos anymore. I couldn't wait to get to the finish line to thank them for helping me through this crazy journey.

*I am almost home. I have only a half mile to go.*

I could hear the announcer, Mike Reilly, congratulating people as they crossed triathlon's most famous finish line in the world—the one I had dreamed about on my parents' living room floor two years ago. "You are an Ironman," he told each of the finishers. Mike had been standing at that finish line every year since 1989, announcing the names of thousands of finishers as they crossed the threshold. How many times I had played this scene in my mind. What would it be like when he announced my name? That moment was almost here.

I thought, *I'm actually going to make it. I'm going to finish this thing. Mike Reilly is going to say, "Scott Rigsby, you are an Ironman."*

I had finished the last nine or ten miles 25 percent faster than I had run the previous sixteen. You're not supposed to get faster as you go along, but I wasn't stopping to take care of my prosthetics. Now I was paying for it, because I had burned two-inch-wide rings around my knees; the flesh was completely gone. I didn't care. I was going to be an Ironman.

It was like that instant when a woman is giving birth and realizes that she's about to see her baby for the first time. All the pain she's been in suddenly doesn't matter because she knows the big moment is just a few minutes away.

For me, those last few hundred meters were a time of joy and reflection. It had been just under two years since I had begun training, and those two years came back to me in a series of mental snapshots. The first was of me running before dawn in the vacant parking lot, back when I had been too embarrassed to run on streets or tracks for fear that people would see the guy with no legs having to stop and walk.

I thought about my first triathlon, my first road race, my first half-Ironman. I thought about breaking my back and all the despair that had caused. I thought about the people who'd be cheering me on to finish . . . and the ones who were hoping I wouldn't finish. I pictured my brother Tim. Everything I had gone through to get to this moment washed over me. The surgeries, the training, the fights, the hardships.

I was overwhelmed, both visually and emotionally, by the sight of the enormous crowds on both sides of the street. On the left sidewalk next to the seawall, there were thousands of people several rows deep. On the right side, people crowded in front of and inside the restaurants, and some even climbed on the roofs. The closer I came to the finish line, the louder the crowd roared. It was louder than any University of Georgia football game I had ever attended.

People pointed at me and elbowed their friends. Jaws dropped. Some spectators jumped up and down and screamed. A few even ran alongside me like they do in the Tour de France.

Then there was the famous finish line, right in front of me.

In those last seconds, the catastrophic accident, the anger at myself and everyone else, the consuming depression, all the pain from the surgeries, the frustration of being in and out of hospitals for years, the hopelessness of addiction, and the twenty agonizing years of living in the suffocating grip of fear . . . it was all washed away!

"He's going to do it! He's going to do it!" Mike Reilly called out as I came into view.

*Wow*, I thought. *I wish I had run a little slower, to savor this magical moment.*

When I was a little kid, I used to stand on the side of the bathtub where I could see myself in the mirror and flex my muscles, hoping to one day get bigger. As I crossed the finish line, I stood and flexed my muscles—just like when I was a kid, except this time I had an audience of fifty million friends from around the world who would see this moment on television. Then I lifted both arms above my head, pointed my fingers skyward to acknowledge God for making this dream come true, and blew a kiss to the screaming crowd, just like my favorite professional wrestler did when I was a kid.

"Scott Rigsby, you are an Ironman," Mike Reilly said. "The first double amputee in the world to finish the Hawaiian Ironman."

The crowd erupted into the kind of cheering you feel in your bones. I had been in an all-day prizefight, and I was still standing.

It's humbling to see grown men and women with tears in their eyes, filled with emotion over your accomplishment. I wanted to stop and thank every one of them. I settled for giving Mike Reilly a big hug. Partly because of his unwavering support of my journey and partly because of sheer exhaustion, I didn't let go for what might have been a long time.

God had opened a door for me, and I had held up my end of the bargain. I had kept the faith and fought the good fight, and he had done his part to see me through. My team got together in a huddle and sent our thanks up to heaven.

Then they hauled me off on the much-anticipated stretcher and got me to a medical tent for IV fluids.

Sixteen hours, 42 minutes, 46 seconds. That's how long it took me to make history.

Twenty-six cups of Coke, twenty-six cups of Gatorade. I wasn't going to sleep for a very long time.

One thought that left a smile on my face: *Tonight, I changed the world.*

# CHAPTER 12

"I'm having a hard time finding out on the Internet. Did you get it done?" Mike McClain asked me on the phone.

"I got it done," I said. "Only seventeen minutes to spare, but I got it done. I am officially an Ironman."

Mike cried.

Twenty-one years earlier, he had held my head in his lap while my blood ran down his leg. He didn't know if I was going to live, let alone walk, let alone do triathlons. A world record wasn't anywhere on the radar.

My friends called one another, wrote to one another, and had their own emotional celebrations across the country. It was one of those nights when you look at the stars and wonder how many other people are looking at those same stars, and you feel connected to everyone and everything.

After all that caffeine, sugar, and adrenaline, I didn't fall asleep until about 3 a.m., and I didn't get up the following day until just about lunchtime. Muscles and body parts that I didn't even know I had hurt. Thirty minutes after I had finished the race, my stumps had swollen to twice their normal size, so managing to sit upright in a wheelchair the next afternoon counted as a good enough effort for the day.

My mom congratulated me and told me she loved me. My dad wouldn't get on the phone.

That night, there was an awards ceremony, and the male and female world champions of the race both gave speeches. Chrissie Wellington was the female winner and the first-ever British winner. She captivated me as I listened to her heartfelt and eloquent speech.

At the end, she said, "The biggest crowd was at midnight to watch the final people come across, and that's something I will never forget and a memory I will treasure forever. I want to say congratulations to all the other professionals for making it such an awesome race, but I want to save the last words for the 1,600 or so age-groupers who swam, biked, ran, walked, and crawled their way over the finish line, from the youngest to the oldest; to Scott Rigsby; to Katie Bolling; and all the others who've fought against adversity and won. You are the true Ironmen and women, and you're an inspiration to me. *Mahalo*."

Her voice cracked with emotion. Her inner beauty and class shone more brightly than any medal the World Triathlon Corporation could have given her. I hadn't met Chrissie before, but she hugged me after her speech, and that was the birth of one of my closest friendships today.

I wasn't expecting to be called to the stage that night, but a familiar voice called out, "Scott Rigsby, 16 hours and 42 minutes." It was Mike Reilly. Mike Lenhart quickly pushed me up to the stage. I didn't have my prosthetics with me, though, so I just stayed seated in my wheelchair.

"How does it feel to make history?"

"I feel like Neil Armstrong after a bar fight," I said.

"What was it like for you out there on the course yesterday?" Mike Reilly asked.

"It was everything everyone said it was going to be."

Just finishing the competition earned me a medal. I bit it to make sure it was real. I also received an *umeke*—a traditional Hawaiian wooden bowl given to all the physically challenged athletes who finished the race. I couldn't wait to fill it with sugary Cap'n Crunch cereal and eat it in front of Scott Johnson.

That day, four former world champions didn't get a medal because they didn't finish the race. But I did.

And so did Charlie Plaskon, a sixty-five-year-old grandfather of three who has been legally blind all his life.

And so did Brian Boyle, who had been in a horrible car accident in 2004. His heart was knocked across his chest, he lost 60 percent of his blood, he had numerous broken bones and nerve damage, and he died on the operating table eight times before he was finally revived.

And so did my friend and training partner, Karen O'Riordan, who log-rolled across the Ironman finish line for Team Blazeman, in honor of Jon Blais, who had finished the 2005 Hawaiian Ironman despite having ALS.

*We are "the Unthinkables,"* I thought with a smile. We were also Ironmen, along with all the other athletes that day who had been counted out for various reasons—too old, too fat, too slow, not athletic, disabled, broken—but had finished the race anyway. The world had told each of us in some way that we just didn't measure up to its standards, but that day we proved the world wrong. We had each done something unthinkable, and today belonged to us.

"What can you do with a man who has an invincible purpose in him; who never knows when he is beaten; and who, when his legs are shot off, will fight on the stumps?" writes Orison Swett Marden in his book *How to Succeed*. "Difficulties and opposition do not daunt him. He thrives upon persecution; it only stimulates him to more determined endeavor. Give a man the alphabet and an iron will, and who shall place bounds to his achievements! . . . *The world always listens to a man with a will in him."*

When I got back to Atlanta the next day, I was physically and emotionally spent. There was no ticker-tape parade waiting for me, no key to the city from the mayor. Just overdue bills in my mailbox. It had been pretty heady to be in a place where almost everyone on the island and nearby islands knew my name and my story after seeing my face featured across giant television screens, worldwide coverage by triathlon media, and the local news in Kona. I even received an invitation to the set of the television show *Lost*—the cast and crew had watched me cross the finish line. Now I was just the legless guy in the grocery store again.

The cashier said, "Haven't seen you in here lately. What have you been up to? Anything interesting?"

"Not much, really," I said.

What I wanted more than anything was to use my victory to inspire people, but I didn't know how, in a practical way, to make that happen. I had hoped that, after the Ironman, television producers would be calling, reporters would knock on my door, and Oprah would ask me out to lunch.

*Maybe I missed her call. Would Oprah's name show up on my caller ID?*

While I waited for the phone to ring, I kept working on my speaking presentations. I had already begun speaking at churches, schools, and organizations over the last year, and I was more in demand as a speaker after completing the Ironman.

I've never met a kid who wasn't fascinated by my prostheses. Every kid who sees me wants to know, "What are those things?" When they ask their parents, 95 percent of parents—and I am being generous with that estimate—have no clue how to give a good answer to that question, especially because kids never ask just one question. If a parent answers that first question, a series of tougher questions will follow.

"Mommy, look at that! What are those?"

"Sweetie, those are artificial legs."

"What happened to him?"

"I don't know. Don't stare! Let's go."

"How does he walk on those things? How do they work?"

"I don't know. Now, let's go."

"Does he wear them to sleep?"

"Let's go!"

This is why I speak to thousands of kids each year. I want them to stare as much as they want and to know that no question is off-limits. With my one life, I hope to educate a whole generation of kids who can later answer their own children's questions about prosthetics with educated ease.

When I get asked, "What audience is the most challenging to speak to?" my answer is always the same: kindergartners, by far!

Kindergartners' little brains go into sensory overload when they see me. There are so many questions racing through their heads that it's tough to settle on one. They blurt out whatever last thought finally makes it to their vocal cords. Usually it's, "You're a robot!"

The first time a child said this to me, I did what every guy with no kids does when a small child says something absurd: I ignored it. Well, we all know what that does—nothing! It takes only one child to make that statement, and then the whole roomful of kids is convinced that I actually am a robot, and nothing I say can dissuade them. But I'm a smart guy who learns from his mistakes. Now when I speak to a group of kindergartners, I tell them the truth right off the bat: "Hey, kids! My name is Mr. Scott, and I'm a robot."

My manager helped me to get bookings with larger companies and universities to continue spreading my message: "Do the Unthinkable." I wanted to reach out to people and tell them that they could overcome even the most difficult obstacles and achieve their craziest dreams. I worked on my presentation through trial and error, and the biggest rewards came when people approached me afterward with their personal stories.

What I found was that people were remarkably open with me about their lives, their fears, and their hopes because I had been so transparent about mine. Often, the people who reached out to me did so because they needed some extra encouragement. It was rewarding for me to get to be that encourager.

Martin Luther King Jr. once said, "Life's most persistent and urgent question is, 'What are you doing for others?'" My historic Ironman finish would have been hollow were it not for its transcendent effect on other people. It would have been a manly accomplishment and a medal hanging on my wall, but it would have had no real meaning.

I don't believe that God wanted me to do an Ironman just so I could brag at dinner parties. There was a reason he got me through that race, and I think it had something to do with people like Kim Houx.

After I gave a talk at an elementary school in Coeur d'Alene, Idaho, a woman followed me out to my car and told me she was a nurse at a local hospital and had a patient named Kim who had recently lost both of her hands and feet due to a rare infection that had almost killed her.

"Would you come talk to her?" the nurse asked.

I went to the hospital and found a woman who was very lost and lonely in her grief, unable to see a life beyond this tragedy. She thought she was going to spend the rest of her life in a wheelchair. I knew her grief. I knew her fear. They are smothering feelings, and they can steal the fight right out of anyone. I told her to keep fighting—God had a plan for her, too. Just a few months later, there was a newspaper article about her.

In it, she said, "When I saw Ironman walking in, I knew I could do this. He said, 'You're going to get there. You're going to get [there] just like me.'"

It was really cool to find out that my visit had had an impact on her outlook, and I craved the chance to do more. I wanted to find more Kims and give them a glimpse of a different future than they might have envisioned for themselves. The Amputee Coalition of America offered training seminars for people who wanted to become peer counselors so I went for my certification. Even though I had been an amputee for more than twenty-two years, I was only now learning key principles on how to be a great listener and an effective communicator with, for example, wounded military veterans who had lost a limb or mobility. More than 1,200 American soldiers have already come home as amputees from Operation Iraqi Freedom, and in my new role as a certified peer counselor, I can spend time with them and their families in the hospital as they are preparing for or recovering from additional surgeries.

Suicide rates among soldiers are at an all-time high, and that's a travesty. It's also, I believe, related to the fact that so many soldiers are coming home with undiagnosed traumatic brain injuries and life-changing physical impairments. Many go from being in phenomenal physical shape to having a body that is scarred and missing some or many of its original parts. These are people who once were dependent on no one and who enjoyed the sense of pride that came from the admiration their uniform generated in public. Now some of them have people feeding them, bathing them, and sometimes helping them learn how to get dressed again. The looks they are receiving aren't those of admiration. In fact, they aren't looks at all. They are stares of pity or uncomfortable glances.

Seeing these wounded soldiers brings us face-to-face with our deepest fears. *What if that were me? How would I handle it? How do they?* There are good therapists who try to help these vets get reintegrated into society, but those therapists generally have all their limbs. As much as they may try to help, there's no way they can really understand.

As I made speaking appearances all across the country, I would call up my buddy Peter Harsch, the director of prosthetics and orthotics at Naval Medical Center San Diego (NMCSD), and he would find out if there were wounded soldiers in the clinics in the area where I'd be who could use a visit. Once I got there, I would visit the prosthetics and orthotics department and then venture over to physical therapy, where I'd spend time talking to the soldiers one-on-one. When I would walk in, they'd look at my legs and then at me in a way that said, "He's one of us!" The connection was instant even though I had never been in the military, which I always made clear.

The first time I went to NMCSD, I met a young seaman, maybe twenty years old, who had recently had both of his legs amputated above the knee. At the time, he seemed content just to be able to walk again. There was no smile, and he said hello kind of bashfully. Peter introduced me and said, "This is Scott Rigsby, and he was the first double amputee on prosthetics to complete the Hawaiian Ironman."

The young man's eyes lit up. I showed him a short video about my journey, and his life changed in those three minutes.

"Do you think I can get some of those running feet?" he asked me at the end of the video.

"I'm sure you can. You can do anything you want."

He had two very expensive and perfectly good artificial walking legs, but they were no longer going to be enough for him. The problem hadn't been the legs; the problem was in his mind, which had seen nothing but limitations. He now saw that his only limits were the ones he was placing on himself.

The next time I visited Peter, I heard that the young seaman was always on the go. On one of my last trips, they told me they couldn't contain him—he was running around the base and scaling the climbing walls in therapy. I thought to myself, *Now why is this kid still around here?*

On that same visit, one of the wounded veterans who had recently had a lower-leg amputation rolled into the therapy room in his wheelchair. The surgery was so recent that his stump was still wrapped in bandages. He seemed nervous about what his life was going to be like.

"Where are you from?" I asked.

"Arkansas," he told me.

"You're a good Southern kid, as I am. So . . . how did you lose your leg?"

"I'm a medic. I was in Iraq and one of my buddies was hurt. I went to pull him to safety when a roadside bomb blew up and blew part of my leg off."

In the course of our conversation, he told me that in high school he had been a cross-country runner.

"Do you want to run again?" I asked him.

He just looked at me a little puzzled, like I had perhaps failed to notice a minor problem—his missing leg.

"Have you ever heard of the Hawaiian Ironman?" I asked. He had. I told him what I had just accomplished, and you could see the wheels turning in his head. "You can run again, just like you did before. You don't have to limit your life just because you're going to have a prosthesis."

It was as if the lights were turned on for him. He wasn't thinking about walking now. In his mind, walking was a given, even though he didn't know what it was going to be like to have a prosthesis. He was fast-forwarding right past that and thinking about what other great things he might do as well.

In December, the NBC special about the Ironman aired for the first time. It featured me quite a bit, along with several other athletes who had overcome great obstacles to finish the race. Even people who had no interest in triathlons told me they were riveted by the stories; the documentary transcended sports and became a story about underdogs achieving greatness.

On the program, the famous sports commentator Al Trautwig introduces me and says, "One thing you notice about him is the barrel chest of a rugby player." This may or may not be a kinder way of saying I'm chubby, but he's right—I sure don't look like the typical triathlete.

There wasn't much about me, in fact, to make me a likely candidate to finish an Ironman, and that's part of what made it unthinkable. Take away that I have no legs, and you're still left with the fact that I was thirty-nine years old and forty pounds overweight; was undertrained; had had a broken vertebra; and, I would later find out, was also verging on diabetes. My insulin levels were through the roof, no doubt aided by all those Gatorades and energy gel packs.

The last thing shown in that television special is the image of me crossing the finish line. The announcer says, "Is it possible to be an Ironman with no legs? Yes, it is, Scott. Anything is possible. And ironically, the two letters you remove from *impossible* to make it so are '*I-M*.' Iron Man."

After the special, my mom called me. "I don't know why anyone would want to do what you did to your body, but I'm proud of you and I love you," she said.

"Did Dad see it?"

"Yes."

"What did he think of it?"

"He didn't say much. You'll have to ask him."

So I did, next time he answered the phone.

"So, Mom said you saw the NBC special. What did you think about it?"

"I didn't think anything about it," he said.

I have to believe that if my dad could see the faces of those soldiers I've met at military hospitals when I walk in and tell them what I've achieved, he would think something about it. I know that my Father in heaven thinks something about it.

At the beginning of 2008, Mike McClain and several others helped me start the Scott Rigsby Foundation, a 501(c)(3) non-profit organization with the primary objectives of helping physically challenged people lead active lifestyles and funding the research to make this a reality. As I write this, it's still an upstart organization, and I've learned that the effort required to establish a nonprofit while initiating fund-raising activities has its own set of unthinkable challenges. I believe the foundation and its mission are really what God intended for me to pursue when he opened that door for me to run through in 2005. My Ironman journey was simply a means to God's ultimate objective. He has surrounded me with a great team, and I'm gaining wisdom from a fantastic group of people with true hearts for servanthood. Much of the early heavy lifting has been provided through the generous pro bono services of the law firm King & Spalding. They actually provided us a key board member, Chris Prince, who has worked countless hours to get the organization ready for prime time. We're off to a great start and have some terrific projects underway in our first year. We now have a global, virtual group of athletes called the Unthinkables, and anyone can sign up to be a member. The athletes join in our fund-raising efforts and raise awareness for challenged athletes at running, cycling, and swimming events.

One of our main fund-raising efforts is to support groups such as Hope for the Warriors. It's an awe-inspiring group whose stated mission is "to enhance quality of life for U.S. service members and their families nationwide who have been adversely affected by injuries or death in the line of duty."

The next partnership came about because someone at World Vision read a magazine article about me. World Vision has been working to address the need for prosthetics care in Angola, where more than thirty-five thousand war veterans and many civilians have lost limbs as a result of the prolonged civil war there. What's worse is that lack of resources and poverty have meant that most of those who have lost limbs either have no prosthetics or have makeshift prosthetics that haven't been fitted or maintained in more than a decade. As a result, their quality of life is typically poor, they're unable to work, and they're dismissed by society.

As part of a peace treaty, the Angolan government has pledged a significant amount of money for rehabilitation and prosthetics for these wounded soldiers and civilians, and World Vision is also pledging to help.

World Vision named me Team World Vision Advocate for Children with Disabilities, and I will be traveling with them to Angola to begin assessing the problem and finding solutions. The plan is for us to build a state-of-the-art prosthetics and orthotics center in Luanda, the main city, with several clinics in smaller cities.

Learning about these injured veterans and civilians—many of them children—has made me think about how blessed I am to have the kind of care I've had. I can visit my prosthetics center anytime to ask for minor adjustments and new parts, which will keep me as comfortable and mobile as possible. I have prosthetics that help me lead an active lifestyle and trained medical professionals who see to it that I have the best products available. The people in Angola have nothing. They're stuck indefinitely where I was right after my accident. I cannot wait to get there and be able to tell these people that they can have hope again—that life is going to change for the better and that they will be able to regain their livelihood and their lives.

If given the opportunity, I would not change anything about my accident. That's right—I do not want my legs back.

It took me more than twenty years to understand the gift I have been given, but I do understand it now. Losing my legs led me to a life that's more meaningful than anything I had planned to do when I still had them. If I had not lost my legs, I would never have received a letter from the wife of a wounded soldier telling me that my story gave her husband his life back. He bought a bike after hearing me speak and found a new purpose. He's going to cycle from his hometown in Kokomo, Indiana, to Camp Lejeune, in North Carolina, in time for the annual Wounded Warrior Run. Along the way, he will raise awareness and funds for programs for wounded veterans.

"Thank you for bringing the life, passion, and drive back into our lives," she wrote. "I had been worried and tried not to convince myself that since my husband sustained his injuries, his true self was probably also lost forever."

I'm not angry with the truck driver anymore. He made a mistake. God wasn't thrown off guard by the accident. He didn't throw his hands in the air and say, "Oh no, what am I going to do with Scott now? That truck driver just ruined my plan!" No, I believe he might have turned to the angels and said, "Look at what I'm going to do with this one!"

I hope that truck driver hasn't wasted years feeling guilty for what happened, and I hope he knows what I've achieved. Someday, I'd love to sit and chat with him and talk about that day.

At times, it was hard to think of a reason to live and to have faith that my life was ever going to amount to anything, and there were times that the best I could do was breathe. But I hung in there one more day, and one more day, and one more day until I reached October 13, 2007.

Today, my life is still a work in progress. My traumatic brain injury still affects me, my apartment is still a wreck, I still have help managing my finances, and I still have battles with my health. In spite of those challenges, my purpose becomes clearer to me every day, and God continues to open new doors of opportunity for me to run through.

Turns out I didn't need a ticker tape parade when I got home from the Hawaiian Ironman; little by little, my message has reached people. Grove Films produced an excellent documentary about me and posted clips from it on Tangle.com, where at least ninety thousand people have watched the trailer. Numerous corporations have booked me as a speaker because of that documentary. In 2008, I won the Physically Challenged Athlete of the Year award from *Competitor* magazine, the Atlanta Sports Hall of Fame gave me its Star of the Year award, and Energizer Battery named me one of the top ten finalists for its "Keep Going" awards. I've also appeared on numerous news programs and talk shows. Each time I speak and each time an article appears about me, I know that God is being glorified and that I have a real chance to make a lasting difference in someone's life.

What I've found is that, too often, people seem to be waiting for everything to be perfect before they attempt to achieve their goals. And what I want to teach is that you can do it now, as imperfect as the circumstances may be. You can do it without family support. You can do it even though you're not in the right job, or not in the right relationship, or your health isn't great, or your house is a mess. Don't wait for the "right time." There may never be a right time. Just do something great now.

Never quit. No matter how long it takes, no matter how great the obstacles, no matter what. I know you can do it.

My name is Scott Rigsby, and I am an Ironman.

# AFTERWORD

Has my story inspired you in any way to do something extra-ordinary with your life? If you are like most people, doing something huge and life changing might be unthinkable. You may have a circumstance that you feel prohibits you from moving forward. That could be the case, or maybe that's just your perception. Allow me to change your perspective. The more difficult your circumstance, the more the odds seem to be stacked against you, the more you've been told it's not possible, then the more opportunity you have to do the unthinkable.

God can take an ordinary life and do extraordinary things.

Over the past two years, I have been blessed to speak to thousands of kids, soldiers, teachers, athletes, doctors, parents, CEOs, troubled youths, pastors, celebrities, and government leaders. Able-bodied and physically challenged alike, we all share common emotional and physical challenges. We also share a passion to find our true purpose in this world.

As you may have learned through my story, I am truly just an ordinary guy whose life experience has been magnified by a roller coaster ride of obstacles and miracles. I'm no scholar—or as my friends like to say, I "ain't the sharpest knife in the drawer." So, when I address an audience during a speaking engagement, I speak only from my own failures, accomplishments, and experiences. But I also speak from my heart.

If you're ready to begin your unthinkable journey, I want

to encourage you to contemplate the five key steps that I took to cross my finish line and change the world.

### 1. HAVE A DREAM

Nothing can happen until you have something big in your heart that drives you. Your dream is yours alone, and it doesn't matter whether or not the dream seems unattainable right now. In fact, searching for your dream may be a process you need to go through before it is fully revealed. Whatever the path, you must be willing to try, and you will know you're on the right course when that dream becomes bigger than yourself. It will become your passion. Just spend some time thinking about what you'd really love to achieve, and pray for God to begin the process of discovery for you by opening new doors.

### 2. BUILD A GOOD SUPPORT TEAM

Big dreamers take big risks, and going it alone means almost certain failure. Your support team doesn't have to include your family, and it may not even include your friends. Find people who can help you on your journey, and then ask them to join you. You'd be surprised how often people will step up to help someone achieve a dream. Don't be afraid to approach the people you admire and ask them for advice or help along the way. If they don't know you need help, they can't help you. In my case, finding my support team actually became part of the journey. When you're doing the unthinkable, those in your camp actually share in the ultimate journey with you.

### 3. CHOOSE FAITH OVER FEAR

In every situation, you can choose to make decisions out of either faith or fear. We all play self-defeating mind games that define our thinking and perceptions of ourselves and others. When I started my Ironman journey, I had no money and no experience. I was overweight, too old, and going through difficult relationship issues. What it all boils down to is that poor self-image and personal negativity are really just expressions of our own fears. Fear is the leading cause of the death of our dreams. The only antidote I know is to choose faith. Faith will lead you to face your fears and point you straight to the core of how to withstand the doubt and uncertainty. Martin Luther King Jr. said, "Faith is taking the first step, even when you can't see the whole staircase."

### 4. EXPECT AND OVERCOME OBSTACLES

Anything worth doing will present some challenges; otherwise you'd have done it already! However, no matter how much faith you exhibit, the "day of trouble" will come. According to Jeremiah 16:19, that is precisely when God becomes our *strength*, our *fortress*, and our *refuge*. Expect that you're going to face some difficulties along the way, plan for how you are going to address them mentally and physically, and commit to reaching for your goal in spite of them. There will be days when you won't feel like putting in the effort, or the conditions may be such that you want to give up. Those are the days when you must push past the fear or pain, for it is the strength you have gained during those days of difficulty that you will rely on when the unanticipated obstacles appear. Training breeds perseverance and instills confidence that you will be able to move past the obstacles, no matter what.

### 5. CROSS YOUR FINISH LINE

Somewhere along your journey, you envisioned what the experience was going to be like when you approached your finish line. Your dream may have taken months, years, or decades to achieve, but the finish line is always there for you to cross. If your mission is truly "unthinkable," then your finish line will be characterized by the following truths:

- *Your "unthinkable" finish line was originally inconceivable and unimaginable.*
- *The line that you must cross cannot be moved closer in or lowered to make it easier.*
- *Pursuit of your goal will scare you out of your comfort zone.*
- *Your goal will cause you to doubt yourself, and others will tell you that your goal is crazy.*
- *The mountain you must climb will be taller than anything you have ever done.*
- *You will experience many setbacks and failures on your way to success.*

Your finish line is where you've placed it, and once you get there, you may find that it was the experience of getting there that has made you stronger and more capable of taking on additional finish lines.

You might even find—as I did—that your dream becomes a *mission*, and your mission changes the world.

I wish you all the best in living your own "unthinkable" dreams.

*Resources Mentioned in This Book*

**All3Sports** (www.all3sports.com)

**American Society for Plastic Surgeons** (www.plasticsurgery.org)

**Athletic Training Services** (www.athletictrainingservices.com)

**Atlanta Sports Medicine & Orthopaedic Center** (www.atlantasportsmedicine.com)

**Body Vision Studio** (www.bodyvisionstudio.com)

**Carole Sharpless** (www.carole-sharpless.com)

**55nine Performance** (www.55nineperformance.com)

**Freedom Innovations** (www.freedom-innovations.com)

**Georgia Sports Chiropractic** (www.georgiasportschiropractic.com)

**Georgia Sports Massage** (www.georgiasportsmassage.com)

**Hope for the Warriors** (www.hopeforthewarriors.org)

**Ironman** (www.ironman.com)

**King & Spalding** (www.kslaw.com)

**Paces Plastic Surgery** (www.pacesplasticsurgery.com)

**ProCare-Prosthetic Care, Inc.** (www.procareprosthetics.com)

**Puako Bed and Breakfast** (http://bigisland-bedbreakfast.com/hosts.php)

**Rick Gunther/Coldwell Banker Real Estate** (www.rggunther.com)

**The Scott Rigsby Foundation** (www.scottrigsbyfoundation.org)

**Robideaux Motors** (www.robideauxmotors.com)

**Skyline Northwest** (www.skylinenw.com)

**SRM** (www.srm.de/index.php?lang=us)

**SwimAtlanta** (www.swimatlanta.com)

**Tri4Health.com** (http://tri4health.com)

**Vertical Earth** (www.verticalearth.com)

**YourDay E.T.C.** (www.yourdayetc.com)

**Zoot Sports** (www.zootsports.com)

## Acknowledgments

***Jenna would like to thank*** her funny, huggable little girl, Sarina, for making every day together a wonderful day. She also thanks Lori, Mark, and Paul Glatzer; Lisa and Chris Fries; Pat Alch; and Keith Potter for their support. And she gives a big thanks to Victor Legarreta for the fact-checking help.

---

***Scott would like to acknowledge the following people*** for helping him along the way of his unthinkable journey. Without their help, none of this would have been possible.

***To my neighbors in the Pebble City community and the church members at Pebble City Baptist Church.*** You have always shown my family and me your love, generosity, and kindness. Your dedicated support and faithful friendship allowed me to weather the terrible storms in my life. My only regret is that I did not show you the proper gratitude for your unconditional love and thoughtful service to me in my greatest time of need.

***To the wonderful people of Camilla, Georgia.*** There's nothing like growing up in a small town. I was blessed to never fear violence from gangs or drug dealers. There was no need to shut windows or lock doors. I loved that almost everybody knew my family, and it made me want to honor that good name. The disadvantage of small towns, some critics would say, is that everyone knows your business. I didn't mind everyone knowing my business when I was lying in a hospital bed in my home for months, trying to piece my life back together. It was your support in bringing food to the house and your neighborly visits that helped to pull me through. If you need help in a small town, there's always somebody there to chip in. Thank you.

***To my former classmates and fellow Wildcats at Westwood School in Camilla.*** I always looked forward to going to school with you every day. It's a special place that taught me so many life lessons that I continue to share with thousands of people around the country, even to this day. I will always be proud to be a Wildcat.

***To my childhood friend, Ken Sirmons, and his never-ending patience*** in teaching me how to ride a bike when we were kids. Ken, I'm sorry for all the profanity I taught you that day. It's no wonder you became a pastor. You, sir, have the patience of Job.

***To Dudley McClain, father of my best friend from high school.*** Mr. Dudley, you took me to my first college football game. You were the chaperone of a memorable weekend with Mike and a few of our buddies. Whenever we spoke, you were always encouraging and supportive. You gave me my best friend from high school in your son Mike. He turned out to be a successful businessman, a faithful husband, and a great father to your grandkids. You would be proud.

***To Ms. Daphine Bass.*** Thank you for not only giving me a ride to school almost every weekday until I could drive but also for being a shining example of a Christian woman. I treasure the friendships I made with your sons, Bobby and Reagan. I'm not sure what life would have been like in a small church without their friendship.

***To Aunt Elvie King Rigsby.*** I wish I would have had the privilege of knowing you. I think you would have been like a second mom to me. I look forward to meeting you in heaven.

***To Aunt Veda Rigsby.*** You never once said anything discouraging to me. You were always in my corner. Even though as a kid I was very unsure of myself, after talking with you, I always felt I could take on the world. You always asked, "How is it going?" I miss hearing that, and I miss you.

***To my cousins, Dean, Deannie, Murray, Clair, Miley, Brent, and Bruce.*** I want to thank each of you for affecting my life in some profound way. Dean, it was a blessing for me when your mom married my Uncle Rudy, because I felt like I gained a brother, and I did. I appreciate that you had the same faith and belief in me that your mom did. Deannie and Murray, thank you for your constant support and for always taking care of Tim. I never had to worry about him when he was in your hands. Clair and Miley, I appreciate your faithful prayer and Christian witness in my life. Even when there were reasons to give up on me and judge me, you didn't. Bruce and Brent, we had some crazy, memorable times growing up, but what I will remember most about you two is your commitment and devotion to helping me lead a normal life after the accident. We had some very frank discussions that were filled with tough love, and you never let me "waller" in self-pity for very long. For that I am thankful.

***To Ray Dixon, brother-in-law.*** I miss the holiday football games we played when I was a kid. You were one of the adults who were always interested in talking with me about my favorite subject: sports. I appreciate the time we spent together.

***To Stanley Warren, brother-in-law.*** Even now, I struggle to write about you. I keep thinking that when I go home for the holidays, you will walk in the door of my parents' home with that contagious smile and infectious laugh. When I get to heaven, it will be easy to find you because it will be where everyone is gathered around a table laughing about life's simple pleasures. Thank you for being a great husband to my sister; an encouraging father to my nephew and nieces—Sam, Jay, and Whitney; and a faithful son-in-law to my parents. I am eternally grateful for your example of forgiveness. You were not just a brother-in-law to me, you were a brother. I will always miss you.

***To Bill Butler, brother-in-law.*** I loved beating you at cards; more important, I didn't mind losing to you, either, because I got to see the same competitive nature in you that is in me. You were a good husband to my sister Elizabeth, and a wonderful dad to Heather and Chris. I know that when I find you in heaven, you will be sitting at a table somewhere, trying to be the king of Phase 10. I miss you, man.

***To Coach Lowe.*** I would like to share "a couple or three" things with you, as you would say. Yes, very much like Cool Hand Luke, I did have a failure to communicate with you at times in high school, but God opened my ears and let my heart hear his purpose for my life. You had as much to do with that as anyone. You put God first in your life and led by example. I appreciate you more than you will ever know for being a Christlike witness as a coach. I now treasure the prayers you prayed over me before high school football practice. They have all been answered.

***To Brooks Mulliford.*** I'm sorry we were not able to be better friends, and I wish you could have seen the completion of this book. Our lives were brought together by tragedy, and part of this book would not have been possible without your eyewitness account of the accident. Also, you helped save my life by your quick thinking and your paramedic training. Your act of kindness was not in vain, and my only regret is that you are not here to see that the life you saved is being used by God to touch millions of lives around the world.

***To Dr. George Cierny, my orthopedic surgeon*** at the time of my accident. I appreciate being, as you said, "your best work of the 1986 year." I am grateful that you did the best you could to make me a functional foot, but I am more grateful to you for your bedside manner and for showing me the quality of person you were outside the hospital.

***To Dr. Foad Nahai, my plastic surgeon*** at the time of the accident. I will never forget your calm demeanor and attentive bedside manner. I looked horrible with third degree burns, missing parts, open wounds, and tubes coming out of everywhere, and yet you would say to me, "You look great, and you will be fine." You were right, because you saw me as I would be, not as I was. I am humbled to still know you and to be friends with your son, Farzad R. Nahai. He and I will continue your good work and make you proud.

***To Steve Singletary.*** How can I possibly express enough thanks to the guy who started my journey of faith in God by introducing me to Jesus? I appreciate your willingness to be led by God's Spirit and the way you conveyed the good news about Jesus in such a simple but profound way that even a knucklehead like me could get it.

***To Jay DeMott, college friend and fraternity brother.*** Jay, when I didn't get into the fraternity on my first try, you told me to rise above the politics, hold my head high, be true to who I was, and things would work themselves out in my favor. They did, and I have used your advice throughout the years, especially on the Ironman journey when I have had to deal with all the politics that surround disabled sports.

***To Jeff Cook.*** You shared with me about God's mercy and forgiveness when all I could see was his wrath.

***To Stephanie Gamble.*** I am thankful for our friendship and for how God used you to teach me that he is always faithful to keep his word.

***To Sherry E. Little.*** God used you to teach me one of his most valuable lessons: that you don't end a friendship just because you don't see eye to eye on issues of faith. You have been in my thoughts and prayers constantly over the years. God allowed the writing of this book to bring healing to me from living with years of regret for my painful mistake. I was so thrilled to find out that life has brought you such great reward for all your hard work. My prayer is that God would continue to richly bless you.

***To Tyler Hutchison.*** You know that, as a farm kid, I loved seeing for the first time that surfboard of yours hanging up on the wall in our living room in our college apartment. I admire your willingness to leave the comforts of the States and go to serve others around the world with the love of Jesus.

***To Clay and Stephanie Powell.*** College can be a challenging experience for most freshmen, but for a kid who was dealing with being a new amputee and the craziness that comes with a TBI, the experience was overwhelming at times. It was your love, kindness, and friendship that allowed me to weather so many tough storms.

***To Dr. Moses Hardin.*** I once heard that we as Christians need to walk what we talk because we might be the only representation of Christ that someone ever sees. I have met very few Christians, even to this day, who beam with the radiant presence of God's Spirit the way you do. Thank you for being a friend and big brother and for making such a great spiritual investment in me.

***To Chuck Carswell.*** I can't believe all the cool things God allowed us to see while we were leading a Bible study with several members of the University of Georgia football team back in college.

***To Lee and Lisa Mason.*** I appreciate the time that you spent with me in college and the spiritual investment you made in me to help me grow as a young Christian. God bless you and your ministry in Athens.

***To Ferrell and Rita Brown.*** I'm not sure what would have happened to me if you hadn't opened your home and helped me get back on my "feet." I am so grateful to you for loving and caring about me when no one else knew what to do to help me. I was paralyzed with fear and despair, and you nursed me back to faith and prosperity.

***To Jeff and Gwen Falkowski.*** I know there were times when I gave no reason for anyone to love me, but you two looked past all the darkness in my life and loved me in spite of myself.

***John and Deb Herron.*** You have seen both my mountaintop and my valley experiences during this long journey, and you have stood by me through many cheers and even more tears. Thank you for helping me cross my finish line. Your friendship is priceless.

***To my college friends/roommates and their wives,*** including Craig and Karen Burnsed, Scott and Kristen Lees, Dru and Natalie Preston, Jamie and

Lindsay Vinson, Brian and Rachel Cox, Joel and Rosemary McElhannon, Mark Preston, Jennifer Stewart Norris, and George Freelin. I thank all of you for always believing in me, against all odds. I am forever humbled by your compassion as my closest confidants. It was your unwavering support and continual prayers that helped me through my darkest days. It was the thoughtful generosity of many of you in loaning me literally thousands of dollars over the years so that I could pay my rent, keep the power on, and still have money left over for food and water that allowed me to stay on this Ironman journey and see it to the very end.

***To Pastor Mike and Patty Atkins.*** I am so fortunate that God allowed our paths to cross, even though it was at a time of great uncertainty for us. Thank you so much for your healing and life-altering words of wisdom in one of my greatest times of need. I love you two.

***To Dr. Scott D. Gillogly.*** I know that my freedom from being a professional patient began when you took off my second leg. Your wisdom, vision, and skill as a surgeon gave me a new life and hope for a bright future. Thank you for making all this possible.

***To my friends at Buckhead Church and all the guys from my former small groups.*** I love and appreciate your acceptance of me just as I am with all my many faults. I appreciate all the prayers.

***To Pastor Andy Stanley.*** You won't remember having met me, but I'll never forget how you stared at my legs and said in shock, "What happened?" What happened was that God gave me a gift, and I am using it to share his love with a world that desperately needs love; hope; and a sense of a real, God-given purpose. Your profound sermons of biblical wisdom and insight into God's truths from the Bible helped carry me through many difficult days. I am taking your advice and doing God's will by just trying to "do the next right thing"—unthinkable thing, that is—and change the world.

***To Mark Sisson.*** I know it had to be tough for you to bail me out of one situation after another after we became friends, but I hope I've shown you that your investment was well worth it. You are a trusted friend, and I am so grateful to have you as a brother.

***To Thomas and Elizabeth Duttera.*** I am so blessed to know you. It seems like only yesterday that we met on a church beach retreat. You both have been a great source of strength and support for me through some very difficult times, and I love you for it.

***To David and Monique Almire.*** I lost my way after George Hyder died, and I am so thankful that you two were there to help me pick up the pieces. I appreciate all that you have done for me and the friendship that we will always have.

***To Ron Smith.*** You were surprised to meet a guy like me, who was 5′8″ tall with an artificial leg in 1988; it is still humorous to me to know that I freaked you out fourteen years later when you saw me on a church beach retreat and I had two prosthetic legs and was 6′1″. You are a great personal trainer and one of my best friends. It was your constant belief and relentless encouragement that gave me the courage to keep following my dreams.

***To Tony and Nancy Myers.*** I know that you could have crushed my Ironman dreams when I spoke to you on the phone for the first time, but true to your character, you always pulled for the underdog. None of this would have been possible without you. It started with you. Tony, you acted as a loving and supportive father figure, guided me through insurmountable odds, and believed in me when very few others did. I love you and Nancy and am so blessed to still have you two in my life.

***To George Hyder, personal trainer.*** You were one of the best personal trainers and friends I've had. I believe that God planted a desire for an unthinkable journey in my heart many years ago while we were training together. I lost my way after you left, but I finally found it again. I wish you could have been there to see me cross the finish line in Hawaii. Whenever bad things happened in the race and I got frustrated, I would remember your words: "Do what you can, do the best that you can, and never quit!" George, I didn't quit. I look forward to seeing you again one day. I'm sure that, even in heaven, I will hear you before I see you.

***To Pete Higgins.*** I treasure the time we spent together. Thank you for teaching me how to swim and for being so incredibly patient with me. I still miss my "Sundays with Pete."

***To Kate McDonald.*** I always wanted a younger sister, but my parents had seven kids and I couldn't talk my mom and dad into having still another one. If I'd had a younger sis made to order and delivered by the stork all the way from South Africa to the United States, and if she had turned out just like you, I would not have changed a thing. I am thankful for all your help as my physical therapist and my beloved friend; and even though I argue with you constantly, and occasionally do not listen to your helpful instructions, I still love hearing your point of view. I love you and your family and could not imagine my life without you in it.

***To Marie Duginski.*** When I came to you at Body Vision Studio, my core was the weakest thing about me. I desperately needed help because this weakness would have been a constant hindrance during my Ironman journey. Through your Pilates instruction, you strengthened and toned me into the best shape of my life. I will always remember your kindness.

***To Chuck and Kristin Dunlop.*** Thank you so much for your love and support as I started my Ironman journey. It was through your Tri-the-Parks triathlons that I was able to experiment with new prosthetic devices in a safe, healthy, and encouraging environment. Through your help, I was able to improve my transition times significantly, which set me on my road to success.

***To Carla Loureiro.*** Thank you for your memorable support for me at Worlds 2006. It may have seemed like a small act of kindness to the average observer, but it made a lasting impression on me. It gave me a sweet voice of confidence to replay in times of doubt and trial. It also birthed a lasting friendship. I wish you and Tristan much happiness.

***To Terry and Jennifer Hunt.*** I never would have made it to Hawaii without your sacrificial personal financial donation to my Ironman journey. Your investment not only changed my life but is also now changing the world.

***To Chris Prince and my King & Spalding family.*** Thank you so much for your time, talent, resources, and friendship. I am forever grateful for your support.

***To Mike Lenhart.*** I won't repeat your nickname out of respect for you, but you know who you are and will always be to me. You are a great brother. I am glad that God brought us together on this crazy journey. Thank you for showing me that God was doing something in me that was bigger and more profound than simply Scott Rigsby and that God's calling on my life was to transcend further and wider than "the most famous finish line in the world."

***To Victoria Seahorn.*** I admire your heart for helping challenged athletes everywhere and assisting them in reaching all their finish lines. I am grateful for your constant support of me and your investment to help me reach my future goals.

***To my coaches at the Concourse Athletic Club:*** Pete, Robin, Diana, and Heidi. Thank you for working with me and helping me become a better swimmer during my Ironman journey.

***To my Multisports.com family.*** I am thankful for all of you—Huddle, Paul, Heather, and Roch. I appreciate the love, support, and constant encouragement every time I see you.

***To Beth Brown.*** Your research on amputee running helped change the world—literally. Thank you for allowing me to be involved in your historic research. I look forward to reaching more historic advancements in prosthetic running with you.

***To my "ridin' dirty" crew***—Scott Burkhardt, Lindsay Janke Bergman, and Pastor Mike Terry. Thank you for loving and supporting me on this journey.

***To Carole Sharpless.*** Sharpie, you are one of the most caring and compassionate friends I have. I appreciate all you did to help me get to my finish line. It was your constant love, encouragement, and belief in me that willed me to that line.

***To the towns of Coeur d'Alene, Hayden, and Post Falls, Idaho.*** Your outpouring of generosity and kindness toward me has always been overwhelming. It started my love affair with the citizens of your towns. Many people there are like family to me—Rick and Roxanne Gunter, Mike and Jenni Gaertner of Vertical Earth, John Robideaux of Robideaux Motors, Nigel and LaDonna Beaumont, Jim and Pam Headley, Pam Houser, Andy and Leslie Emberton, Martin and Vicki Scates, Paul and Katie Burke, Scott and Donna Wemple, Michelle Goal Haustein, Bret Bowers, Kim Gibson, and so many others. I will always be in debt to the generous citizens of Coeur d'Alene and many fantastic businesses there. Thank you, everyone, for all you have done to support me and all the Ironman participants who come there every year. You have very much to be proud of.

***To K.O.*** I was in such a bad place when we became training partners, but your constant encouragement and unwavering belief in me and what I was trying to accomplish gave me the faith to continue on when the future looked so grim. I can never repay your love, support, and kindness, and I will never forget the sacrifices you made for me to make my dream become a reality.

***To Puna.*** Your hospitality was humbling and overwhelming. Thank you for allowing me to share your home while in Kona. *Ke Akua Ho'omaika'I Oe!*

***To Scott Chapman.*** Brother, thank you, first and foremost, for serving your country faithfully and going back again into harm's way to protect our freedom. I appreciate the time you spent in helping me train for the Hawaiian Ironman and for your friendship.

***To Bob Babbit.*** You are triathlon's greatest ambassador; but more important, you are one of the greatest advocates for challenged athletes in the United States. One of the things I admire most about you is your ability to rise above the politics that permeate disabled sports and stay focused to your true passion: the challenged athlete. You are not a respecter of persons, and you treat all challenged athletes with dignity and respect. It's an honor to consider you a friend and role model.

***To Mike Reilly, "the Voice of Ironman."*** Thank you for saying those magical words that will ring in my ears for a lifetime: "Scott Rigsby, you are an Ironman!" It was one of the greatest moments of my life to hear you shout that to me. I am grateful for your support and, most of all, your friendship.

***To Jon "the Blazeman" Blais.*** Jon, I'm sorry I never met you. I think we would have been great friends. However, I have had the privilege of meeting your parents, Bob and Mary Ann. They are wonderful people, and you would be proud of the work they have done with the Blazeman Foundation and its ongoing war against ALS. Thanks for being such an inspiration to all the underdogs out there like me.

***To Henry Forrest, 1978 Ironman finisher.*** Thank you for being there to greet me at my first half-Ironman and for being so supportive of my efforts. I always looked forward to seeing your great smile at all the races. You are dearly missed.

***To Blair and Phillip Lahaye.*** I am grateful for your friendship and for how you eased my worries before the race. There was so much to think about before that historic event, and I was a bundle of nerves. You alleviated all those worries with your kindness, love, and support. Thank you for all the memorable experiences and the birth of a lifelong friendship.

***To Peter Harsch and Lauren McVey.*** I am so grateful for your friendship. You loved me through the disappointments at the Coeur d'Alene Ironman and the triumphs at the Hawaiian Ironman. I am so thankful for all you have done for me.

***To Diana Bertsch, Linda Jane Kelley, and the rest of my Ironman family at the Kona office.*** I love you and thank you so much for your vital role in helping me make October 13, 2007, a historic and unforgettable moment.

***To my ProCare-Prosthetics family***—Tammy, Pam, Rusty, Andy, Laura, and Tom. Thank you for all your help. To Stephen and Mariamne Schulte. I came to you without any running feet, no money, and just a dream. Your belief in me, your innovative, outside-the-box thinking, and your sacrificial support helped us make history. I am forever indebted to you for going beyond the call of duty to see me reach my dream.

***To Maynard, Roland, Megan, Kurt, Celisa, and all my family at Freedom Innovations.*** When my prosthetic running feet were taken from me and not returned, you saved me by giving me new running feet to carry on my Ironman journey. I love you and thank you for your constant support in helping me get to my finish line. I look forward to crossing many more with you in the future.

***To my Zoot family***—Brian, Eli, Heather, and the rest of the gang at Zoot Sports. I had no money to buy clothes to run in the Hawaiian Ironman (and no one would have wanted to see that!), but you clothed me and took care of all my triathlon needs. I love you, and I appreciate all your help in getting me to the finish line.

***To Joey O'Connor and family and Virginia Dixon and family.*** Thank you so much for your love, support, and faith in God's vision for me. I know that God divinely brought our lives together to share his love with the world through the arts and media and through sharing our heritage of God's faithfulness with others. I treasure you and my Grove Center for the Arts & Media family.

***To Josh and Collette Glass.*** You were such a huge part of my success. Every week, I would beat my body up, but between the two of you, I was put back together somehow for another week of training. You are such great people. I love you and value our friendship.

***To Chrissie Wellington.*** I am humbled to know you and so blessed to be your friend. Your unbelievable athletic talent pales in comparison to your internal strength and radiant beauty, which comes from your compassion to help the world be a better place. God has used you as a wonderful role model to show the world that, in spite of your unmatched talent, you acknowledge what is truly important in life: the grace to hold our heads high while smiling in victory and in defeat, the strength to give our all in every event, and the unselfish service of others.

***To Jamie Williams Carter.*** I love you and your family. Ever since we were in high school, you have been a faithful and encouraging friend. Our friendship proves that God's timing is perfect. With all the challenges with my TBI, I could never have written this book without you and your careful guidance, constructive feedback, and meticulous attention to detail. I also want to thank your husband, Scott, and your daughters, Malorie and Rebecca, for their support and for allowing you to spend time away from them to work on the book.

**To Christi Williams Marsh.** Thank you for your friendship and your support in helping Jamie edit the book.

***To Daryn Kagan.*** This book was your idea. I can still remember the conversation we had in which you said, "You should write a book." Thank you for your friendship, your support, and your continued encouragement to me, even when I doubted this would ever be a reality.

***To Saint Day Adeogba and my family at YourDay E.T.C.*** I appreciate you so much for persevering with me to "reveal, recreate, and revitalize my habits." It is through you that I am learning "C.H.A.R.A.C.T.E.R. Fitness" and "Balance Excellence."

***To Scott Johnson, the magic man.*** The Bible says, "A friend loves at all times, and a brother is born for adversity" (Proverbs 17:17). You are the brother who was born for my adversity. If I am the James J. Braddock, "Cinderella Man," of triathlon, then you are my Joe Gould. You have always been in my corner, you never threw in the towel, and you have never given up on me. My getting to and finishing the Hawaiian Ironman, the Scott Rigsby Foundation, this book, and all the wonderful upcoming projects we have together would not be possible without your strategic vision, critical thinking, unselfish sacrifice, and hard work.

***To Beth Johnson.*** I am forever in your debt for your love, support, and sacrifice to make this book, and all the great things that happened to me since I met Scott, a precious reality.

***To Jenna Glatzer.*** I know in my heart that God handpicked you to help write his story and the role that I played in it. You did an amazing job. I could not have done it without you. I treasure the time we spent together.

I am so blessed to have worked with you, but I am even more blessed to have made a friend in you for life.

***To my sisters and brother—Elizabeth, Ann, Susie, Emily, and Jim.*** I love you, and I'm sorry for all the heartache I caused you over the years. I am grateful and thankful for your love and support and for not giving up on me.

***To my brother Tim.*** The doctors said you wouldn't live past infancy, and now here you are in your forties. One of the greatest moments of my life was when I was able to put my Ironman medal around your neck. One day, when you get to heaven, you will be able to hear; you will be able to speak; you will be able to walk; and greatest of all, you will be able to run, if you want to. You are the reason I finished those *excruciatingly* painful last three miles of the Hawaiian Ironman. I love you, and you are my inspiration.

***To Mom.*** Thank you for the nine months you carried me; for the nights that you sat up with me, whether it was caring for me when I was sick, watching a pet who was dying, nursing the pain of my broken heart, or wiping away the tears from my cheeks as I faced the fear and uncertainty of an unknown future without legs; for doctoring me; for teaching me the Bible; and for kneeling by your bed and praying for me every night. I am so sorry for all the time, tears, and pain I cost you through the years. For the nights filled with worry, I apologize. I am grateful for your godly advice and the sound wisdom you have shared with me. Always know that I will remember what you prayed most for me: "Train up a child in the way he should go: and when he is old, he will not depart from it" (Proverbs 22:6, KJV). I am doing my best to honor the ways you taught me. I love you.

***To Dad.*** Though we have never seemed to see eye to eye on things, if it weren't for the tenacity you passed on to me, I would not have finished this race, inspired millions, and fulfilled God's plan for my life. I am grateful for your provision—that I've always had plenty to eat, clothes to wear, a car to drive, and a roof over my head. I love you because you're my dad, and I don't regret that God gave you to me. You are a blessing!

***To Jesus.*** I want to thank you for coming to this earth, living a sinless life, and dying on the cross for my sins. When I received you, you forgave me all my past, present, and future sins; you gave me purpose for living; and you gave me hope for a future spent with you. You are not only my Savior but also my Lord. Most important, you are my friend.

***To God, my heavenly Father.*** This book is your story, not mine. I am humbled that you would invite me to play a role in the beautiful masterpiece that you have been writing since the beginning of time; for that I will be eternally grateful. Thank you, Father, that I am not a cosmic mistake. You formed me in my mother's womb, and you know even the hairs on my head. Thank you for watching over me and sending all these wonderful people my way to help me fulfill your purpose for my life. You continue to keep your end of our bargain, so I will continue to keep mine. Open doors for me, Father, that I might bring honor to you in this life and the life to come. I love you, and I am yours.

# *About the Author*

**Scott Rigsby** is a professional speaker and certified counselor who encourages people to "Do the Unthinkable." He has completed more than twenty triathlons, and in 2007, he became the first double amputee to complete the Ford Ironman Triathlon World Championship using prosthetics to swim, bike, and run the 140.6-mile course. He is the founder of the Scott Rigsby Foundation, a Georgia-based nonprofit organization that exists to inspire and enable physically challenged individuals and athletes. In 2008, he was named World Vision's Advocate for Children with Disabilities. Scott lives in Atlanta, Georgia.

**Jenna Glatzer** is the author of seventeen books, including *Celine Dion: For Keeps*; *Bullyproof Your Child for Life*, with Joel Haber; and *The Marilyn Monroe Treasures*. She has written hundreds of articles for magazines such as *Woman's World*, *Prevention*, *Women's Health & Fitness*, *Contemporary Bride*, and *Physical*. She is also a contributing editor for *Writer's Digest*.

## *Notes*

1. http://www.theodoreroosevelt.org/life/quotes.htm.
2. When asked about his decision to roll across the finish line at the Hawaiian Ironman in 2005, Jon Blais said, "During a radio show with Mike Reilly, I said that if I got close enough to the finish line, they could just log-roll me across. I was able to do my own log roll across the line." At subsequent races, representatives of the Blazeman Warriors have honored Jon's memory by log-rolling across the finish line. See http://ironman.com/columns/ironmanlife/ironmanlife.com-32.
3. "From the Inside Out," by Joel Houston (HillsongUnited, 2006).